## YOUR GUIDE TO THE

# Federal Census

## for genealogists, researchers, and family historians

INCLUDES INFORMATION ★★★★ 1930 CENSUS ★★★ ON THE NEWLY RELEASED

### Kathleen W. Hinckley

**BETTERWAY BOOKS**

CINCINNATI, OHIO

www.familytreemagazine.com

## About the Author

Kathleen W. Hinckley, owner of Family Detective <www.familydetective.com>, is a professional genealogist and private investigator. She is executive director of the Association of Professional Genealogists and a trustee for the Board for Certification of Genealogists. She has been certified as a genealogical records specialist since 1982.

Kathleen appeared as an expert in the PBS television series *Ancestors* and is a frequent lecturer at genealogical conferences and workshops across the country. She authored *Locating Lost Family Members & Friends* and is nationally recognized for her expertise in nineteenth- and twentieth-century genealogical research.

**Your Guide to the Federal Census.** © 2002 by Kathleen W. Hinckley. Manufactured in the United States of America. All rights reserved. No part of this book may be reproduced in any form or by any electronic or mechanical means including information storage and retrieval systems without permission in writing from the publisher, except by a reviewer, who may quote brief passages in a review. Published by Betterway Books, an imprint of F&W Publications, Inc., 4700 East Galbraith Road, Cincinnati, Ohio 45236. (800) 289-0963. First edition.

Other fine Betterway books are available from your local bookstore or on our Web site at www.familytreemagazine.com. To subscribe to Family Tree Magazine Update, a free e-mail newsletter with helpful tips and resources for genealogists, go to http://newsletters.fwpublicat ions.com.

06  05  04  03  02     5  4  3  2  1

**Library of Congress Cataloging-in-Publication Data**

Hinckley, Kathleen W.
  Your guide to the federal census / Kathleen W. Hinckley.
    p.  cm.
  Includes bibliographical references and index.
  ISBN 1-55870-588-0 (alk. paper)
    1. United States. Bureau of the Census. 2. United States—Census. 3. United States—Census—Methodology. I. Your guide to the federal census.
  HA37.U6H556   2002
  317'.3—dc21                                                         2002018264
                                                                              CIP

Editor: Sharon DeBartolo Carmack, CG
Production editor: Brad Crawford
Production coordinator: John Peavler
Cover designer: Wendy Dunning
Interior designer: Sandy Conopeotis Kent
Icon designer: Cindy Beckmeyer

DEDICATION
*To my sister,*
*Karen Westberg Rossow,*
*1970 census enumerator*

# Acknowledgments

The support and assistance I received while writing this book was astounding. As proud as I am of the resulting text, I am more honored that my colleagues and friends gave their time and talent in order to assist in this contribution to the genealogical field.

The donations of case studies and anomalies, detailed on the next page, typify the sharing nature of genealogists. The variety of examples enhanced this book beyond any expectation I had when proposing it. I never could have gathered these examples alone and am forever grateful to everyone who contributed.

Jim Hansen, Roger Joslyn, and Elizabeth Mills, who are all authorities on census records, answered my technical inquiries and contributed in ways invisible to the reader, but which I certainly appreciated.

Birdie Holsclaw and I met several times to analyze the case studies and develop editorial styles to present the information clearly and concisely. I always left our four- to six-hour meetings full of renewed inspiration and motivation. Thank you, Birdie.

Jan Prater offered to be my personal elf at the Denver Public Library and the National Archives' Rocky Mountain regional facility. Weeks turned into months as I wrote this book, and Jan became more than an elf. She was my angel and cheerleader and always my friend. I cannot imagine how I could have completed this book without Jan's assistance and support.

Sharon Boatwright listened to my daily groans or celebrations. The highlight of this entire writing process was when she personally delivered a box of chocolates.

Maureen Taylor (Massachusetts) and Kay Ingalls (California) were my long-distance support team. They not only read the entire book and gave valuable critiques, but they also shared their own writing experiences with me so I knew it was *normal* to feel overwhelmed, frustrated, or unable to write for a few days.

Julie Miller and Alvie Davidson were unwavering in their assistance. They never stopped asking "How can I help you?" and never hesitated to research those little details that I needed or to photocopy a page for my reference. Their fingerprints are hidden throughout the book.

The maps beginning on page 240 were adapted with permission from Ani-Map County Boundary Historical Atlas. The AniMap Plus software is available from The Gold Bug Store <www.goldbug.com>. A special thank-you to Adrian Ettlinger, who customized the maps for print format.

My daughters, Shauna and Jessica, are impressed that their mother is an author. I am more impressed with them as young women establishing their own career paths with energy and dynamic goals. A special thank-you to my son, Joshua, for helping me appreciate today, learn from the past, and have hope for the future.

My mother and father taught me to believe in myself and to face challenges with courage and determination. Their unconditional love and support made it possible to step outside my envelope and devote energy to writing. They think this book will sell a million copies. How lucky am I to have such big fans?

Twelve friends/colleagues read my manuscript during the writing process and helped polish the text. Thank You to Sharon Boatwright, Alvie Davidson, Roger Dudley, Sherril Erfurth, Gordon Gray, Jim Hansen, Birdie Holsclaw, Kay Ingalls, Julie Miller, Jan Prater, Pat Stamm, and Maureen Taylor.

## Contributors

# Table of Contents At a Glance

# Table of Contents

*Incarceration: Massachusetts; Reasons for Incarceration: Iowa; North Dakota Artist • Duplicate Entries; Case Study: Same City, Different Addresses and Dates; Case Study: Same Address, Different Dates; Case Study: Same Family, Adults' First and Middle Names Reversed; Case Study: Same Person in Two Different Households; Case Study: Same Family in Two Different States; Case Study: Neighborhood Double-Counted • Three Swedish Families Without Names; Court Case Against Enumerator; Male Reported as Female; Born "on the Plains"; 1880 Seminole Indian Village Includes Adopted Black Female; Unorganized Census Pages; Slaves Listed in Free Schedule in 1850 for Collin County, Texas; Incomplete, Confusing, and Peculiar Census Entries in 1810 for Columbus County, North Carolina; 1820 Census Marshal Added Identifiers • Discovering More Census Anomalies*

**For an exclusive update on using the 1930 census after these records are released on 1 April 2002, go to <www.familytreemagazine.com/ articles/1930 census.html>.**

# Icons Used in This Book

 **Brick Wall Buster**
How to turn dead ends into opportunities

 **Case Study**
Examples of this book's advice at work

 **Citing Sources**
Reminders and methods for documenting information

**\di'fin\** *vb*
**Definitions**
Terminology and jargon explained

 **For More Info**
Where to turn for more in-depth coverage

 **Idea Generator**
Techniques and prods for further thinking

 **Important**
Information and tips you can't overlook

 **Internet Source**
Where on the Web to find what you need

 **Notes**
Thoughts, ideas, and related insights

 **Printed Source**
Directories, books, pamphlets, and other paper archives

 **Quotes**
Useful words direct from the experts

 **Reminder**
"Don't-Forget" items to keep in mind

 **Research Tip**
Ways to make research more efficient

 **Sources**
Where to go for information, supplies, etc.

 **Step By Step**
Walkthroughs of important procedures

 **Timesaver**
Shaving minutes and hours off the clock

 **Tip**
Ways to make research more efficient

 **Warning**
Stop before you make a mistake

# Introduction

I remember the first time I viewed a census record—twenty-five years ago. I lived in Waseca, Minnesota, and used my local library's interlibrary loan program to borrow the 1880 census microfilm. My five-year-old daughter was with me with her crayons and coloring book as I cranked the microfilm reader handle. After nearly an hour of reading each census page, I finally found a familiar name. The handwritten page listed my Swedish great-grandparents on their Minnesota farm, and for the first time, my ancestors seemed like real people. I wanted to shout out loud that I'd found my family, but the quiet library restrained me.

My quest to learn more about my ancestors has not diminished since that unforgettable day. But census research *has* changed—dramatically. In 1977 the 1910, 1920, and 1930 censuses were not yet available to the public because of privacy laws. Printed indexes were just beginning to be published, and microfilm was the only format available. Who could have imagined that twenty-five years later you could view census images on a computer screen in your own home?

Although technology has improved the format and accessibility of census records, the research methodology has *not* changed. You still need to compare and analyze information and merge the census data with your other research in order to make sound genealogical conclusions. The census remains the most valuable record resource to document families, communities, and social history. The census is the most complete and democratic record available, as it includes everyone, regardless of race, age, wealth, or occupation. Both the famous and the infamous will be found in census records.

For example, American painter Georgia O'Keeffe (1887–1986) is listed on line 86 in the 1920 census (see next page). She was thirty-two and living at 114 East Fifty-Ninth Street in New York City. This census entry verifies the accuracy of Susan Wright's remark in *Georgia O'Keeffe: An Eternal Spirit* (Todri, 1996), page 24: "O'Keeffe painted all day, living and working on the top floor of a brownstone on Fifty-Ninth Street."

O'Keeffe's Manhattan neighborhood was a true melting pot with immigrants from Africa, Austria, Germany, Greece, Holland, Ireland, Poland, Russia, Scotland, Sweden, and Switzerland. There were fourteen other persons residing in O'Keeffe's brownstone. Wouldn't it be interesting to find out if their descendants know that their ancestor lived near such a famous artist? Census research gives insight into such possibilities.

Enjoy your exploration into census records, and savor each morsel of information. And when you receive a census questionnaire in 2010, be sure to complete the form and return it according to the instructions. When the census is released according to privacy laws in 2082, there may be a genealogist in your family who will want to see your answers.

9–137

DEPARTMENT OF COMMERCE—BUREAU OF THE

FOURTEENTH CENSUS OF THE UNITED STATES:

STATE _New York_
COUNTY _New York_
TOWNSHIP OR OTHER DIVISION OF COUNTY _15ᵗʰ Assembly District_
NAME OF INCORPORATED PLACE _____
NAME OF INSTITUTION _____
ENUMERATED BY ME ON TH[...]

The census schedule (partial, Georgia O'Keeffe household) records names, relation, personal description, citizenship, education, and nativity columns for residents enumerated at sheet 11B.

Georgia O'Keeffe lived in a brownstone on Fifty-ninth Street in Manhattan when she was enumerated in the 1920 census.

Georgia O'Keefe [sic] household, 1920 U.S. census, New York County, New York, population schedule, Fifteenth Assembly District, Manhattan borough, supervisor's district (S.D.) 1, enumerator district (E.D.) 1066, sheet 11B; National Archives micropublication T625, roll 1213.

: CENSUS     [D1—576]

## 1920—POPULATION

**SUPERVISOR'S DISTRICT No.** *1st*     **SHEET No.**

**ENUMERATION DISTRICT No.** *1066*     *11* **B**

*Manhattan Borough*

**WARD OF CITY** _____ *92*

E ___ *13* ___ DAY OF *January* , 1920. *Harry Dreyfach* ENUMERATOR. *624*

| Place of birth (Father) 21 | Mother tongue (Father) 22 | Place of birth (Mother) 23 | Mother tongue (Mother) 24 | Whether able to speak English 25 | Trade, profession 26 | Industry 27 | 28 | 29 | |
|---|---|---|---|---|---|---|---|---|---|
| many | German | Germany | German | Yes | Manager | Household duties | W | | 51 |
| many | German | Germany | German | Yes | none | | | | 52 |
| many | German | Germany | German | Yes | Chauffer | Private family | W | | 53 |
| antry | German | Tennessee | | Yes | Teacher | Piano | W | | 54 |
| tria | Austrian | Austria | German | Yes | Developer | Moving Picture | W | | 55 |
| v York | | New York | | Yes | Engineer | Club House | W | | 56 |
| ssia | Russian | Russia | Russian | Yes | Watchman | club | W | | 57 |
| rmany | German | Germany | German | Yes | Caterer | Club | In | | 58 |
| many | German | Germany | German | Yes | none | | | | 59 |
| many | German | Germany | German | Yes | School | | | | 60 |
| many | German | Germany | German | Yes | School | | | | 61 |
| many | German | Germany | German | Yes | | | | | 62 |
| many | German | Germany | German | Yes | Porter | Club | W | | 63 |
| issed | Polish | Island | Polish | Yes | Porter | Club | W | | 64 |
| and | Polish | Island | Polish | Yes | Porter | Club | W | | 65 |
| zirland | German | Switzerland | German | Yes | none | | | | 66 |
| zirland | German | Switzerland | German | Yes | Governess | Private family | W | | 67 |
| and | English | Ireland | English | Yes | Caretaker | Public Library | W | | 68 |
| and | English | Ireland | English | Yes | none | | | | 69 |
| land | English | Ireland | English | Yes | Clerk | Express Co | W | | 70 |
| land | English | Ireland | English | | | | | | 71 |
| land | English | Ireland | English | | | | | | 72 |
| eland | English | Ireland | English | Yes | Motorman | Street car | W | | 73 |
| US | | US | | | | | | | 74 |
| US | | US | | | | | | | 75 |
| ssia | Russia | Russia | Russian | Yes | keeper | Restaurant | En | | 76 |
| ssia | Russia | Russia | Russia | Yes | none | | | | 77 |
| ssia | Russian | Russia | Russian | Yes | Bookkeeper | Music | W | | 78 |
| ssia | Russian | Russia | Russian | Yes | none | | | | 7 |
| rmany | German | Georgia | | Yes | Artist | Studio | OA | | 8 |
| eden | Sweden | Sweden | Swedish | Yes | Dealer | art | Sa | | 8 |
| edish | Swedish | Sweden | Swedish | Yes | School | | | | 8 |
| nnecticut | | New York | | Yes | Student | Medical | | | 8 |
| eland | English | Ireland | Eng Art | Yes | Nurse | | W | | 8 |
| York | | New York | | Yes | Student | Medical | | | 8 |
| consin | | Wisconsin | | Yes | Artist | At home | OA | | 8 |
| ryland | | Maryland | | Yes | Lawyer | Insurance | W | | 8 |
| nectient | | New York | | Yes | none | | | | 8 |
| aryland | | New York | | Yes | School | | | | 8 |
| aryland | | New York | | | | | | | 8 |
| consin | | Wisconsin | | Yes | Artist | Decorator | OA | | 8 |
| chigan | | Massachusetts | | Yes | Teacher | High School | W | | 8 |
| eland | English | Ireland | English | Yes | Keeper | Lodgers | OA | | 8 |
| eland | Dutch | Holland | Dutch | Yes | Teacher | Music | OA | | 8 |
| gland | English | England | English | Yes | Manager | Hall Cafe | W | | 8 |
| w York | | New York | | Yes | Artist | Leisure | OA | | 8 |
| eland | English | Ireland | English | Yes | Keeper | Lodgers | OA | | 8 |
| eden | Swedish | Sweden | Swedish | Yes | none | | | | 8 |
| rmany | German | Germany | German | Yes | Buyer | Jewelry | OA | | 8 |
| ece | Greek | Greece | Greek | Yes | Waiter | Restaurant | W | | 8 |

# PART ONE

---

# Introduction
# to the Census

# ONE

# Census Content

American citizens have grumbled about personal questions in the federal census ever since Congress mandated counting the U.S. population to determine representation in the House of Representatives. The 2000 census was no exception, with many accusing Uncle Sam of invading their privacy.

In the beginning, the government merely counted the population and placed individuals into age categories by head of household. Each successive census had more questions to gather statistics for government planning such as military pension expenses, housing needs, and economic predictors.

The cartoon in the 18 August 1860 issue of *The Saturday Evening Post* (see page 6) captured the nation's reaction to the 1860 census questions, yet put a humorous spin on the situation.

Questions such as those in the 1860 cartoon continued every ten years. By 1900, Uncle Sam required immigrants to report their year of immigration and whether they could speak English. In 1930, the government wanted to know if the family owned a radio set; and thirty years later, Uncle Sam asked if there was a flush toilet in the house or building.

The census questions may seem odd or even intrusive, but in the process Uncle Sam inadvertently created a record group that is *the* most important source in American genealogy and history. As outlined in the following sections, the census provides information or clues fundamental to genealogical research.

## HOW THE 1790–1930 CENSUSES HELP GENEALOGISTS

*Note: Less than 1 percent of the original 1890 population census schedules survived a fire in 1921. See chapter three for more information.*

### Name

The 1790 through 1840 census enumerations listed only the head of household by name, whereas the 1850 and later returns included the name of each individ-

**Figure 1-1**
"I jist want to know how many of yez is deaf, dumb, blind, insane and idiotic—likewise how many convicts there is in the family—what all your ages are, especially the old woman and the young ladies—and how many dollars the old gentleman is worth!" *The Saturday Evening Post*, Aug. 18, 1860.

ual residing in a household. It was not until 1870 that everyone was named in the census record, i.e., former slaves and Indians not taxed were named individually for the first time.

**Tip: The name of an individual shown on a census return often varies from census to census.** For example, the 1850 census may report J.E. Anderson; the 1860 census, John E. Anderson; and the 1870 census, John Edward Anderson. One year the census may report Jack (a nickname for John), or the first and middle name may get reversed to read Edward J. Anderson.

Comparing how a name was reported census by census is a valuable technique to gather the full name of an ancestor. The census can sometimes be the only source for finding a middle name or nickname.

## Address

The 1880 census was the first enumeration to report the street name and house number. All census records since then provide space for this information, but the enumerator does not always record it.

Earlier census returns report the county of residence and often the name of a post office, city, district, township, and/or parish.

It is not uncommon for the post office listed to be that of the enumerator rather than of the people enumerated. It is most noticeable when the post office listed is the same for an entire township or district in an era when the nearest post office in settled areas was rarely more than a few miles away. This can be misleading when you presume a location within the district because of the post office listed in the census.

Tip: There are always exceptions to the rule. For example, the 1790 Philadelphia census gives the street addresses and occupations of individuals—information not normally found in that census.

## Age or Date of Birth

The 1790 through 1840 census enumerations divide family members by sex and age ranges, such as 0–10, 10–16, 16–20, etc.

The 1830 census was the first census to include an age category of over one hundred years; prior to that, the oldest age category was over forty-five, and 1790 merely divided men and women by age under sixteen or over sixteen.

The 1850 through 1930 returns report the age of each member of the household. In 1900, the month and year of birth is also reported for each individual.

Tip: Sometimes the date of the enumeration can give a clue as to the date of birth when the calculated age varies from one census to the next. Also remember that knowing one's age was not as important as it is today, and aging inconsistencies flourish in the census. Ages that end in zero or five, such as forty or forty-five, may be estimates rather than exact ages.

The 1870 and 1880 censuses report the month of birth, but only for persons who were born "within the year," meaning in the twelve months prior to the date of the census rather than in the current calendar year.

Beginning in 1850, young children's ages are often reported as fractions, such as $5/12$ (five months), or $1\,1/12$ (one year, one month).

For ages of Indians, see "Indians" at page 12.

## Place of Birth

The 1850 through 1930 census schedules report the place of birth (state or country) of each member of the household.

Beginning with 1880, the birthplace of each individual's mother and father is also listed. If the birthplace was a foreign country, it was to be named as specifically as possible. For example, England, Scotland, or Wales was to be reported rather than Great Britain. Instead of Germany, they were to specify the state such as Prussia, Baden, Bavaria, Württemberg, Hesse, or Darmstadt.

Tip: In 1900 and 1910, enumerators were instructed to report the birthplace by its *current* region rather than the name of the place at the time of the birth. This is why you might find for an individual West Virginia, North Dakota, South Dakota, or Oklahoma as the state of birth even though the state had been created after the date of birth.

If a person was born outside of the United States, the 1900 and 1910 census instructions were to report Germany rather than Prussia or Saxony. They were to record Ireland, England, Scotland, or Wales rather than Great Britain, and Hungary or Bohemia rather than Austria. They were told to write Finland rather than Russia for persons born in Finland. The 1910 instructions added

## PRE-1850 CENSUS BIRTH DATE CALCULATION TABLE

This chart can be used to calculate, based on the indicated age group, the approximate period in which a person was born. The math is simply a matter of subtraction of the age group spans from the census year. For example, for the 1810 census, one age column was "of 16 and under 26." This means the person was already sixteen years old by census day in 1810 and, therefore, was born no later than 1794. If the person was "under 26," or at most twenty-five, then the birth was no earlier than 1785. However, the twenty-sixth birthday could have occurred after census day in the census year, in which case the birth could have been in 1784.

| Census Year | Age | Year of Birth |
|---|---|---|
| 1790 | Over 16<br>Under 16 | 1774 or earlier<br>1774–1790 |
| 1800 | Under 10<br>10–16<br>16–26<br>26–45<br>45+ | 1790–1800<br>1784–1790<br>1774–1784<br>1755–1774<br>1755 or earlier |
| 1810 | Under 10<br>10–16<br>16–26<br>26–45<br>45+ | 1800–1810<br>1794–1800<br>1784–1794<br>1765–1784<br>1765 or earlier |
| 1820 | Under 10<br>10–16<br>16–18<br>16–26<br>26–45<br>45+ | 1810–1820<br>1804–1810<br>1802–1804<br>1794–1804<br>1775–1794<br>1775 or earlier |
| 1830 | Under 5<br>5–10<br>10–15<br>15–20<br>20–30<br>30–40<br>40–50<br>50–60<br>60–70<br>70–80<br>80–90<br>90–100<br>100+ | 1825–1830<br>1820–1825<br>1815–1820<br>1810–1815<br>1800–1810<br>1790–1800<br>1780–1790<br>1770–1780<br>1760–1770<br>1750–1760<br>1740–1750<br>1730–1740<br>1730 or earlier |
| 1840 | Under 5<br>5–10<br>10–15<br>15–20<br>20–30<br>30–40<br>40–50<br>50–60<br>60–70<br>70–80<br>80–90<br>90–100<br>100+ | 1835–1840<br>1830–1835<br>1825–1830<br>1820–1825<br>1810–1820<br>1800–1810<br>1790–1800<br>1780–1790<br>1770–1780<br>1760–1770<br>1750–1760<br>1740–1750<br>1740 or earlier |

Used with permission from Roger D. Joslyn, CG, FASG

---

**CENSUS TRIVIA**

The census is rich in genealogical information beyond the simple list of names, addresses, and ages. Chapter one demonstrates the depth of genealogical data that can be gleaned from census records. **A resourceful genealogist uses census statistics and trivia to enhance her knowledge of an ancestor's life.**

Life expectancy in 1790 was about thirty-five years for the total population. By 1900 it had reached 46.3 years for men and 48.3 years for women, and by 1950 it had jumped to 65.6 years for men and 71.1 years for women.

---

that if a person was born in Turkey, *Turkey in Europe* should be distinguished from *Turkey in Asia*.

The government advised the enumerators in 1900 to 1930 to report "at sea" if a person was born at sea.

## Date of Marriage

The 1850 through 1890 censuses asked if any person had married within the past year, meaning the twelve months prior to the date of the census. If this column was checked, you can estimate the date of the marriage to within one year.

The marital status (single, married, widowed, or divorced) was first reported in 1880 and continued through 1930. The 1900 and 1910 censuses asked for the length of the present marriage. In 1910, enumerators were instructed to ask married persons whether they had been married before. For a first marriage, the enumerator wrote "M1," but for second or subsequent marriage, he wrote "M2" (meaning married more than once). A third marriage may therefore be reported as M2 rather than M3.

The 1900 and 1910 Indian Schedules asked the number of times married and if the Indian man was living with more than one wife (polygamy). In 1910, they also asked if the wives were sisters.

In 1930, married persons were asked to report their age at their *first* marriage. Enumerators were to be cautious with this question. When it was evident to the enumerator that it was a first marriage, he was to ask for "age at marriage" rather than "age at first marriage," or to ask the question on this form and then make certain that the parties had not been married before.

**Tip: You can approximate the year of marriage of a couple based on the year of birth of the eldest child,** but be careful to allow for second marriages and stepparenting.

The approximate date of marriage can also be estimated by noting the last census year when an individual was single and the first census year in which they were married. This can only be done beginning with the 1880 census since that was the first year marital status was reported.

## Number of Children

Prior to 1850, children were counted within age categories and not named individually. Beginning with the 1850 census, each child is listed separately with age, birthplace, and whether he attended school.

The 1890 through 1910 censuses reported how many children were born to each female and how many of those children were still living at the time of the census.

Tip: **Compare the total number of children for each given census year with your family data to ascertain if you have recorded all children.** Remember that there may have been stillbirths or infant deaths between census years.

## Date and/or Cause of Death

The 1850 through 1880 and 1885 (Colorado, Dakota Territory, Florida, Nebraska, and New Mexico Territory only) censuses include a mortality schedule that gives information about persons who died in the twelve months preceding the census. Information gathered includes the month of death and name of the disease or cause of death. See chapter four for a complete discussion of mortality schedules.

In 1880 persons were asked if they were sick or temporarily disabled on the day of the enumeration, and if so, the reason.

The 1890 census asked if anyone was suffering from an acute or chronic disease, and if so, the name of the disease and length of time afflicted.

Tip: **You can approximate the date of death of some individuals within ten years by noting their appearance in one census and nonappearance in the following census.** The nonappearance, however, is not solid proof but merely a clue that the person was deceased. Seek other records to prove the death date.

For a woman listed as a widow with children under the age of ten, you can approximate her husband's death date as between the date of conception of the youngest child and that of the census.

Beginning with 1880, a person's marital status is reported; therefore, if an individual was a widow or widower, you can approximate the death date of the spouse. Some persons reported that they were widowed when in fact they were divorced. And some divorced persons may have reported that they were single. Be aware of these possibilities.

## Relationship to Head of Household

Household relationships were first reported in the 1880 census.

Tip: **Stepchildren are not always clearly identified in the census.** For example, stepchildren of a male head of household may be reported with the stepfather's surname and listed as his children. But other information, such as the children's ages and the couple's date of marriage, may suggest that they were stepchildren. Carefully analyze ages, birthplaces, and marriage dates to properly compile family relationships.

Tip: **Do not dismiss boarders as nonrelatives.** Often a boarder was actually a distant relative such as a cousin or nephew. For all census years, beware of making incorrect relationship conclusions or assumptions.

# Race

The first census to report the number of "colored" persons was in 1820. "Free colored" were listed in the 1820 to 1840 censuses by name if they were the head of household and counted statistically as "other free persons" or "slaves" in the 1790 to 1810 censuses.

A free Negro was an individual whose ancestors had never been slaves, such as a descendant of indentured servants; who was born of a free parent(s); who had been manumitted; who had bought his own freedom; or who was a successful runaway.

Beginning in 1850, the color of each person was to be reported as follows:
- 1850: White, black, or mulatto
- 1860: White, black, or mulatto
- 1870: White, black, mulatto, Chinese, or Indian
- 1880: White, black, mulatto, Chinese, or Indian

Enumerators were cautioned to be careful reporting mulatto because it was a generic term and included quadroons, octoroons, and all persons having any perceptible trace of African blood.
- 1890: White, black, mulatto (one-half Negro blood), quadroon (one-quarter Negro blood), octoroon (one-eighth Negro blood), Chinese, Japanese, or Indian
- 1900: White, black (Negro or of Negro descent), Chinese, Japanese, or Indian

The 1910 and 1920 censuses defined *mulatto* as all persons having any trace of Negro blood.

Special instructions in 1910 noted that for persons who did not fall into one of the predefined races, the enumerator was to write "Ot" (for *other*) in the race column and write the race on the left-hand margin of the schedule.

The 1930 instructions were specific:
- A person of mixed white and Negro blood was considered Negro, no matter how small the percentage of Negro blood.
- A person who was part Indian and part Negro was also to be listed as Negro unless the Indian blood predominated and the person was generally accepted as an Indian in the community.
- A person of mixed white and Indian blood was to be reported as an Indian, except where the percentage of Indian blood was very small or where he or she was regarded as white in the community. American Indians were to report the degree of Indian blood and the tribe in the column intended for birthplace of the father and mother.
- Persons who were born in Mexico or to parents born in Mexico and were not definitely white, Negro, Indian, Chinese, or Japanese were classified as Mexicans. Any mixture of white and any other race was to be reported according to the race of the parent who was not white. Mixtures of colored races—except Negro-Indian, which is discussed above—were to be listed according to the father's race.

**Tip:** Although these specific instructions on reporting race were given to the enumerators, **many persons were reported as white when, in fact, they should have been reported as mulatto, Indian, Negro, or another race.**

Because of the limitations of the early census form, which had no "Red" or "Indian" category, Native Americans or persons of mixed white and Native American origin were often reported as black or mulatto.

It is not unusual for the racial identification of a person to vary from census to census. Different enumerators made conflicting judgments, and society's racial attitudes influenced the responses from individuals.

## Slaves

From 1800 to 1840, slaves appeared only as counts by age under the name of the slave owner.

Slaves were counted in 1850 and 1860 in separate slave schedules, but again only under the name of the slave owner. The individual names of the slaves were not reported. The schedules did, however, ask for the age, sex, and color of each slave; whether he was deaf-mute, blind, insane, or idiotic; and whether he was a fugitive from the state.

The slave schedule was not intended for use in the free states, yet schedules exist for 1850 for New Jersey and 1850 and 1860 for the District of Columbia.

**Tip: Researching court, property, and probate records of the slave owner sometimes reveals specific information about the names and ages of slaves.**

See chapter ten for more on researching black persons in the census.

## Indians

Very few Indians were named or counted in early census reports because the enumerators were instructed to include only Indians who were taxed, meaning those who did *not* live on the reservations. Indians not taxed included the few who had severed their tribal affiliations and mingled with the white population by, for example, marrying into white families or residing in huts or tepees on the outskirts of towns or settlements.

Indians were counted for the first time in 1860 and in the category "civilized Indians," meaning those living among the general population and paying taxes. Indians retaining tribal connections were estimated in number.

The 1880 census was the first to instruct enumerators to use a race classification of "Indian."

**Tip: Check census indexes for the surname Indian.** Chapter ten gives examples of Indians enumerated under that surname, plus it gives other information on locating Native Americans in the census.

The government warned the census enumerators in 1900 through 1920 that ascertaining the exact age of Indians may be difficult because they frequently reckoned their age from notable events that occurred in the history of their tribes. The enumerator was to try to determine when those events occurred and then calculate the Indians' ages accordingly.

Special instructions were given in 1930 regarding Indians. Enumerators were instructed to report the degree of Indian blood (whether full or mixed) and the name of the tribe. Since there was not a designated column for this information, enumerators were told to place the data in the column normally used for place of birth of the parents of the individual.

## Citizenship, Ethnicity, and Nationality

The 1820 census asked for the number of persons not naturalized, thus giving a clue about foreign-born family members.

In 1830 and 1840, the census asked for the number of aliens.

The 1870 census indicates if a person had foreign-born parents, although it does not report the country of their birth.

The schedules in 1870 also include columns checked if male citizens over age twenty-one could vote (column 19) or if their right to vote had been denied or abridged on grounds other than rebellion or other crime (column 20).

Tip: If citizenship was not checked for a foreign-born individual, this is a clue to search for immigration and naturalization records for the individual. Foreign-born persons who were naturalized were citizens and could vote.

The 1880 through 1930 censuses asked for the birthplace of the mother and father of each person, thus giving clues or direct information on ethnicity or nationality of the family.

Instructions in 1920 and 1930 called for reporting the birthplace of a person born abroad to American parents and adding "Am. cit." to indicate American citizenship.

The 1930 census asked what language a person spoke in the home before coming to the United States—an excellent clue to ethnic origins.

Tip: Research the boundaries of countries and obtain maps specific for each time period of the census. Birthplaces such as Germany, Austria, Switzerland, Turkey, and Poland can be confusing unless you consult maps.

## Year of Immigration

For the 1900 through 1930 censuses immigrants were to report their year of immigration to the United States.

Tip: Immigrants sometimes unintentionally gave incorrect dates. Therefore, search immigration records for the period from five years before to five years after the date reported.

## Naturalization

In 1890, persons were asked if naturalization papers had been filed.

The 1900 through 1930 censuses indicate the person's naturalization status: "Al" for alien, "Pa" for first papers (Declaration of Intention) filed, and "Na" for naturalized. "NR," indicating "not reported," is often added to the Soundex cards.

The 1920 census also asked for the year in which a person was naturalized. Remember that the year may not be correct, just as ages and year of immigration are not always accurate.

Tip: The 1870 census asked males over age twenty-one if they were citizens of the United States. If foreign-born people checked this column, they had become naturalized by 1870.

| 1920 AND 1930 CENSUSES: FOREIGN LANGUAGES | |
|---|---|
| The enumerators were given the following list of foreign languages that were likely to be reported in the 1920 and 1930 censuses as the mother tongue or native language of foreign-born persons: | |
| Albanian | The Indo-European language of Albania. |
| Arabic | A Semitic language, consisting of numerous dialects, that is the principal language of Arabia, Jordan, Syria, Iraq, Lebanon, Egypt, and parts of northern Africa. |
| Armenian | The Indo-European language of Armenia. |
| Basque | The language of the Basques, of no known linguistic affiliation. The Basques are a people of unknown origin inhabiting the western Pyrenees in France and Spain. |
| Bohemian | See "Czech." |
| Breton | The Celtic language of Brittany, which is a region of northwestern France. |
| Bulgarian | The Slavic language of Bulgaria. |
| Chinese | Any of the dialects spoken by the Chinese people. |
| Croatian | The Slavic language of Croatia. |
| Czech | The Slavic language of the Czechs, who are defined as natives or inhabitants of Czechoslovakia, especially Bohemians, Moravians, or Slovaks. |
| Dalmatian | The language of Dalmatia, a seaside region of Croatia. |
| Danish | The North Germanic language of Denmark. |
| Dutch | The West Germanic language of the Netherlands. |
| Egyptian | The language of Egypt. |
| English | The West Germanic language of England, the United States, and other countries that are or have been under English influence or control. |
| Estonian | The Finno-Ugric language of Estonia. |
| Finnish | The Finno-Ugric language of Finland. |
| Flemish | The Low German language of Flemings. A Fleming is a native of Flanders or a Belgian who speaks Flemish. |
| French | The Romance language of France, Switzerland, parts of Belgium, and other countries formerly under French influence of control. |
| Frisian | The West Germanic language of the Frisian Islands or Friesland. |
| Fujian | A dialect of Chinese spoken in Fujian Province, eastern Guangdong Province, and Taiwan. |
| Gaelic | The language of Scotland, Ireland, and the Isle of Man. |
| Georgian | The language of Soviet Georgia. |
| German | The West Germanic language of Germany, Austria, and part of Switzerland. |

| | |
|---|---|
| **Great Russian** | The language of central and northeastern Russia. |
| **Greek** | The Indo-European language of Greece. |
| **Gypsy** | The Indic language of Gypsies. |
| **Hebrew** | The Semitic language of the ancient Hebrews or later forms of this language, especially the language of the Israelis. |
| **Hindi** | The language spoken in India, especially northern India. |
| **Icelandic** | The North Germanic language of Iceland. |
| **Irish** | The language of Ireland. |
| **Italian** | The Romance language of the Italians and one of the three official languages of Switzerland. |
| **Japanese** | The language of Japan. |
| **Korean** | The language of Korea. |
| **Kurdish** | The Iranian language of the Kurds. |
| **Lappish** | The Finno-Ugric language of Lapland. |
| **Lettish** | The Baltic language of the Latvians. |
| **Lithuanian** | The Baltic language of Lithuania. |
| **Little Russian** | The East Slavic language spoken in Ukraine and in Ukrainian communities in neighboring Belarus, Russia, Poland, and Slovakia. |
| **Macedonian** | The Slavic language of modern Macedonia. |
| **Magyar** | The Finno-Ugric language of the Magyars. It is the official language of Hungary. |
| **Montenegrin** | The language of Montenegro, a Slavonic principality on the east of the Adriatic. |
| **Moravian** | See ''Czech.'' |
| **Norwegian** | The North Germanic language of Norway. |
| **Persian** | The language of Persia and Iran. |
| **Polish** | The Slavic language of Poland. |
| **Portuguese** | The Romance language of Portugal and Brazil. |
| **Romansch** | The Rhaeto-Romantic dialects of eastern Switzerland and neighboring parts of Italy. |
| **Rumanian** | The Romance language of Rumania. |
| **Russian** | The Slavic language of Russia. |
| **Ruthenian** | The Ukrainian dialect of the Ruthenians. |
| **Scotch** | The language of Scotland. |
| **Serbian** | The language of southern Slavic people in Serbia and adjacent republics of Yugoslavia. |
| **Slovak** | The language of Slovakia. |
| **Slovenian** | The Slavic language of Slovenia. |

| Spanish | The Romance language of Spain and most of Central America and South America. |
|---|---|
| Swedish | The North Germanic language of Sweden. |
| Syrian | The language of Syria. |
| Turkish | The language of Turkey. |
| Ukrainian | The Slavic language of the Ukraine. It is closely related to Russian. |
| Walloon | A dialect of French spoken by the Walloons. A Walloon is one of a French-speaking people of Celtic descent inhabiting southern and southeastern Belgium and adjacent regions of France. |
| Welsh | The Celtic language of Wales. |
| Wendish | The Slavic language of the Wends (of Saxony and Brandenburg). |
| White Russian | The East Slavic language of Belarus. |
| Yiddish | A High German language with many words borrowed from Hebrew and Slavic that is written in Hebrew characters and spoken chiefly as a vernacular in Eastern European Jewish communities throughout the world. |
| Finno-Ugric | A subfamily of the Uralic language family that includes Finnish, Hungarian, and other languages of Eastern Europe and northwestern U.S.S.R. |
| Indo-European | A family of languages consisting of most of the languages of Europe as well as those of Iran, the Indian subcontinent, and other parts of Asia. |
| North Germanic | A subdivision of the Germanic languages that includes Norwegian, Icelandic, Swedish, Danish, and Faeroese. |
| Romance | Languages that developed from Latin. |
| Slavic | A branch of the Indo-European language family that includes Bulgarian, Belorussian, Czech, Polish, Russian, Serbo-Croatian, Slovak, Slovene, and Ukrainian. |
| West Germanic | A subdivision of the Germanic languages that includes High German, Low German, Yiddish, Dutch, Afrikaans, Flemish, Frisian, and English. |

## Occupation

The 1820 and 1830 censuses give statistics on number of persons engaged in agriculture, commerce, or manufacturing within each family.

The 1840 census reports the number of persons engaged in mining; agriculture; commerce; manufacturing and trade; navigation of the ocean; navigation of canals, lakes, and rivers; learned professions; and engineering.

The 1850 census was the first to report exact occupations. The marshals were instructed to record the occupation of all males (white and free black) over age fifteen. Women's occupations were *not* reported. The denomination of clergymen was to be noted.

Beginning in 1870, the census asked the profession, occupation, or trade of every male *and* female. This census was essentially the first to report child labor. The enumerators were told that if an individual, regardless of age, was working and earning money regularly and contributing to family support, the occupation was to be stated.

The 1880 census reported the number of months each worker was employed during the census year.

In 1910, 1920, and 1930, the type of industry was reported as well as the occupation. If a person was unemployed, the enumerator recorded the number of months in 1900 or number of weeks in 1910. In 1930 enumerators asked if people were at work "yesterday." An unemployment schedule was completed in 1930 for those without jobs, but the schedules were later destroyed and are not available for research.

**Tip: The occupation may be listed as "DO," meaning "ditto"**: the same as stated above. For example, if the occupation for the first entry is "farmer" and all others have "DO" in that column, those people also were farmers. "DO" may also occasionally appear in the name or birthplace column, particularly in the 1850 and 1860 censuses.

The Census Bureau coded occupations for their statistical evaluation of the population. You'll often see these numbers in the margin of the 1900 through 1930 census enumerations. The National Archives has not located master lists to decipher the occupation codes. See <www.ipums.umn.edu/~pipums/volii/toc ccode.html> for a full discussion of occupation coding by the University of Minnesota's Integrated Public Use Microdata Series.

See chapter four for information on manufacturing and agriculture supplemental schedules for the 1810, 1820, and 1850 through 1880 censuses.

## Migration

Beginning in 1850, the birthplace of each household member was reported, thereby providing information to track a family's migration from their homeland to the United States and from state to state.

**Tip: If a family had one or more children born in their homeland and additional children born in the United States, you can estimate the family's date of arrival into the United States as being between the dates of birth of the last foreign-born child and the first United States–born child.**

## Neighbors

Most census reports were completed by going door-to-door; therefore, the census can provide valuable information on neighbors. Advanced research methodology involves studying neighbors as another tool in developing more complete genealogical data. Neighbors, especially in rural areas, sometimes shared common ancestral roots and were related or later became related through marriages of children or grandchildren.

Households next door in the census were not necessarily physically next door to each other. After ending his count for the day, the enumerator may have started counting the next day in a different part of his district. One listing may be across the road, a mile down the valley, or over the hill from the previous listing. This means that families listed on the same page as your ancestors may have been their neighbors, but they were not technically next door.

See chapter eight for an example of plotting an 1830 neighborhood in Jefferson County, Alabama, and tracking the path of the enumerator. Families on lines 17 and 25 turned out to be neighbors, rather than families on lines 17, 18, and 19.

As discussed in chapter five, some surviving census manuscripts are not the original gathering of residential data, but handwritten copies where the community is rearranged alphabetically by last name, and sometimes by first name. This type of record, of course, destroys any analysis or information on specific neighborhood reconstruction.

Some 1790 census enumerations were not conducted door-to-door. The census marshal announced he was going to be at some central location in his district, and residents were supposed to come to him. This procedure was also followed sporadically in other areas or time periods.

**Tip: Every time you locate a family member in the census, photocopy three pages: the page with your family and one page before and after it.** You can then consult this partial record of neighbors during future research.

## Real Estate/Land Ownership

The 1850 through 1870 censuses recorded the value of real property (land) owned by each person. The cash value of farms was reported on the agriculture schedules in 1850 through 1880.

The 1900 through 1920 censuses asked whether a person owned or rented the home or farm, and if owned, whether mortgaged.

In 1930, the value of the home was also reported. If the home was rented, the amount of monthly rent was reported.

**Tip: Search for deed and mortgage records for anyone who owned a home or farm.**

See chapter four for information on agriculture schedules for 1840 through 1880.

## Personal Estate

The 1860 and 1870 censuses asked for the value of personal estate such as stocks, bonds, mortgages, notes, livestock, plates (china), jewels, and furniture, but not wearing apparel. In 1860 only, the value of slaves was included in the personal estate total. The column was left blank if the total property was worth less than one hundred dollars.

**Tip: Compare the value of personal estate among families to get an indication of their financial status.** Families with high personal estate values are more likely to have written wills that can be found in county probate records.

## Military Service

The names and ages of Revolutionary War or other military pensioners, or their widows, were reported in the 1840 census.

In 1880, all soldiers of the U.S. Army, civilian employees, and other residents at posts or on military reservations were to be enumerated in the district in which they normally resided.

Sailors temporarily at a sailors boarding or lodging house who acknowledged any other home within the United States were to be reported at their land home, not the boarding house.

The 1890 census asked whether a person was a Union or Confederate soldier, sailor, or marine during the Civil War or the widow of such a person.

The 1890 Special Union Veterans and Widows supplemental schedules gave a veteran's rank, company, regiment or vessel, dates of enlistment and discharge, length of service, post office address, and nature of any disability. Schedules survive for Washington, DC; about half of Kentucky; and all states alphabetically from Louisiana through Wyoming.

**Tip: For some Confederate soldiers mistakenly listed and then crossed out in the special schedule, the listings are still readable.** Do not eliminate researching this record if a family was Confederate.

In 1900, military personnel, even if they were on assignment, were to be enumerated with their families. This was also the first census to count American citizens abroad, including armed forces personnel and civilian government employees.

The 1910 census enumerators were instructed to ask all males over fifty years of age who were born in the United States and all foreign-born males who immigrated to the United States before 1865 if they were survivors of the Union Army ("UA"), Union Navy ("UN"), Confederate Army ("CA"), or Confederate Navy ("CN").

The 1930 census asked if a person was a veteran of the U.S. military or naval force and excluded persons who only served during peacetime. Persons who served in a war or expedition were asked which one: World War ("WW"), Spanish-American War ("Sp"), Civil War ("Civ"), Philippine Insurrection ("Phil"), Boxer Rebellion ("Box"), or Mexican Expedition ("Mex").

## Education/Illiteracy

The 1840 census was the first to ask for the number of persons attending school and the number of persons over age twenty-one who could not read and write. This was continued in 1850; however, the age changed from twenty-one to twenty for those who could not read and write.

The 1860 through 1930 census schedules reported whether persons attended school and if they could read and write.

**Tip: Local or state governments sometimes took a school census which usually included names and ages (or exact dates of birth) for the children and names, occupations, and addresses of the parents.** Content and availability varies among states. Check the state archives or library in your area of interest to determine if a school census exists.

## Disabilities (Deaf, Deaf-Mute, Blind, Dumb, Idiotic, or Insane)

The 1830 census was the first to identify persons as deaf and dumb or blind.

In the 1840 through 1870 censuses, the categories were deaf and dumb, blind, insane, or idiotic. Insane persons were described as suffering from mental impairment, including mania, melancholia, paresis (general paralysis), dementia, epilepsy, or dipsomania.

The 1850 and 1860 slave schedules did not list slaves individually, but they did ask for the number of slaves deaf-mute, blind, insane, or idiotic.

**Tip: In 1870, the government intended that only persons with total blindness and undoubted insanity be included in this section.** Deafness without the loss of speech was not to be reported.

In 1880 the government asked if anyone was permanently disabled and, if so, the nature of the disability. The 1880 census is the only enumeration that also has a separate schedule (Defective, Dependent, Delinquent Classes, aka DDD Schedules) that gives additional information about each individual marked in this category. See chapter four for details on these special schedules.

In 1890 the terminology was changed to ask if anyone was defective in mind, sight, hearing, or speech and whether crippled, maimed, or deformed (with name of defect).

The 1900, 1920, and 1930 censuses did not include questions regarding these afflictions.

In 1910, persons were asked if they were blind in both eyes. If a person was not blind in both eyes, the column was left blank. If a person was both deaf and dumb, the enumerator wrote "DD." For persons who were deaf but not dumb or dumb and not deaf, no such disability was reported.

**Tip: Remember to consider the time frame and medical knowledge for each census.** For example, a person who was having fits or was considered insane may have been an epileptic.

See chapter four for details regarding the 1850 through 1880 social statistics schedules that gave more information about this special population.

## Paupers and Convicts

The 1850 census asked if free persons or slaves were fugitives from the state.

The 1860 census indicates whether a person was a pauper or convict. If persons convicted of a crime during the year were residing with their families, the enumerator was to consult county records for information rather than ask the family.

In 1870, questions about paupers and convicts were removed from the population schedule because they were considered offensive; however, the questions reappeared one more time in the 1890 population schedule.

The 1880 non-population schedule Defective, Dependent, and Delinquent Classes (commonly known as DDD schedules) names homeless children and prisoners. See chapter four for more details.

**Tip: County court records may provide additional information on paupers, convicts, and homeless children.**

## EXTRA INFORMATION IN THE CENSUS

Uncle Sam obviously generated a gold mine for genealogists. The preceding pages cover nearly every type of information needed to compile a family history.

But sometimes enumerators listed extra information that not only is fun to find, but can be important to your research. The following section describes the types of surprises you might find.

## Place of Birth

Some enumerators added the county, or exact village in an immigrant's homeland, in the place of birth column. See chapter eleven for examples.

Occasionally, an enumerator added special comments, such as when the census marshal reported in 1830, "Sarah Wilder 103 years old born in Dunwoody [*sic*; should be Dinwiddle] County, Va." Sarah was in the household of Hardin Wilder, Washington Co., Virginia (National Archives micropublication M19, roll 200, pg. 299, line 23).

## Marriages

Sometimes we assume our ancestors married only once. The census may uncover other marriages or a family skeleton such as a man maintaining two households with his different wives.

## Medical

An enumerator might have added medical information such as the reason for the loss of a limb or that the family was quarantined for smallpox.

An enumerator's sense of humor, prejudice, or frustration shows up occasionally. In 1880 Oxford County, Maine (page 69B), Horace Morrill's occupation was reported as "chronic loafer." In 1880 Baker County, Oregon (page 9A), fifty-eight-year-old Stephen Cogsdale's occupation was listed as "drinks bad whiskey."

Often we can laugh at oddities found in records, but sometimes we also uncover hurtful items or family skeletons. Information found in the census, as in all genealogical research, must be balanced with an understanding of the circumstances and time period.

Most census research is tedious and uneventful, but discovering every possible piece of information about your ancestors is fun and necessary for a complete family history.

The census is the backbone of genealogy. It is one of the first records you should consult when beginning a research project, and you should continue to use it as your research progresses. We are fortunate that the federal government not only asked those personal questions every ten years, but also preserved the records for public examination.

# TWO

# History of the U.S. Federal Census

The U.S. federal census was mandated in 1787 by Article 1, Section 2 of the Constitution. The number of seats for each state in the House of Representatives was to be based upon population, as well as each state's tax assessments for Revolutionary War expenses. When President George Washington signed the Census Act in March 1790, the United States became the first country in the world to implement a comprehensive and regular count of its population.

## COUNTING THE POPULATION
### Who to Count and How to Count

From 1790 through 1860, Uncle Sam counted free males and their households who paid taxes and had the right to vote. Indians living on treaty land were not counted because they did not pay taxes or vote. Slaves were counted as three-fifths of a person. This mathematical equation was created for the benefit of states such as Virginia and South Carolina where slaves represented approximately 40 percent of the population.

Although the government established these specific rules for how to count

---

**CENSUS TRIVIA**

Herman Hollerith, a former Census Bureau employee, developed an electrical enumerating machine with punch cards for the 1890 Census. Using 105 of Hollerith's machines, the 1890 census count was completed in three years instead of the seven years it took to hand count the previous census. Hollerith went on to establish the Hollerith Tabulating Company, which was renamed International Business Machines (IBM) in 1924.

---

## HOOVER'S NAME COUNTED IN FEDERAL CENSUS

WASHINGTON, April 2 (AP)

Hardly had President Hoover been counted Wednesday in the fifteenth decennial census, upon which will be based a redistribution of the seats in the House of Representatives, before widely separated communities of the country began to report that they had finished their task.

A Missouri district, an Idaho district, and one from New Jersey reported to census headquarters here before the offices closed at 5 P.M. Wednesday that they had finished the tally of their residents.

Centertown, Cole County, in the exact geographical center of Missouri, by telegram to Director William M. Steuart, claimed the honor of being the first incorporated municipality to finish, and called a noon town meeting to celebrate.

President Hoover followed the census director's advice, given to everybody by press and by radio, to have answers to questions already prepared when the enumerator arrives.

The president had his typed. He also took advantage of Director Steuart's admonition that all information given to a census enumerator should be considered strictly confidential and made public only a few of his replies to census queries—that he was 54 years old; that he had been married at the age of 25; that his birthplace was West Branch, Iowa, his father's, Miami County, Ohio, and his mother's Ontario Province, Canada, although his mother's parents were born in Wooster, Ohio.

The president again expressed the hope that enumerators everywhere would be given the assistance "they deserve."

*Birmingham Age-Herald*, Birmingham, Alabama, Thursday, April 3, 1930, 1:5

---

the population, the rules were not always followed or understood. Rhode Island, for example, named all whites, Indians, and slaves in the 1890 census.

Congress modified Article 1, Section 2 of the Constitution in 1868 so that all persons who resided in the United States on census day would be counted, regardless of taxpayer status.

The greatest increase in population occurred between 1900 and 1910, one of the largest periods of immigration from Eastern Europe (see page 24).

## When to Count

Congress specified an official date for each census and allocated a time limit to gather the information (see page 26). Enumerators were instructed to record information from a household as if time had stopped on the census day, even though he may not have visited the home until days or weeks after the specified

| HOW MANY HAVE BEEN COUNTED | | |
|---|---|---|
| Year | Population (in millions) | Increase |
| 1790 | 3.9 (21 percent slaves) | — |
| 1800 | 5.3 (20 percent slaves) | 36 percent |
| 1810 | 7.2 (20 percent slaves) | 36 percent |
| 1820 | 9.6 (18 percent slaves) | 33 percent |
| 1830 | 12.9 (18 percent slaves) | 34 percent |
| 1840 | 17.1 (17 percent slaves) | 33 percent |
| 1850 | 23.2 (16 percent slaves) | 36 percent |
| 1860 | 31.4 (14 percent slaves) | 35 percent |
| 1870 | 38.6 | 23 percent |
| 1880 | 50.2 | 30 percent |
| 1890 | 63.0 | 25 percent |
| 1900 | 72.6 | 15 percent |
| 1910 | 92.2 | 27 percent |
| 1920 | 106.0 | 15 percent |
| 1930 | 123.2 | 16 percent |

**Important**

date. **Someone born after the census day was not to be counted. Similarly, persons who died after the census day were to be counted as living persons.** Although this was the rule, enumerators often recorded information as of the day they visited the families. Some families also misunderstood the questions and gave inaccurate answers.

## What They Asked

The first census was a relatively simple head count. As the government's desire for more exact information on a wide range of topics increased, so did the content of the census. The 1890 census contained a total of 13,161 questions—the highest in any census year. Note that 233 separate schedules covered twenty-two subjects such as agriculture, crime, insurance, mines and mining, manufacturing, and transportation. The majority of households answered about forty-five questions. Unfortunately only one percent of this enumeration survived a fire in 1921.

See Appendix B for lists of questions and maps for each census year of the population schedules. See chapter four for non-population schedules such as agriculture, mortality, and veterans.

## HISTORY OF PRIVACY

From 1790 through 1840 the census was a public record. Congress directed that the completed census schedules be posted "in two of the most important places" in the enumeration district. Copies of the schedules were therefore

## MOST COMMON SURNAMES
## A TWO HUNDRED–YEAR COMPARISON
## 1790 THROUGH 1990

| Rank | 1790 | 1990 |
|---|---|---|
| 1 | Smith | Smith |
| 2 | Brown | Johnson |
| 3 | Johnson | Williams |
| 4 | Davis | Jones |
| 5 | Jones | Brown |
| 6 | Clark | Davis |
| 7 | Williams | Miller |
| 8 | Miller | Wilson |
| 9 | Moore | Moore |
| 10 | Taylor | Taylor |

Comparing the two lists, the only common surname that appears for 1790 and not 1990 is Clark, which dropped to number 21 in 1990. Otherwise, the top ten surnames are basically the same with slight variations in rank. Wilson, number eight in 1990, was eleventh in 1790. To determine the ranking of your surname or first name in 1990, go to <www.census.gov/genealogy/www/freq names.html>.

Ed Hamrick developed software that graphically illustrates the distribution of the fifty thousand most common surnames in the United States in 1850, 1880, 1920, and 1990. The color of each state indicates how frequently persons with a specific surname reside within that state. Go to <www.hamrick.com/names> and experiment with your family's surnames. This may give you a fresh idea on places to research.

posted in public areas such as the courthouse, church, or saloon. Residents examined the census for accuracy and, if needed, made corrections. See chapter five for discussion on the survival of these extra copies.

In 1850, the secretary of the interior established the policy that census returns would be used exclusively by the government and "not to be used in any way to the gratification of curiosity, the exposure of any man's business or pursuits, or for the private emolument of the marshals or assistants."

Privacy was further assured when the 1880 Census Act required enumerators to take an oath not to disclose any information to anyone except their supervisors. The census returns were filed with the Department of the Interior rather than given to local officials, as was done in the past. Business information was protected, but information related to individuals was not. The director of the census could release personal information at his discretion for a standard fee.

In the early 1900s, the Census Bureau realized that businesses might analyze pieces of information from the census and be able to identify and obtain informa-

**Notes**

**CENSUS TRIVIA**

In 1790, a twenty-dollar fine (nearly ten times that in today's dollars) was levied against anyone who refused to answer the enumerator's questions. The government and the enumerator shared the money equally.

| CENSUS DAY | | |
|---|---|---|
| **Census Year** | **Census Day** | **Time Allotted** |
| 1790 | 2 August | nine months (took eighteen months) |
| 1800 | 4 August | nine months |
| 1810 | 6 August | ten months |
| 1820 | 7 August | thirteen months |
| 1830 | 1 June | twelve months |
| 1840 | 1 June | eighteen months |
| 1850 | 1 June | five months |
| 1860 | 1 June | five months |
| 1870 | 1 June | five months |
| 1880 | 1 June | one month |
| 1890 | 1 June | one month |
| 1900 | 1 June | one month |
| 1910 | 15 April | one month |
| 1920* | 1 January | one month |
| 1930 | 1 April<br>1 October 1929<br>(Alaska only) | one month |

*The Department of Agriculture requested the date change from the traditional April or June to January. Its reasoning was that harvests would be completed and information about the harvests would be fresh in the farmers' minds and that more people would be at home in January than in April. As it turned out, major snowstorms in January created serious delays in the enumeration.

## THE WOMEN'S BUREAU

The Women's Bureau was established in 1920 under the Department of Labor to develop policies and programs to economically benefit working women and improve their working conditions. In 1930, the government produced a motion picture called *Within the Gates* showing women working on farms and in factories, offices, and stores; in 1931, the film *Behind the Scenes in the Machine Age* depicting technological changes affecting female factory workers. These films are archived in Record Group 86 at the National Archives in Washington, DC.

tion about their competitors. Therefore the 1910 Census Act prohibited the Census Bureau from publishing any data that could be used to identify businesses.

Civil War veterans were able to obtain information from the director of the census to help them prove their eligibility for receiving a pension.

Since widespread requirement for birth certificates did not occur in most

---

## NEW FIREPROOF VAULT FOR 1930 CENSUS FACTS

WASHINGTON, March 29 (AP)

An immense fireproof vault is being completed at the Census Bureau to receive the 1930 "secrets" which everybody will be telling enumerators within three days.

"Strictly confidential" is the stamp placed by the president's proclamation on every item the people may tell to the 120,000 census takers who will start circulating through city and countryside on Wednesday morning.

Any one of a possible 20,000 questions may be answered freely and frankly, because all answers will be locked in the vault.

"There need be no fear that any disclosure will be made regarding any individual person or his affairs," President Hoover's census proclamation read.

He could make that assurance because of the way the Census Bureau keeps secrets. The bureau itself is being housed, pending completion of a new Department of Commerce building, in temporary wartime structures down on the Mall. The only fireproof structures on the lot are for the census schedules.

Back to the very first census in 1790 the reports are kept under lock and key in steel cases within cement structures. These are guarded by caretakers who give them anti-moth and anti-mold treatments. Miss Mary C. Oursler, for twenty-one years in charge of records, would not permit even one peek at a 1910 volume lying on a repair table.

A census official explained that schedules were considered sealed for fifty or sixty years until they ceased to be personal and became genealogical.

The 1930 vault under construction is larger than any built heretofore. It will receive all original records just as soon as the first tabulation squeezes out the "human interest" and substitutes "cold statistics." One trip through an amazing machine, and each individual becomes an abstraction—just so many code perforations punched in a piece of cardboard, to be tabulated as literate or illiterate, gainfully employed or unemployed, or whatever happens to be in the compilation.

*New York Times*, March 30, 1930, II, 3:1

---

states until about 1915, the Census Bureau supplied federal officials with names and ages of individuals eligible for the World War I draft. Conversely, men who were too young to be drafted often contacted the Census Bureau in order to prove their age.

In 1921, private institutions promoting literacy used the census records to identify illiterate individuals in the United States. At about this time the desire

**Figure 2-1**
1790 U.S. census, Washington County, Pennsylvania, page 143; National Archives micropublication M637, roll 9.

---

**CENSUS TRIVIA**

The federal government did not provide forms or paper for the enumerators until 1830. However, the state of Massachusetts furnished printed blanks to its marshals and assistants. The census schedules for all other states were recorded on nonstandardized books and hand-lined sheets or scraps of paper. Some were bound together in newspaper or in printed broadsides. Col. Presley Nevill covered his 1790 enumeration of Washington and Allegheny Counties, Pennsylvania, in pink orchid wallpaper (see page 28).

---

for protection of privacy among individuals was increasing. In 1930, the Women's Bureau (see page 26) requested the names, addresses, and occupations of some women, but the Census Bureau refused to release the information.

In 1942, the War Department requested as part of the relocation program the names and addresses of Japanese families residing in the United States. The Census Bureau refused to provide specific names and addresses but did identify geographic locations of heavy concentrations of Japanese residents.

It was not until 1954 that access by private and public entities to census records was restricted by Title 13 of the U.S. Code <www.4.law.cornell.edu/uscode>. This section mandates that all individual responses to censuses are to be held confidential for seventy-two years. This is why the 1930 census was not released to the public until 1 April 2002 and the 1940 census will remain confidential until 2012.

Three laws now govern the privacy and confidentiality of census enumerations: Title 13 of the U.S. Code, the Privacy Act of 1974, and 92 Stat. 915; Public Law 95-416; October 5, 1978. The Privacy Act provides individuals with certain rights regarding access to information, restricts the type of data that can be collected, and limits the circumstances under which information can be disclosed.

## AVAILABILITY OF THE CENSUS

- Microfilm copies of the original population schedules for 1790 through 1930 (only 1 percent of the 1890 census survived a 1921 fire) are available at the National Archives in Washington, DC <www.nara.gov>; its thirteen regional archives; and many libraries throughout the United States, including the Family History Library in Salt Lake City, Utah, and its more than 3,400 Family History Centers worldwide.
- Digital images of the original census schedules for 1790 through 1920 are available online at <www.ancestry.com>, <www.genealogylibrary.com>, and <www.heritagequest.com> with payment of a subscriber fee. The 1930 images were added soon after the release of the census in April 2002. Digital images are also available for purchase on CD-ROM from genealogical vendors.

# THREE

# Population Schedules

The U.S. federal census is the foundation of genealogical research. It provides basic data needed throughout a genealogical project such as place and date of birth, relationship to others, changes in residence, citizenship status, and ethnic origins. The census is usually the first record type outside the home you would examine when beginning your family history search and continues to be a touchstone as your research progresses.

## CENSUS HIGHLIGHTS

Census enumerations vary in length and content. With each succeeding census, the government added questions to predict the nation's needs in education, retirement, housing, and health care. Even the 1790 census, with the least amount of information, provided statistics on future military capabilities.

- From 1790 through 1840 only the heads of household were named, and all other family members and slaves were listed statistically. Some early Spanish and British colonial censuses do name every member of the household—even slaves.
- Beginning in 1850 each household member was named with accompanying data.
- The place of birth (state or country) of each person was first reported in 1850, and this continued through 1930.
- The post–Civil War, 1870 census is especially important if you are researching black ancestors. Prior to 1870, free blacks were named individually; slaves were reported only by age and sex.
- Reporting the place of birth of the parents of each person named in the census began in 1880 and continued through 1930.
- The 1880 census is the first to identify the relationship of each person to the head of household.

- Only the 1900 and 1920 census schedules have a Soundex index for *all* families in *all* states.
- The year of immigration to the United States is reported only in the 1900 through 1930 census schedules.

## CENSUS FACTS, MAPS, AND QUESTIONS

Maps of the United States for each census year begin on page 240 in appendix B. Each map is accompanied by the respective list of questions, thereby providing you a quick-reference section while you research the census. Other facts about each enumeration follow:

### The Census of 1790
**The First Census of the United States**

- Census Day: 2 August 1790 (first Monday in August).
- Time Allotted: nine months.
- Population: 3.9 million (21 percent slaves).
- U.S. marshals and their assistants (later called enumerators) were given nine months to complete the census, but it actually took eighteen months to count the 3.9 million residents. President George Washington felt the count was too low, but Congress accepted the data and apportioned the number of representatives accordingly.
- The original 1790 schedules for Delaware, Georgia, Kentucky, New Jersey, and Virginia are lost.
- The 1790 census was actually taken in 1791 in Vermont since it did not become a state until 1791. Some families who moved from another state into Vermont between 1790 and 1791 may appear in the census twice—once in their state of origination and once in Vermont.
- The 1790 census for Virginia was compiled using state enumerations from 1782, 1783, 1784, and 1785 plus the tax lists of Greenbrier County from 1783 to 1786.
- The Census Bureau published transcripts of the extant (surviving) census schedules as *Heads of Families at the First Census of the United States Taken in the Year 1790* (twelve volumes; Washington, D.C.: Government Printing Office, 1907–08, reprinted 1965–75). Each state volume includes an index. Confirm the accuracy of your family's data by viewing the original census record.
- Debra L. Newman compiled *List of Free Black Heads of Families in the First Census of the United States, 1790* (Washington, D.C.: National Archives and Records Service, 1973).

### The Census of 1800
**The Second Census of the United States**

- Census Day: 4 August 1800 (first Monday in August).
- Time Allotted: nine months.
- Population: 5.3 million (20 percent slaves).

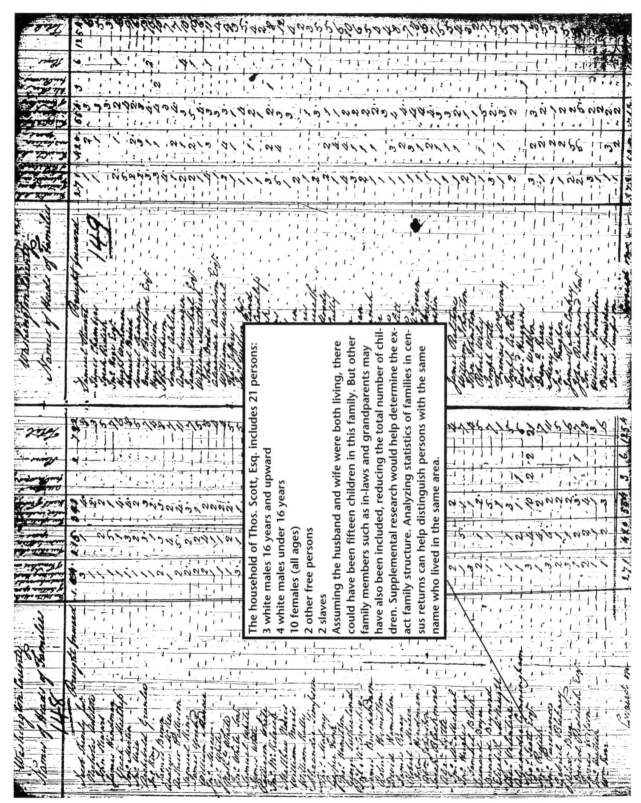

The household of Thos. Scott, Esq. includes 21 persons:

3 white males 16 years and upward

4 white males under 16 years

10 females (all ages)

2 other free persons

2 slaves

Assuming the husband and wife were both living, there could have been fifteen children in this family. But other family members such as in-laws and grandparents may have also been included, reducing the total number of children. Supplemental research would help determine the exact family structure. Analyzing statistics of families in census returns can help distinguish persons with the same name who lived in the same area.

**Figure 3-1**
1790 U.S. census, Washington County, Pennsylvania, pages 148–149; National Archives micropublication M637, roll 9.

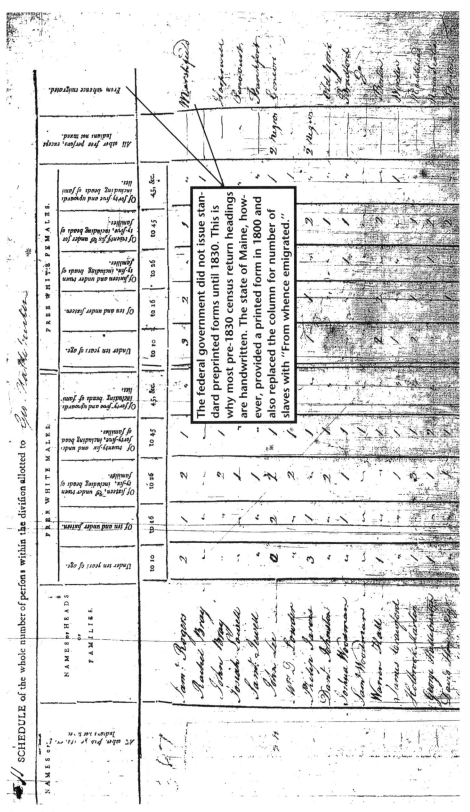

**Figure 3-2**
1800 U.S. census, Hancock County, Maine, page 11, part 1; National Archives micropublication M32, roll 7.

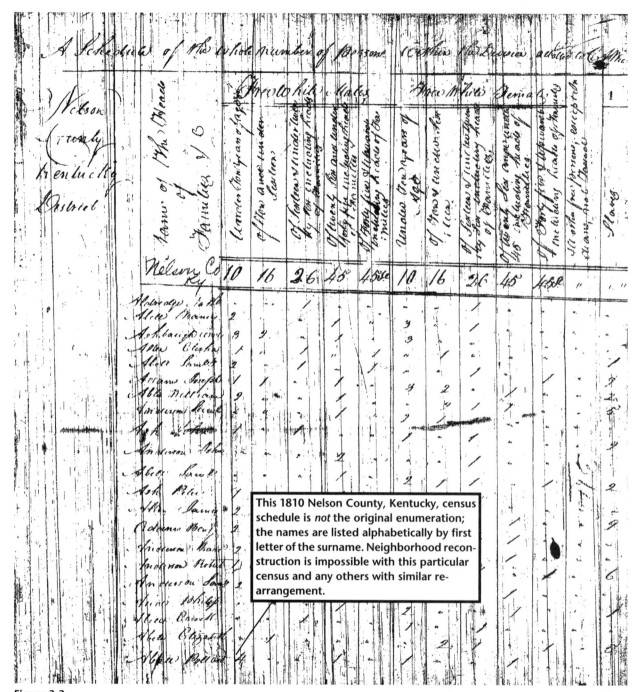

This 1810 Nelson County, Kentucky, census schedule is *not* the original enumeration; the names are listed alphabetically by first letter of the surname. Neighborhood reconstruction is impossible with this particular census and any others with similar rearrangement.

**Figure 3-3**
1810 U.S. census, Nelson County, Kentucky, page 1; National Archives micropublication M252, roll 8.

- The questions and age categories in the 1800 and 1810 censuses are identical.

# The Census of 1810
### The Third Census of the United States
- Census Day: 6 August 1810 (first Monday in August).
- Time Allotted: ten months.

- Population: 7.2 million (20 percent slaves).
- The questions and age categories in the 1800 and 1810 censuses are identical.
- As expected, the center of the U.S. population, gradually moved westward:

| Census Year | State of Population Center | Specific Location |
|---|---|---|
| 1790 | Maryland | 23 miles east of Baltimore |
| 1800 | Maryland | 18 miles west of Baltimore |
| 1810 | District of Columbia | 40 miles northwest by west of Washington, DC |
| 1820 | Virginia | 16 miles east of Moorefield |
| 1830 | Virginia | 19 miles west-southwest of Moorefield |
| 1840 | Virginia | 16 miles south of Clarksburg |
| 1850 | Virginia | 23 miles southeast of Parkersburg |
| 1860 | Ohio | 20 miles south by east of Chillicothe |
| 1870 | Ohio | 48 miles east by north of Cincinnati |
| 1880 | Kentucky | 8 miles west by south of Cincinnati |
| 1890 | Indiana | 20 miles east of Columbus |
| 1900 | Indiana | 6 miles southeast of Columbus |
| 1910 | Indiana | the city of Bloomington |
| 1920 | Indiana | 8 miles south-southeast of Spencer |
| 1930 | Indiana | 3 miles northeast of Linton |
| 2000 | Missouri | approximately 2.8 miles east of Edgar Springs |

*The center of the black population moved, as well:*

| | | |
|---|---|---|
| 1790 | Virginia | 25 miles west-southwest of Petersburg |
| 1880 | Georgia | 10.4 miles east of Lafayette |
| 1890 | Georgia | 15.7 miles southwest of Lafayette |
| 1900 | Alabama | 10.7 miles northeast of Fort Payne |
| 1910 | Alabama | 5.4 miles north-northeast of Fort Payne |

# The Census of 1820
## The Fourth Census of the United States

- Census Day: 7 August 1820 (first Monday in August).
- Time Allotted: thirteen months.
- Population: 9.6 million (18 percent slaves).
- Males and females who were sixteen or seventeen years old might have been counted twice in the 1820 census—once in the category "of 16 and under 18" and again in "of 16 and under 26." This duplication may account for the census's total number of children in your family group not matching your other records or research.
- This census counted the number of persons not naturalized (foreigners).

**Figure 3-4**
1820 U.S. census, Delaware County, New York, town of Tompkins, stamped page 90; National Archives micropublication M33, roll 54.

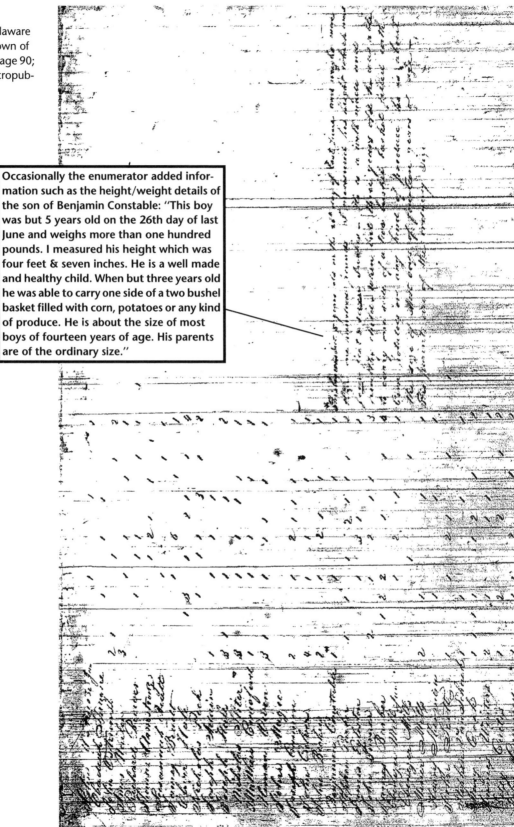

Occasionally the enumerator added information such as the height/weight details of the son of Benjamin Constable: "This boy was but 5 years old on the 26th day of last June and weighs more than one hundred pounds. I measured his height which was four feet & seven inches. He is a well made and healthy child. When but three years old he was able to carry one side of a two bushel basket filled with corn, potatoes or any kind of produce. He is about the size of most boys of fourteen years of age. His parents are of the ordinary size."

# The Census of 1830
## The Fifth Census of the United States
- Census Day: 1 June 1830.
- Time Allotted: twelve months.
- Population: 12.9 million (18 percent slaves).
- This was the first federal census where enumerators were supplied with uniform, printed forms for recording names.
- This was the first census to include an age category of over one hundred years.

# The Census of 1840
## The Sixth Census of the United States
- Census Day: 1 June 1840.
- Time Allotted: eighteen months.
- Population: 17.1 million (17 percent slaves).
- Revolutionary War pensioners and their widows were named in the 1840 census, along with their exact age. The results were published in *A Census of Pensioners for Revolutionary or Military Services, as Returned Under the Act for Taking the Sixth Census in 1840* (1841; reprint, Baltimore: Genealogical Publishing Co., 1954). This report is also reproduced in National Archives micropublication T498, 1790 census, roll 3. An Internet version is posted at <www.usgennet.org/usa/topic/colonial/census/index.html>.

# The Census of 1850
## The Seventh Census of the United States
- Census Day: 1 June 1850.
- Time Allotted: five months (shortened from eighteen months in 1840).
- Population: 23.2 million (16 percent slaves).
- This was the first census to report the name of each household member rather than only that of the head of household.
- The place of birth (state or country) of each individual was first reported in this census.

# The Census of 1860
## The Eighth Census of the United States
- Census Day: 1 June 1860.
- Time Allotted: five months.
- Population: 31.4 million (14 percent slave).

# Slave Schedules—1850 and 1860
The Schedule of Slave Inhabitants was used in the South in 1850 and 1860. Although this schedule was intended for use in southern states only, New Jersey and the District of Columbia also submitted returns.

The only name on a slave schedule is that of the slave owner; however, a personal description including age, sex, and color (black or mulatto) is given

**Notes**

**CENSUS TRIVIA**

In 1850, enumerators were instructed to read information back to the person they interviewed so that errors could be corrected immediately.

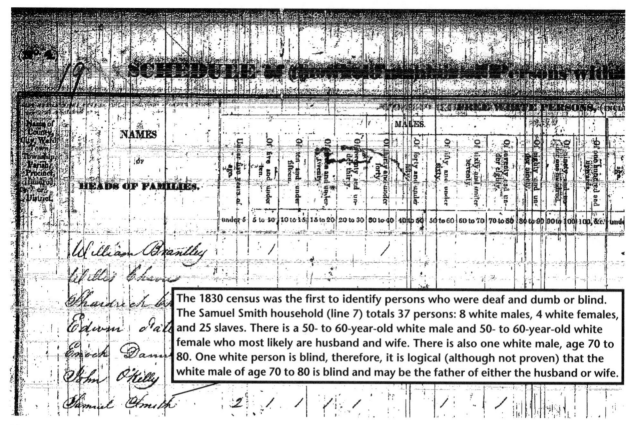

The 1830 census was the first to identify persons who were deaf and dumb or blind. The Samuel Smith household (line 7) totals 37 persons: 8 white males, 4 white females, and 25 slaves. There is a 50- to 60-year-old white male and 50- to 60-year-old white female who most likely are husband and wife. There is also one white male, age 70 to 80. One white person is blind, therefore, it is logical (although not proven) that the white male of age 70 to 80 is blind and may be the father of either the husband or wife.

**Figure 3-5**
1830 U.S. census, Columbus County, North Carolina, page 19, line 7; National Archives micropublication M19, roll 120.

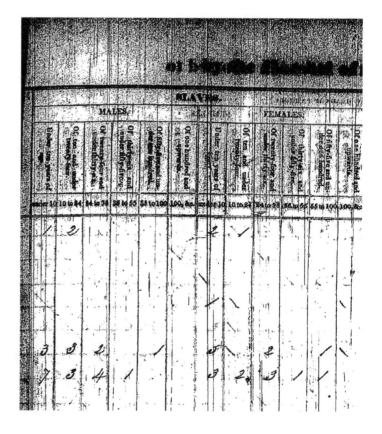

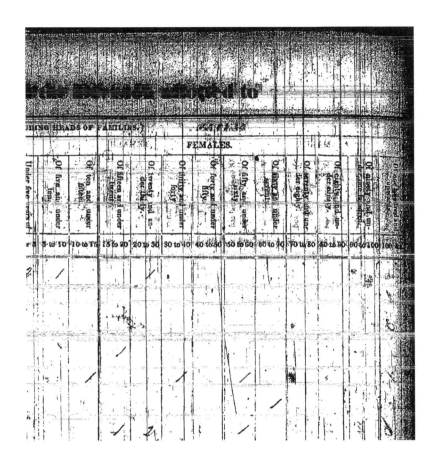

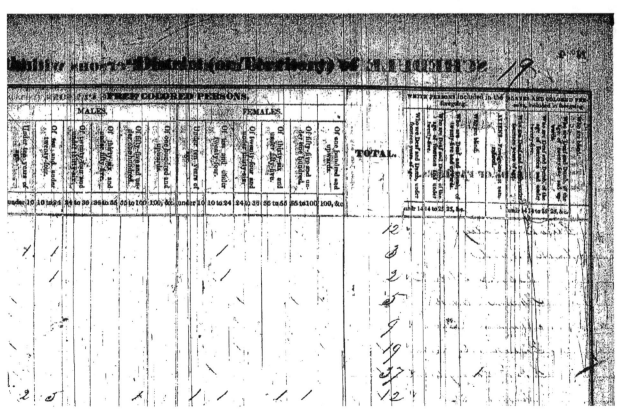

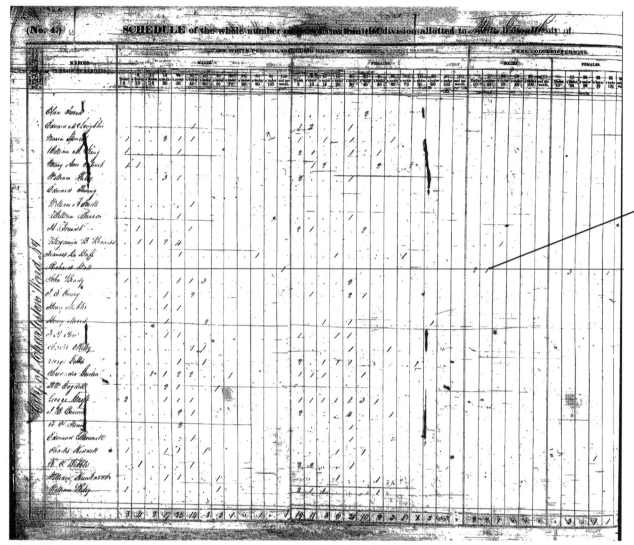

**Figure 3-6**
1840 U.S. census, Charleston District, South Carolina, stamped page 10; National Archives micropublication M704, roll 509.

for each slave. Most slave schedules list the slaves chronologically by age rather than in family groupings. If any slave was deaf and dumb, blind, insane, or idiotic, that fact is stated. Slaves over age one hundred were sometimes named, and occasionally the occupation of a slave, such as blacksmith or carpenter, was reported.

*Slave Schedules—1850 and 1860*

| | |
|---|---|
| Alabama | 1850, 1860 |
| Arkansas | 1850, 1860 |
| Delaware | 1850, 1860 |
| District of Columbia | 1850, 1860 |
| Florida | 1850, 1860 |
| Georgia | 1850, 1860 |
| Kentucky | 1850, 1860 |

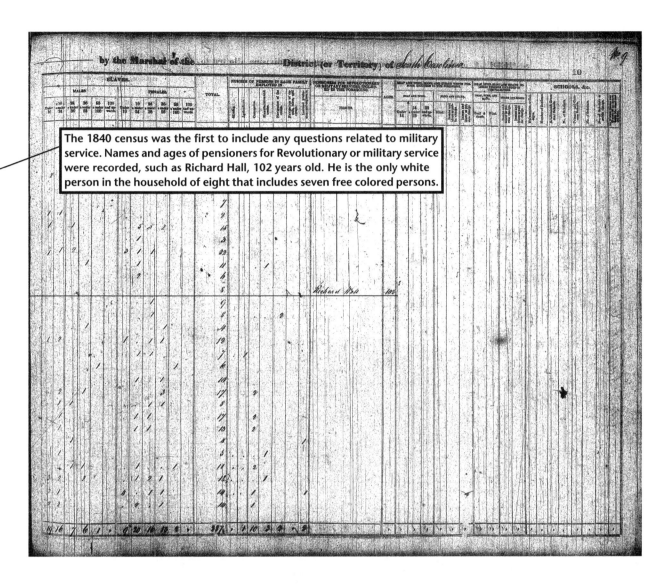

The 1840 census was the first to include any questions related to military service. Names and ages of pensioners for Revolutionary or military service were recorded, such as Richard Hall, 102 years old. He is the only white person in the household of eight that includes seven free colored persons.

| Louisiana | 1850, 1860 |
|---|---|
| Maryland | 1850, 1860 |
| Mississippi | 1850, 1860 |
| Missouri | 1850, 1860 |
| New Jersey | 1850 |
| North Carolina | 1850, 1860 |
| South Carolina | 1850, 1860 |
| Tennessee | 1850, 1860 |
| Texas | 1850, 1860 |
| Virginia | 1850, 1860 |

## The Census of 1870
### The Ninth Census of the United States
- Census Day: 1 June 1870.
- Time Allotted: five months.
- Population: 38.6 million.

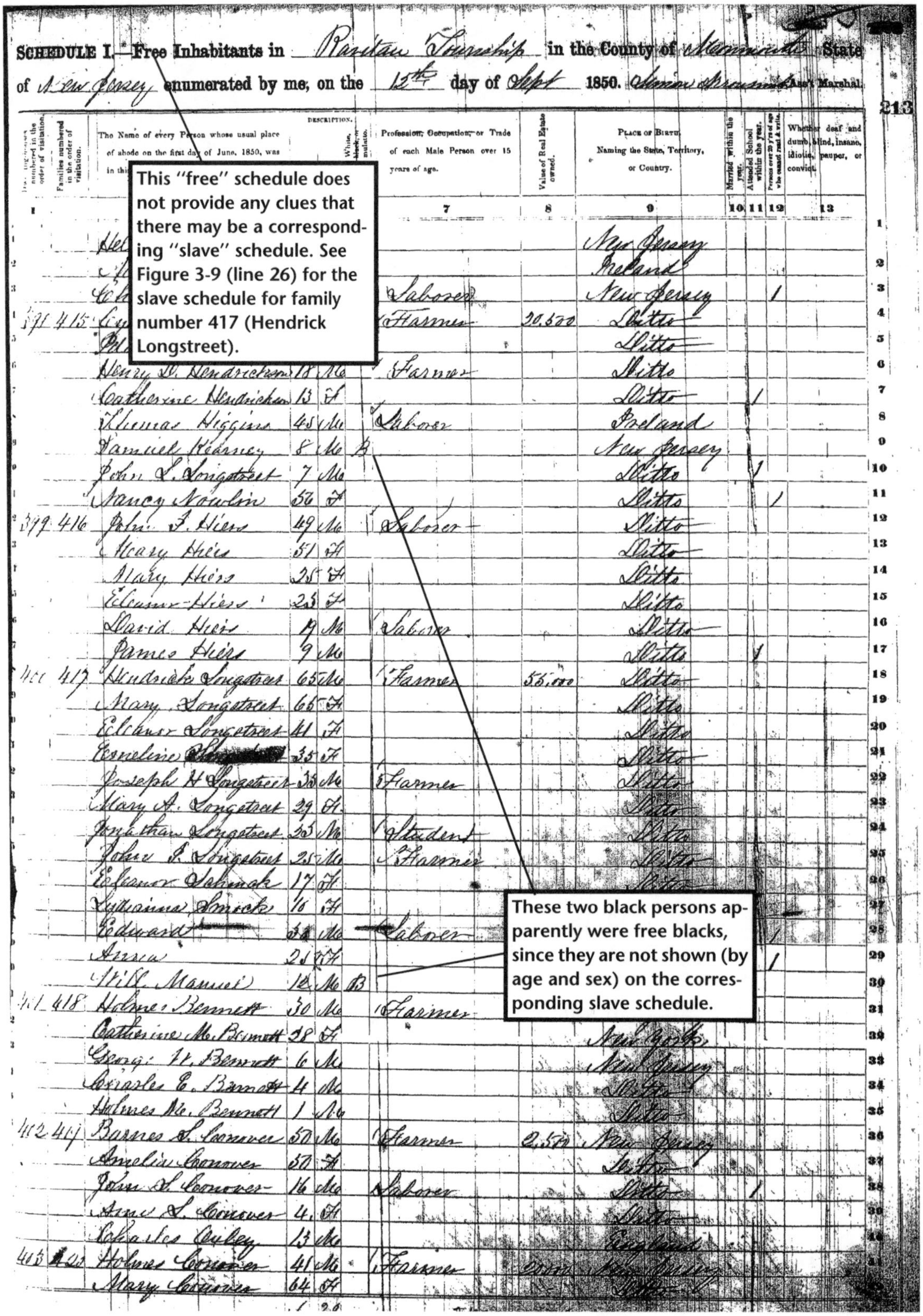
SCHEDULE I.—Free Inhabitants in Raritan Township in the County of Monmouth State of New Jersey enumerated by me, on the 15th day of Sept 1850.
This "free" schedule does not provide any clues that there may be a corresponding "slave" schedule. See Figure 3-9 (line 26) for the slave schedule for family number 417 (Hendrick Longstreet).
These two black persons apparently were free blacks, since they are not shown (by age and sex) on the corresponding slave schedule.
213

**Figure 3-7**

1850 U.S. census, Monmouth County, New Jersey, free schedule, Raritan Township, page 213 (stamped); National Archives micropublication M432, roll 456.

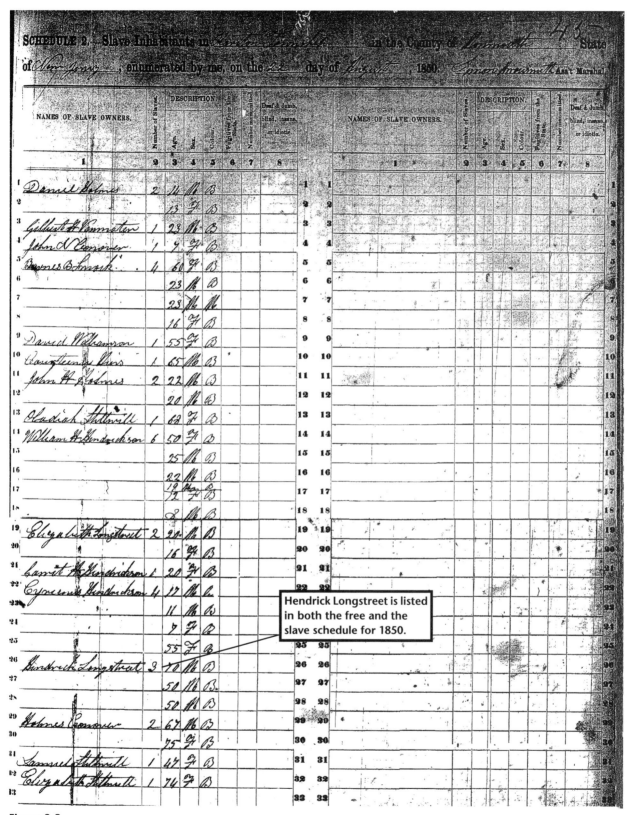

**Figure 3-8**
1850 U.S. census, Monmouth County, New Jersey, slave schedule, Raritan Township, page 45 (handwritten); National Archives micropublication M432, roll 466.

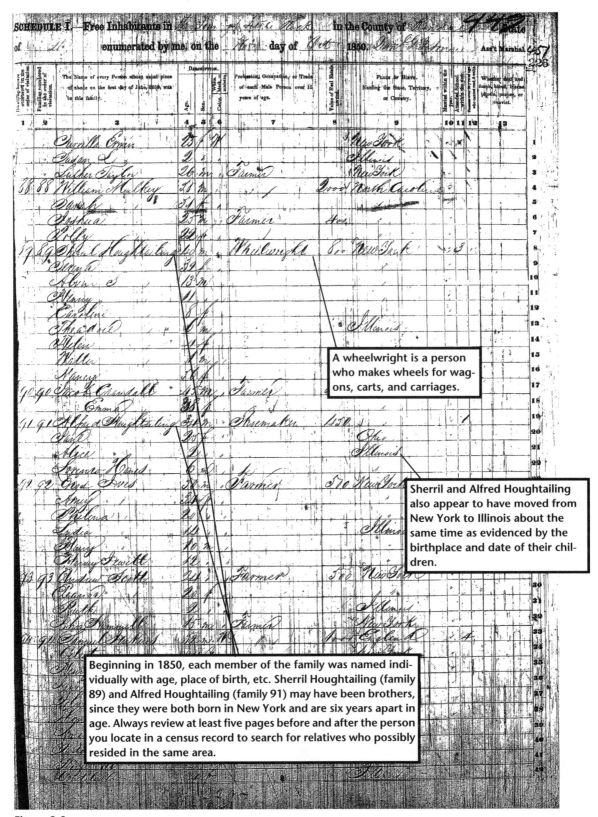

A wheelwright is a person who makes wheels for wagons, carts, and carriages.

Sherril and Alfred Houghtailing also appear to have moved from New York to Illinois about the same time as evidenced by the birthplace and date of their children.

Beginning in 1850, each member of the family was named individually with age, place of birth, etc. Sherril Houghtailing (family 89) and Alfred Houghtailing (family 91) may have been brothers, since they were both born in New York and are six years apart in age. Always review at least five pages before and after the person you locate in a census record to search for relatives who possibly resided in the same area.

**Figure 3-9**
1850 U.S. census, Kendall County, Illinois, free population schedule, town of Little Rock, page 226 (printed), page 451 (handwritten); National Archives micropublication M432, roll 113.

SCHEDULE 1.—Free Inhabitants in _____ District _____ in the County of _Fauquier_ State of _Virginia_ enumerated by me, on the _14th_ day of _August_ 1860. _Geo Calvert_ Asst Marshal.
Post Office _Catlett_

| 1 | 2 | The name of every person whose usual place of abode on the first day of June, 1860, was in this family. 3 | Age 4 | Sex 5 | Colour; White, black, or mulatto 6 | Profession, Occupation, or Trade, of each person, male and female, over 15 years of age. 7 | Value of Real Estate 8 | Value of Personal Estate 9 | Place of Birth, Naming the State, Territory, or Country. 10 | Married within the year 11 | Attended School within the year 12 | Persons over 20 y'rs of age who cannot read and write 13 | Whether deaf and dumb, blind, insane, idiotic, pauper, or convict. 14 | |
|---|---|---|---|---|---|---|---|---|---|---|---|---|---|---|
| 1 | 850 | 777 | John Smallwood | 21 | m | | | | | Va | | | | | 1 |
| 2 | 851 | 778 | Mildred B Lipscomb | 70 | f | | | 250 | 135 | " | | | | | 2 |
| 3 | | | Munroe M " | 21 | m | | Subject to fits at any time & before they come on he is idiotic. The fits are more frequent about the change of the moon | | | " | | | | Idiotic | 3 |
| 4 | 852 | 779 | James Clough | 35 | m | | Black Smith | 2,800 | 1,015 | Yorkshire, England | | | | | 4 |
| 5 | | | Mary A | 34 | f | | | | | " | | | | | 5 |
| 6 | | | Samuel Siddall | 20 | m | | | | | | | | | | 6 |
| 7 | 853 | 780 | Nimrod Mark | 46 | m | | Superior Ct. | | | | | | | | 7 |
| 8 | | | Isabella " | 42 | f | | | | | | | | | | 8 |
| 9 | | | Mary H " | 22 | f | | | | | | | | | | 9 |
| 10 | | | Rebecca F " | 20 | f | | | | | | | | | | 10 |
| 11 | | | Byron " | 19 | m | | | | | | | | | | 11 |
| 12 | | | Martha L " | 18 | f | | Teacher | | | | | | | | 12 |
| 13 | | | George M " | 17 | m | | | | | " | | | | | 13 |
| 14 | | | Emma D " | 16 | f | | | | | " | | | | | 14 |
| 15 | | | Benjamin " | 13 | m | | | | | " | | | | | 15 |
| 16 | | | John N " | 11 | m | | | | | " | | | | | 16 |
| 17 | | | Ellen E " | 10 | f | | | | | " | | | | | 17 |
| 18 | | | Cynthia A " | 8 | f | | | | | Va | | | | | 18 |
| 19 | | | Charles M " | 2 | m | | | | | " | | | | | 19 |
| 20 | 854 | 781 | Susan Mc Redd | 43 | m | | Widow | | 75 | Va | | | | | 20 |
| 21 | | | Richard " | 16 | m | | | | | " | | | | | 21 |
| 22 | | | Polk " | 14 | m | | | | | " | | | | | 22 |
| 23 | | | Bettie " | 13 | f | | | | | " | | | | | 23 |

> In 1860, the enumerators were instructed to report the cause of insanity such as intemperance, spiritualism, grief, affliction, heredity, misfortune, religious excess, jealousy, weight, and disappointment. Perhaps that is why this enumerator added information about the 21-year-old idiot who was "subject to fits at any time and before they come on he is idiotic. The fits are more frequent about the change of the moon."

**Figure 3-10**
1860 U.S. census, Fauquier County, Virginia, free population schedule, page 111, line 3; National Archives micropublication M653, roll 1344.

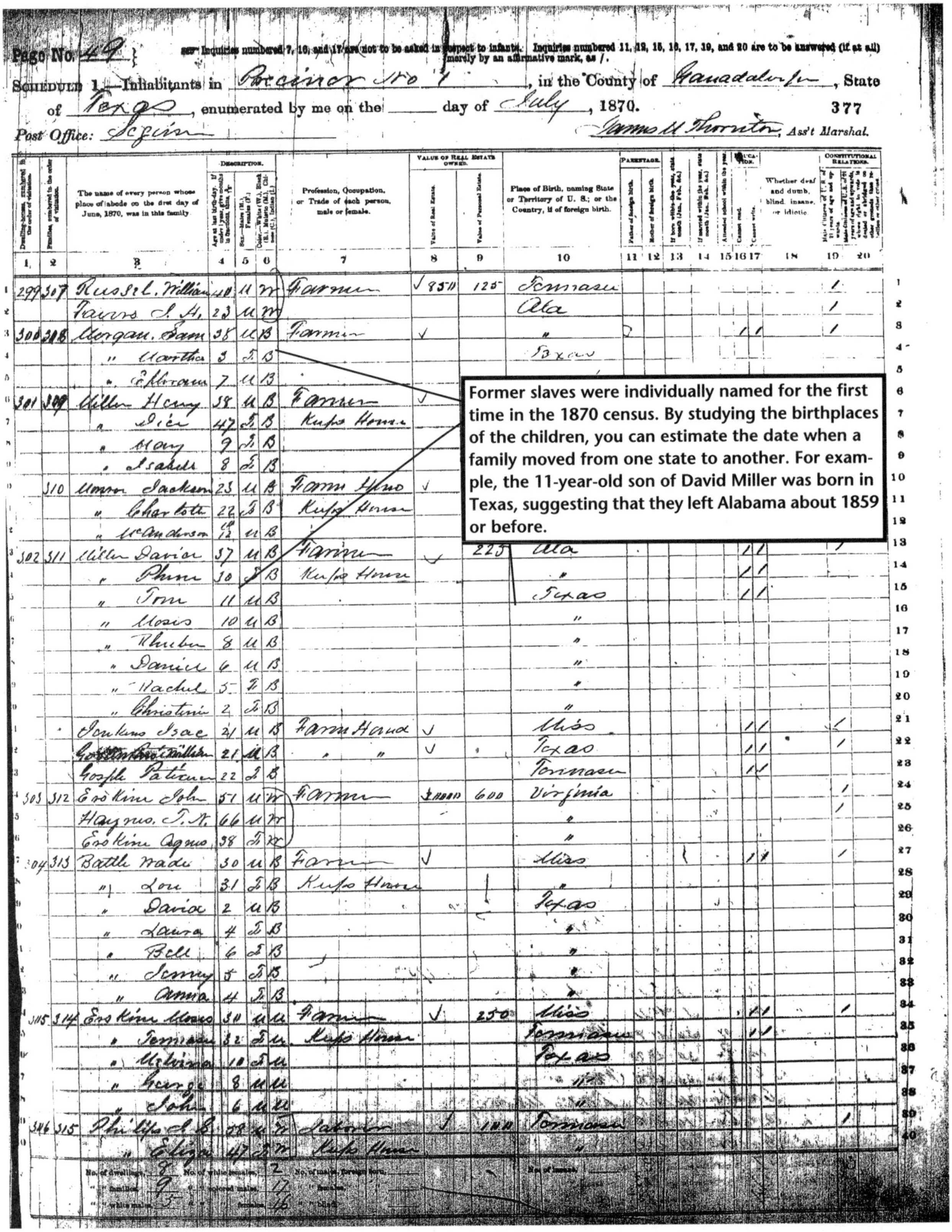

An inset note within the figure reads:

> Former slaves were individually named for the first time in the 1870 census. By studying the birthplaces of the children, you can estimate the date when a family moved from one state to another. For example, the 11-year-old son of David Miller was born in Texas, suggesting that they left Alabama about 1859 or before.

**Figure 3-11**

1870 U.S. census, Guadalupe County, Texas, population schedule, Precinct Number 1, page 377; National Archives micropublication M593, roll 1589.

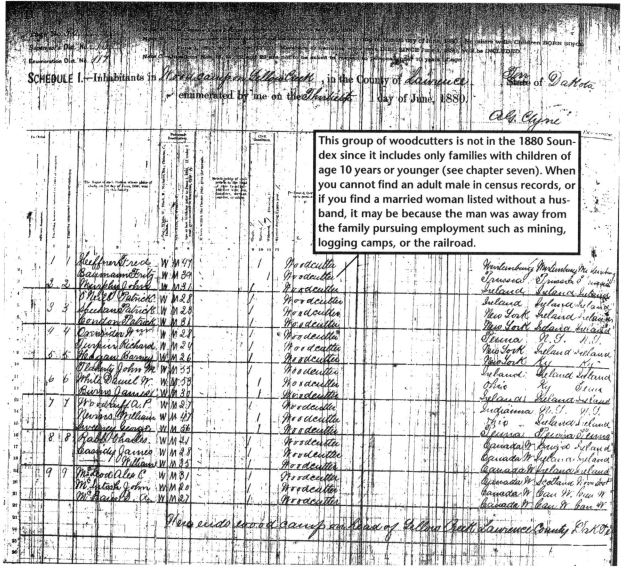

**Figure 3-12**
1880 U.S. census, Lawrence County, Dakota Territory, population schedule, wood camp on Yellow Creek, supervisor's district [S.D.] 15, enumeration district [E.D.] 117, page 30B; National Archives micropublication T9, roll 113.

# The Census of 1880

## The Tenth Census of the United States

- Census Day: 1 June 1880.
- Time Allotted: one month (shortened from five months in 1870).
- Population: 50.2 million.
- The birthplace of the mother and father of each individual was reported for the first time in this census.
- This is the first census to indicate relationship to the head of the household, e.g., wife, son, daughter, grandchild.
- The race classification of Indian was used for the first time in this census.

## CENSUS TAKERS' TROUBLES

Yesterday a *Times* reporter made the tour of several houses on West Forty-seventh Street in company with Mrs. Jenny V.H. Baker, a modest, prepossessing young widow, the niece of Mrs. Dr. Clemence Lozier, of West Forty-eighth Street. The fair census taker, who had just lost her husband, was dressed in black throughout, carried a large portfolio under her arm, and was altogether as quiet and submissive in her demeanor as the most imperious of her sex could demand. She rang the doorbell of a "well" house close to Fifth Avenue, and a white-capped French *bonne* answered the call.

"Who's there, Marie?" cried a voice from the end of the hall. Mrs. Baker timidly explained her errand and displayed her credentials, including the large official blanks prepared by the government. The mistress of the house angrily declined to see her and flounced downstairs into the basement, where a spirited dialogue was carried on between the two, the servant standing at the head of the stairs and repeating the mistress's remarks to the visitor. Mrs. Baker protested in vain that she was an authorized officer, and that the questions she would ask were simple and could be answered in a few minutes, and that a continued refusal would only result in trouble to both. The lady of the house positively refused to stir from her hiding place under the stairs.

"Tell you my age, indeed," she cried, trembling with indignation. "Wait till my husband comes home, and he'll tend to you. That's all!" Mrs. Baker, who had been wearied out by the refusals of several silly householders of the same kind, determined to assert herself and secured from Capt. Mount, of the Fifty-ninth Street Police Station, the services of a policeman, the officer being instructed to be as polite as possible, but to see that the law was obeyed. The sight of the officer made the mistress of the house more tractable, but she still refused to stir from behind the kitchen stairs, and Policeman Smith was compelled to carry on the dialogue from the landing above.

"What is your husband's name, Madame?" asked the enumerator respectfully, holding her pen in hand to note down the answer. The policeman politely repeated the request, which nearly threw the lady into hysterics.

"My husband's name! She wants my husband's name! Oh! The black-eyed minx! What do you want my husband's name for?"

"I must have it, Ma'am," replied Mrs. Baker fiercely. "The law requires it."

"Pray be quiet, Ma'am," said the policeman from the head of the stairs. "You've got to give it to her or be fined $100."

"I won't!" screamed the lady. "What does she want of my husband, the good-for-nothing thing!"

At last, by dint of repeated explanations, the husband's name was elicited, the lady sobbing violently and threatening all sorts of dire vengeance on the heads of the policeman and the enumerator. A similar exhibition followed in each of the remaining 25 queries, and the tumult in the houses and the indignation of the servants was excessive. At least the schedule was filled out, and the plucky little census taker tripped down the steps with a sigh of relief.

"There!" said she, when she regained the pavement where the *Times* reporter had been keeping a wary eye out for the male, and presumably pugnacious, head of the household. "I was afraid to ask her if she had any boarders. I believe she'd have torn my eyes out if I had."

*New York Times,* June 5, 1880, 10:1

## The Census of 1885
### Special Census With Federal Assistance
The federal government offered states and territories partial reimbursement for the expense of taking an 1885 census pursuant to an act of 1879 (20 Stat. 480). Only Colorado, Florida, Nebraska, and the territories of Dakota and New Mexico took the census with four separate schedules:

*Schedule 1: Inhabitants*
- name
- color
- sex
- age
- relationship to head of family
- marital status
- occupation
- place of birth
- place of birth of parents
- literacy
- sickness or disability

*Schedule 2: Agriculture*
- name of farm owner
- tenure
- acreage
- farm value
- expenses
- estimated value of farm products
- number and kind of livestock
- amount and kind of produce

*Schedule 3: Products of Industry*
- name of owning corporation or individual

- name of business or products
- amount of capital invested
- number of employees
- wages and hours
- number of months in operation during the year
- value of materials used
- value of products
- amount and type of power used

*Schedule 4: Mortality*
- name
- age
- sex
- color
- marital status
- place of birth
- place of birth of parents
- occupation
- cause of death

## The Census of 1890
### The Eleventh Census of the United States

- Census Day: 1 June 1890.
- Time Allotted: one month.
- Population: 63.0 million.
- A basement fire in the Commerce Building in Washington, DC, destroyed most of the 1890 population census. Kellee Blake's two-part article titled "First in the Path of the Firemen: The Fate of the 1890 Population Census," *Prologue* (Quarterly of the National Archives and Records Administration), Spring 1996, vol. 28, no. 1 and reprinted at <www.nara.gov/publications/prologue/1890cen1.html> and <www.nara.gov/publications/prologue/1890cen2.html> gives an excellent report on the cause and effect of this historic fire.
- The surviving schedules (about 1 percent of the census), listed below, have been microfilmed (M407, one roll) and alphabetically indexed (M496, two rolls). None of the communities is completely covered by the surviving fragments, and portions of many pages are missing.
  Alabama
      Perry County (Perryville beat number 11 and Severe beat number 8)
  District of Columbia
      Q, thirteenth, fourteenth, R, W, Corcoran, fifteenth, S, R, and Riggs Streets and Johnson Avenue
  Georgia
      Muscogee County (Columbus)
  Illinois
      McDonough County (Mound Township)

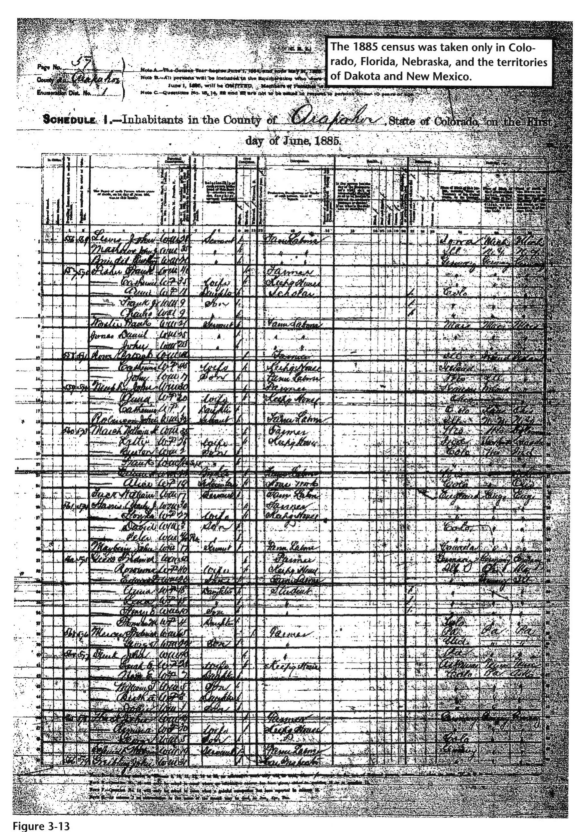

**Figure 3-13**
1885 U.S. census, Arapahoe County, Colorado, population schedule, enumeration district [E.D.] 1, page 59; National Archives micropublication M158, roll 1.

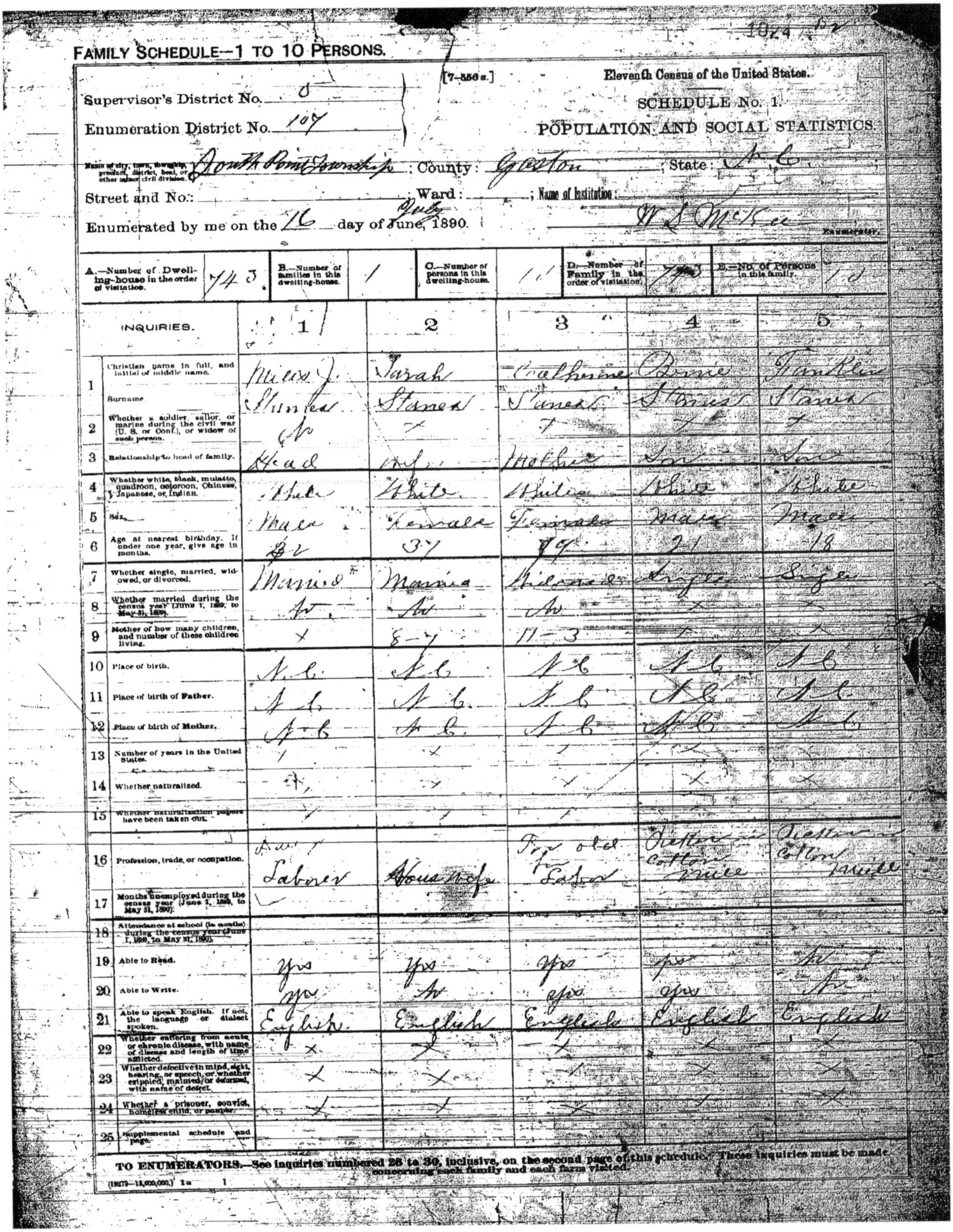

**Figure 3-14**
1890 U.S. census, Gaston County, North Carolina, population schedule, South Point Township, enumeration district [E.D.] 107, page 1024; National Archives micropublication M407, roll 3.

## SCHEDULE No. 1.—POPULATION AND SOCIAL STATISTICS.

| INQUIRIES. | | 6 | 7 | 8 | 9 | 10 |
|---|---|---|---|---|---|---|
| 1 | Christian name in full, and initial of middle name. | Rosanna | Amanda | Emma | Betsey | King |
| 2 | Surname. | Stanes | Stanes | Stanes | Stanes | Stanes |
| | Whether a soldier, sailor, or marine during the civil war (U. S. or Conf.), or widow of such person. | x | | | | |
| 3 | Relationship to head of family. | Daughter | Daughter | Daughter | Daughter | Son |
| 4 | Whether white, black, mulatto, quadroon, octoroon, Chinese, Japanese, or Indian. | white | white | white | white | w |
| 5 | Sex. | Female | Female | Female | Female | Male |
| 6 | Age at nearest birthday. If under one year, give age in months. | 13 | 11 | 9 | 6 | 4 |
| 7 | Whether single, married, widowed, or divorced. | Single | Single | Single | Single | Single |
| 8 | Whether married during the census year (June 1, 1889, to May 31, 1890). | | | | | |
| 9 | Mother of how many children, and number of these children living. | | | | | |
| 10 | Place of birth. | N.C. | | N.C. | N.C. | N.C. |
| 11 | Place of birth of Father. | N.C. | | | | N.C. |
| 12 | Place of birth of Mother. | N.C. | | | | N.C. |
| 13 | Number of years in the United States. | | | | | |
| 14 | Whether naturalized. | | | | | |
| 15 | Whether naturalization papers have been taken out. | | | | | |
| 16 | Profession, trade, or occupation. | Spinner cotton mill | | | | at home |
| 17 | Months unemployed during the census year (June 1, 1889, to May 31, 1890). | | | | | |
| 18 | Attendance at school (in months) during the census year (June 1, 1889, to May 31, 1890). | | 1 | 2 | 5 | |
| 19 | Able to Read. | No | | No | No | No |
| 20 | Able to Write. | No | | No | No | No |
| 21 | Able to speak English. If not, the language or dialect spoken. | English | English | English | English | English |
| 22 | Whether suffering from acute or chronic disease, with name of disease and length of time afflicted. | | | | | |
| 23 | Whether defective in mind, sight, hearing, or speech, or whether crippled, maimed, or deformed, with name of defect. | | | | | |
| 24 | Whether a prisoner, convict, homeless child, or pauper. | | | | | |
| 25 | Supplemental schedule and page. | | | | | |
| 26 | Is the home you live in hired, or is it owned by the head or by a member of the family? | | | | | |
| 27 | If owned by head or member of family, is the home free from mortgage incumbrance? | | | | | |
| 28 | If the head of family is a farmer, is the farm which he cultivates hired, or is it owned by him or by a member of his family? | | | | | |
| 29 | If owned by head or member of family, is the farm free from mortgage incumbrance? | | | | | |
| 30 | If the home or farm is owned by head or member of family, and mortgaged, give the post-office address of owner. | | | | | |

The government created a completely different style of census form in 1890, establishing a column for each family member. Although the majority of the census was lost in the 1921 fire, a few schedules survived. Note that the 11- and 13-year-old children worked in the cotton mill; these notations provided the government with child labor statistics.

TO ENUMERATORS.—The inquiries numbered 26 to 30, inclusive, must be made concerning each family and each farm visited.

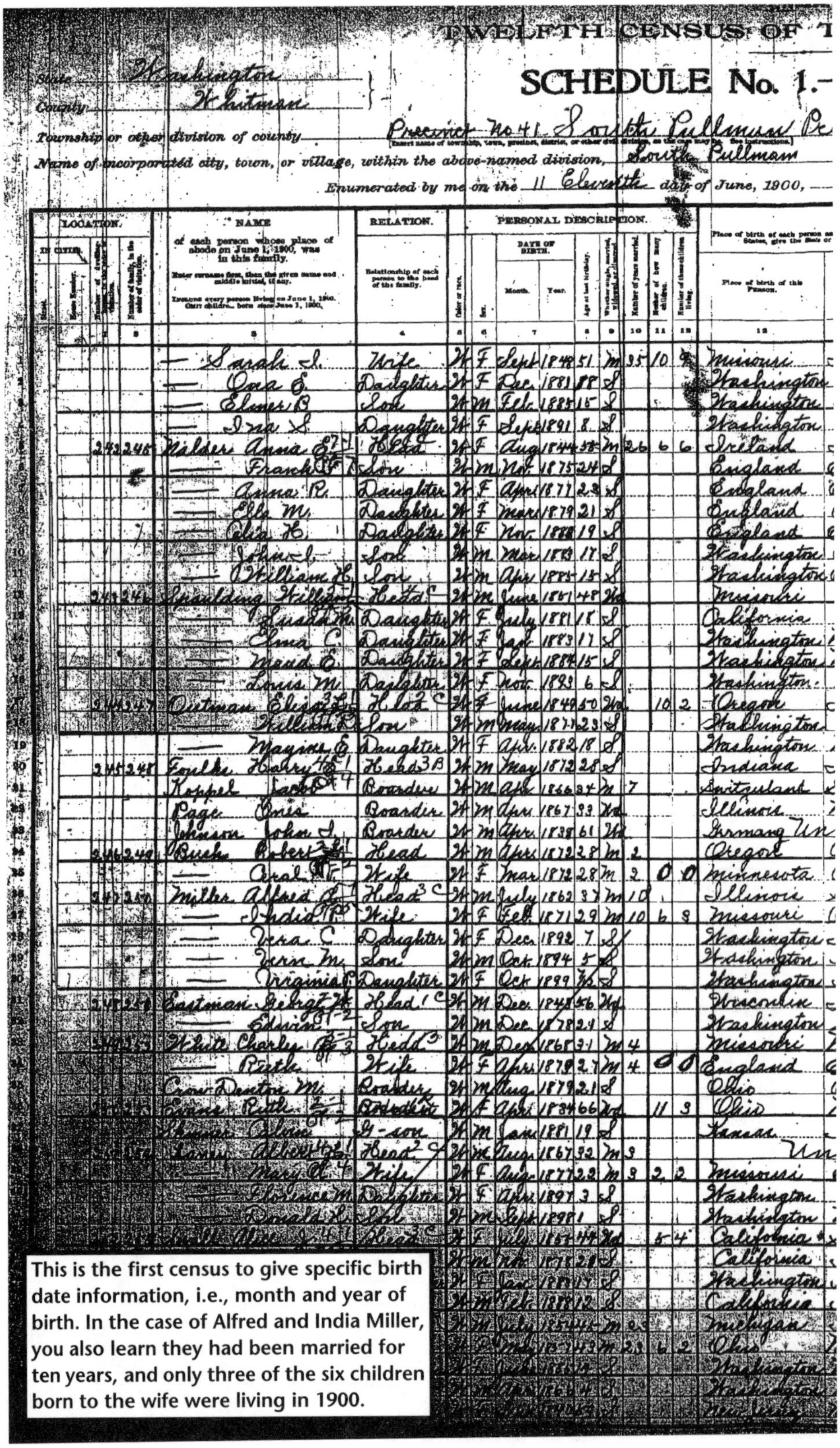

TWELFTH CENSUS OF T[...]

SCHEDULE No. 1.—

State: Washington
County: Whitman
Township or other division of county: Precinct No 41 South Pullman Pc
Name of incorporated city, town, or village, within the above-named division, South Pullman
Enumerated by me on the 11 Eleventh day of June, 1900,

| Dwelling | Family | Name | Relation | Color | Sex | Month | Year | Age | Marital | Years married | Mother of how many children | Number living | Place of birth |
|---|---|---|---|---|---|---|---|---|---|---|---|---|---|
| | | — Sarah J. | Wife | W | F | Sept | 1848 | 51 | M | 35 | 10 | 9 | Missouri |
| | | — Ora E. | Daughter | W | F | Dec | 1881 | 18 | S | | | | Washington |
| | | — Elmer B. | Son | W | M | Feb | 1885 | 15 | S | | | | Washington |
| | | — Ina S. | Daughter | W | F | Sept | 1891 | 8 | S | | | | Washington |
| 243 | 245 | Walder Anna | Head | W | F | Aug | 1844 | 55 | M | 26 | 6 | 6 | Ireland |
| | | — Frank | Son | W | M | Nov | 1875 | 24 | S | | | | England |
| | | — Anna R. | Daughter | W | F | Apr | 1877 | 23 | S | | | | England |
| | | — Ela M. | Daughter | W | F | Mar | 1879 | 21 | S | | | | England |
| | | — Eliz H. | Daughter | W | F | Nov | 1880 | 19 | S | | | | England |
| | | — John L. | Son | W | M | Mar | 1883 | 17 | S | | | | Washington |
| | | — William H. | Son | W | M | Apr | 1885 | 15 | S | | | | Washington |
| | | Spaulding William | Head | W | M | June | 1851 | 48 | Wd | | | | Missouri |
| | | — Luada M. | Daughter | W | F | July | 1881 | 18 | S | | | | California |
| | | — Elma C. | Daughter | W | F | Jan | 1883 | 17 | S | | | | Washington |
| | | — Maud E. | Daughter | W | F | Sept | 1884 | 15 | S | | | | Washington |
| | | — Louis M. | Daughter | W | F | Nov | 1893 | 6 | S | | | | Washington |
| | 247 | Outman Eliza | Head | W | F | June | 1849 | 50 | Wd | | 10 | 2 | Oregon |
| | | — Wilbert R. | Son | W | M | May | 1877 | 23 | S | | | | Washington |
| | | — Maxine E. | Daughter | W | F | Apr | 1882 | 18 | S | | | | Washington |
| 245 | 248 | Foulke Harry | Head | W | M | May | 1872 | 28 | S | | | | Indiana |
| | | Koppel Jacob | Boarder | W | M | Apr | 1866 | 34 | M | 7 | | | Switzerland |
| | | Page Ernie | Boarder | W | M | Apr | 1867 | 33 | Wd | | | | Illinois |
| | | Johnson John J. | Boarder | W | M | Apr | 1838 | 61 | Wd | | | | Germany |
| 246 | 249 | Buck Robert | Head | W | M | Apr | 1872 | 28 | M | 2 | | | Oregon |
| | | — Arval | Wife | W | F | Mar | 1872 | 28 | M | 2 | 0 | 0 | Minnesota |
| 247 | 250 | Miller Alfred A. | Head | W | M | July | 1862 | 37 | M | 10 | | | Illinois |
| | | — India | Wife | W | F | Feb | 1871 | 29 | M | 10 | 6 | 3 | Missouri |
| | | — Vera C. | Daughter | W | F | Dec | 1892 | 7 | S | | | | Washington |
| | | — Vern M. | Son | W | M | Oct | 1894 | 5 | S | | | | Washington |
| | | — Virginia | Daughter | W | F | Oct | 1899 | 7/12 | S | | | | Washington |
| | | Eastman George | Head | W | M | Dec | 1843 | 56 | Wd | | | | Wisconsin |
| | | — Edwin | Son | W | M | Dec | 1878 | 21 | S | | | | Washington |
| | | White Charles | Head | W | M | Dec | 1868 | 31 | M | 4 | | | Missouri |
| | | — Bertha | Wife | W | F | Apr | 1872 | 27 | M | 4 | 0 | 0 | England |
| | | Cone Denton M. | Boarder | W | M | Aug | 1879 | 21 | S | | | | Ohio |
| | | Cone Ruth | Boarder | W | F | Apr | 1834 | 66 | Wd | | 11 | 3 | Ohio |
| | | [illegible] Alvin | G-son | W | M | Jan | 1881 | 19 | S | | | | Kansas |
| | | [illegible] Albert | Head | W | M | Aug | 1867 | 32 | M | 3 | | | [illegible] |
| | | — Mary A. | Wife | W | F | Aug | 1877 | 22 | M | 3 | 2 | 2 | Missouri |
| | | — Florence M. | Daughter | W | F | Apr | 1897 | 3 | S | | | | Washington |
| | | — Donald L. | Son | W | M | Sept | 1898 | 1 | S | | | | Washington |
| | | [illegible] Alice J. | Head | W | F | July | 1855 | 44 | Wd | | 5 | 4 | California |
| | | [illegible] | | W | M | | 1878 | 21 | S | | | | California |
| | | [illegible] | | W | F | Jan | 1882 | 18 | S | | | | Washington |
| | | [illegible] | | W | M | Feb | 1888 | 12 | S | | | | California |
| | | [illegible] | | W | M | July | 1854 | 45 | M | | | | Michigan |
| | | [illegible] | | W | F | May | [illegible] | [illegible] | M | | 6 | 2 | Ohio |
| | | [illegible] | | | | | [illegible] | [illegible] | S | | | | Washington |
| | | [illegible] | | | | | [illegible] | [illegible] | S | | | | Washington |
| | | [illegible] | | | | | [illegible] | [illegible] | | | | | New Jersey |

**This is the first census to give specific birth date information, i.e., month and year of birth. In the case of Alfred and India Miller, you also learn they had been married for ten years, and only three of the six children born to the wife were living in 1900.**

**Figure 3-15**
1900 U.S. census, Whitman County, Washington, population schedule, South Pullman Precinct, supervisor's district [S.D.] 2, enumeration district [E.D.] 104, sheet 12A; National Archives micropublication T623, roll 1754.

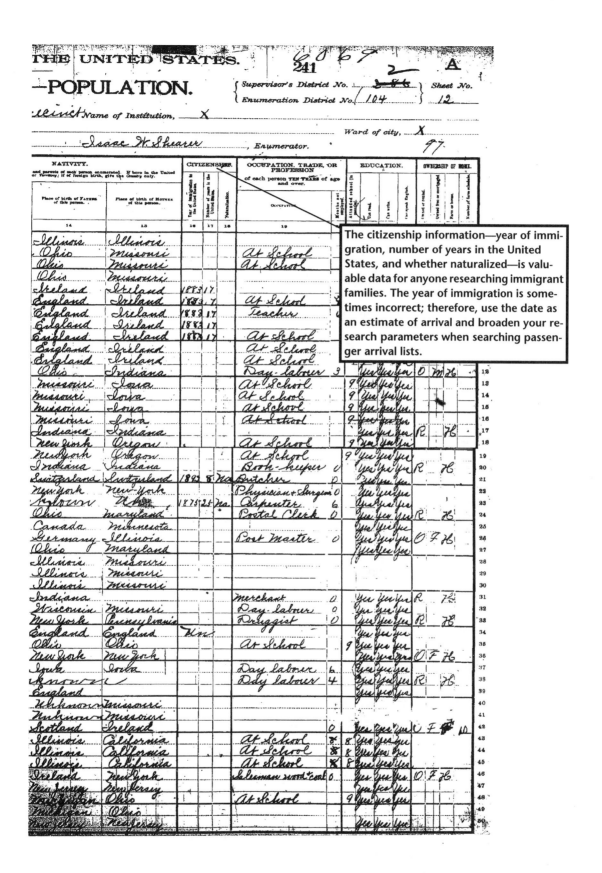

The citizenship information—year of immigration, number of years in the United States, and whether naturalized—is valuable data for anyone researching immigrant families. The year of immigration is sometimes incorrect; therefore, use the date as an estimate of arrival and broaden your research parameters when searching passenger arrival lists.

Minnesota
Wright County (Rockford)
New Jersey
Hudson County (Jersey City)
New York
Westchester County (Eastchester)
Suffolk County (Brookhaven Township)
North Carolina
Gaston County (South Point Township and River Bend Township)
Cleveland County (Township No. 2)
Ohio
Hamilton County (Cincinnati)
Clinton County (Wayne Township)
South Dakota
Union County (Jefferson Township)
Texas
Ellis County (J.P. No. 6, Mountain Peak, and Ovilla Precinct)
Hood County (Precinct No. 5)
Rusk County (No. 6 and J.P. No. 7)
Trinity County (Trinity Town and Precinct No. 2)
Kaufman County (Kaufman)

- See chapter four for information on the 1890 Union Veterans and Widows of Union Veterans schedule.

## 1890 Substitute

Ancestry.com, with the aid of the National Archives and Records Administration and the Allen County (Indiana) Public Library, is creating an online substitute for the 1890 census. They have identified more than twenty million records from fragments of the original 1890 census that survived the fire, special veterans schedules, several Native American tribal censuses for years surrounding 1890, state censuses (1885 or 1895), city and county directories, alumni directories, and voter registration records.

## 1890 New York City Recount

A New York City "police" census (one conducted by the city) was taken as a recount of that year's federal census and survives. In 1890, New York City was in what is today the borough of Manhattan and part of The Bronx.

The original recount is located in the Municipal Archives in New York City; microfilm copies (fifty-nine rolls) are at the Family History Library in Salt Lake City, the New York Public Library, and the New York Genealogical and Biographical Society.

In order to use this census, you must start with an address (obtained from the Wilson Street Directory that is included in the microfilm) and convert it into an assembly district and then the election district. The New York Genealogical and Biographical Society <www.nygbs.org> has two finding aids: *Map Guide to New York County "Police Census" 1890* and *Street Guide to New*

## DIARY OF 1910 CENSUS ENUMERATOR FLETA M. MYERS, MT. ZION TOWNSHIP, MACON COUNTY, ILLINOIS

Nineteen-year-old Fleta M. Myers was the census enumerator for Mt. Zion Township, Macon County, Illinois. Miss Myers kept a diary during her experience, giving personal insight into the responsibility and adventure of interviewing everyone in her community. Fleta Marie Myers died in 1973, and her diary is now in the possession of her grandson, Virgil Durwood Purdue. A full transcription of her census-related entries (5 February through 12 August 1910) is published in the Orange County California Genealogical Society *Journal*, volume 33, April 1996, pages 12–16. Bobbie Purdue gave permission to abstract a few of the entries.

February 5—Saturday
To H. School & took Exam for Census Enumerator from 2 till 6:10.

March 19—Saturday
Received my appointment as Census Enumerator for the 129th district this morning. Vella Patterson got it for the rural district of Lovington township.

March 21—Monday
Went to Dickey's Saturday evening and signed the oath and sent it in.

March 23—Wednesday
Rec'd my supplies yesterday of scedules [*sic*], etc. and took an invoice this morning and sent in.

April 4—Monday
Went to Zion this afternoon and worked till after six o'clock sending out advance farm schedules.

April 8—Friday
Enumerator conference at P.O. building at 10 A.M.

April 14—Thursday
Worked on my map a while.

April 15—Friday
Began working this morning in Mt. Zion. Amount for first day's work about $2.98. No particular trouble. 8 hrs. Harry Nun's first stop!

April 19—Tuesday
Some people surely are afraid other folks will find out their ages. Needn't worry about me telling. Forgot them almost instantly excepting the ones who lied to me & that simply impressed the fact on my mind a little stronger. 8 hrs. 14 min. Amt. $4.27. Just missed one 3¢ per. Ha! Ha!

April 21—Thursday

My first day in the country and "Oh! you farmer." Drove all over one 160 acre field at my second visit this morning and finally succeeded in filling out my schedule, etc. All day. One old lady came running to me, kissed me, and then backed off with, "Well, I don't believe I do know you." Guess she would have acted differently had she known. Yes! Or No! Or Both! And talk about inquisitiveness, what is it when one lady says, "Say, now did Miss <u>Blank</u> (a tolerable old blank too) tell you how old she was?" and I answer, "why certainly." then, in sort of a whisper "well, how old is she anyway." simply laugh and tell her the <u>pen</u> (in stripes) is for me if I tell her. Apologies are forthcoming. 9 hrs. 30 min. Amt $4.83. No dinner hour today. Ate on the road. Had to hunt names for two babies, fill out the farm schedules, listen to an old lady's tale of woe, etc., just when I was in the biggest hurry.

April 25—Monday

My biggest day so far. Worked 9 hrs. 30 min. Amt. $5.73. Have numerous invitations every day to stay to dinner, supper or spend the night. People generally are very courteous to me. One lady whom I had never seen before, insisted that she go to the end of the lot and open the gate for me, and finally won out, going thru quite a little mud too. I wonder if one poor old lady has taken her hair down again since I came home. She was somewhat excited when answering my questions and suppose she did not notice, but four different times she rearranged her hair. But perhaps she couldn't get it up to feel comfortably. Good thing she didn't wear "rats." Mr. Blank said he'd tell his age if I told him some of the elderly spinsters' ages.

May 8—Sunday

Wonder if I am such a funny looking piece. One man flatly refused to see me. Sent word I should go to his wife for any information wanted—he didn't know anything about it—"didn't want to talk to no woman anyway." Ha! Ha! After some persuasion I found out what I wanted from his wife. One woman in Whistleville said, "if you want any information concerning my mother-in-law, better let me tell you as she will run if she sees you coming." Sure, I took the information then and there. One poor silly fellow, wanted to show me his watch, also to look at my "nice big book, great big book" as he called it. Oh dear, the way some people have to live! About the only answer I could get from one old woman was, "L__, G__, child I don't know." Another begged for some old cloths, if I had any I could let her have, and she surely looked as if she needed them.

May 13—Friday

My last day. Oh! Joy. Finished at noon.

May 17—Tuesday

Working on my books this morning.

May 19—Thursday
Took my books to Zion this eve. Called Mr. Bobb & decided to wait a day or two before handing them in.

May 21—Saturday
Took my books to the P.O.

Thursday, August 11
My check came today & false alarm sur nuff when I looked inside the envelope and found a blank.

Friday, August 12
Check came O.K. today.

Miss Myers dealt with long hours, several rainstorms, muddy roads, grouchy and friendly neighbors, and an April snowfall. The dollar amounts reported in her diary totaled $69.37, which is equal to about $1,300 today.

*York County "Police Census" 1890: An Alphabetical List of the Streets in Lower Manhattan and the Bronx Enumerated in the Lowest and Highest Numbered Books.* The census lists
- street and number
- name
- sex
- age
- patrolman and enumerator
- police precinct

# The Census of 1900
## The Twelfth Census of the United States
- Census Day: 1 June 1900.
- Time Allotted: one month.
- Population: 72.6 million.
- This is the only census, modern censuses included, to report the month and year of birth of each person.
- Beginning in 1900 and continuing through 1930, the census requested immigrants to report the year of immigration to the United States.

# The Census of 1910
## The Thirteenth Census of the United States
- Census Day: 15 April 1910 (changed from June 1 since 1830).
- Time Allotted: one month.
- Population: 92.2 million.

# The Census of 1920
## The Fourteenth Census of the United States
- Census Day: 1 January 1920.

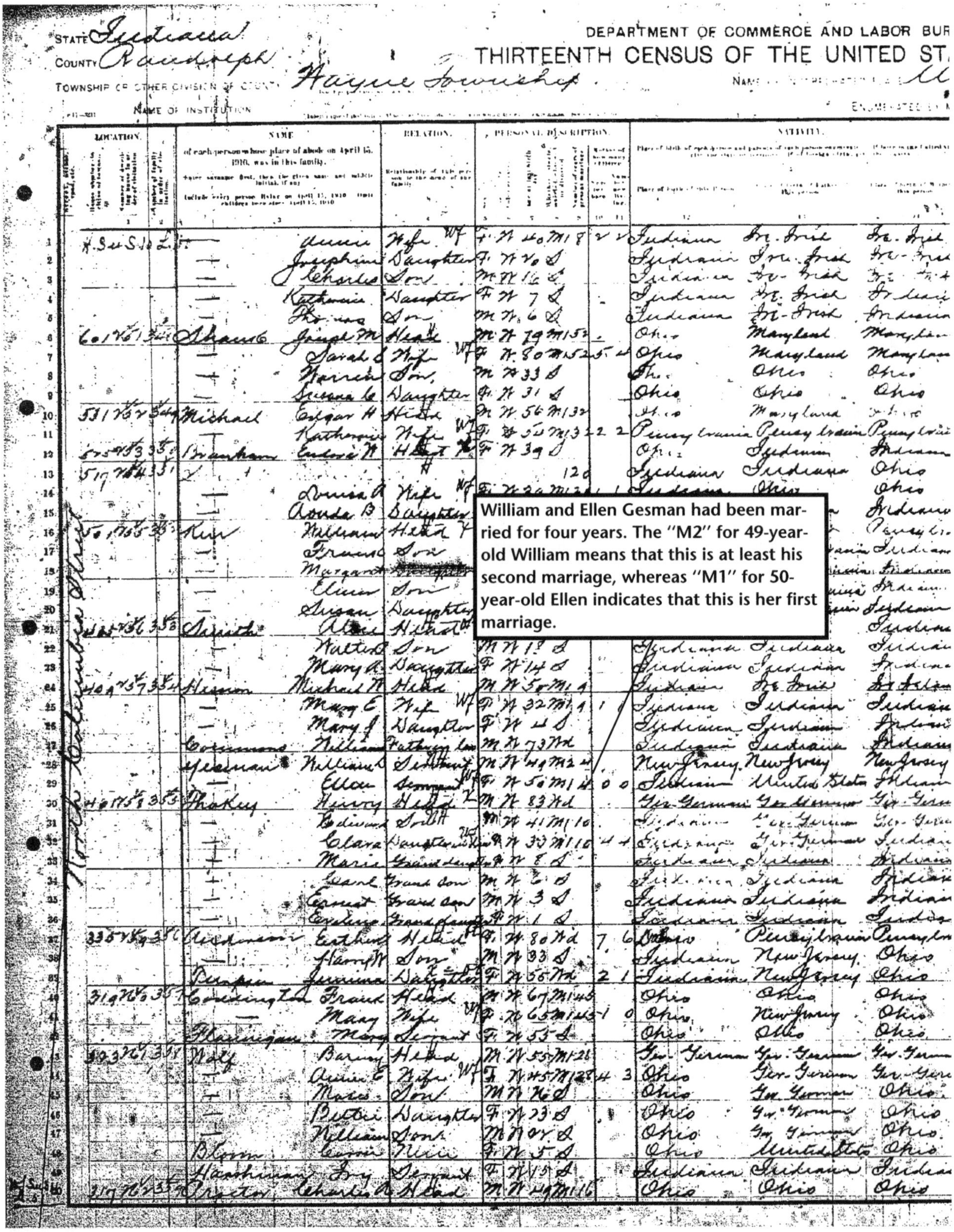
STATE Indiana
COUNTY Randolph
TOWNSHIP OR OTHER DIVISION OF COUNTY Wayne Township
NAME OF INSTITUTION
DEPARTMENT OF COMMERCE AND LABOR BUR
THIRTEENTH CENSUS OF THE UNITED ST
William and Ellen Gesman had been married for four years. The "M2" for 49-year-old William means that this is at least his second marriage, whereas "M1" for 50-year-old Ellen indicates that this is her first marriage.

**Figure 3-16**

1910 U.S. census, Randolph County, Indiana, population schedule, First Ward, Union City, Wayne Township, supervisor's district [S.D.] 8, enumeration district [E.D.] 144, sheet 11A; National Archives micropublication T624, roll 376.

BUREAU OF THE CENSUS
STATES: 1910 POPULATION

SUPERVISOR'S DISTRICT No. **8**  SHEET No. **11 A**

ENUMERATION DISTRICT No.

WARD OF CITY

ENUMERATOR

The quality and readability of this census page is above average. Many 1910 schedules are nearly impossible to read and cannot be remicrofilmed since the originals no longer exist. Congress authorized the destruction of the 1910 census after it was microfilmed more than fifty years ago.

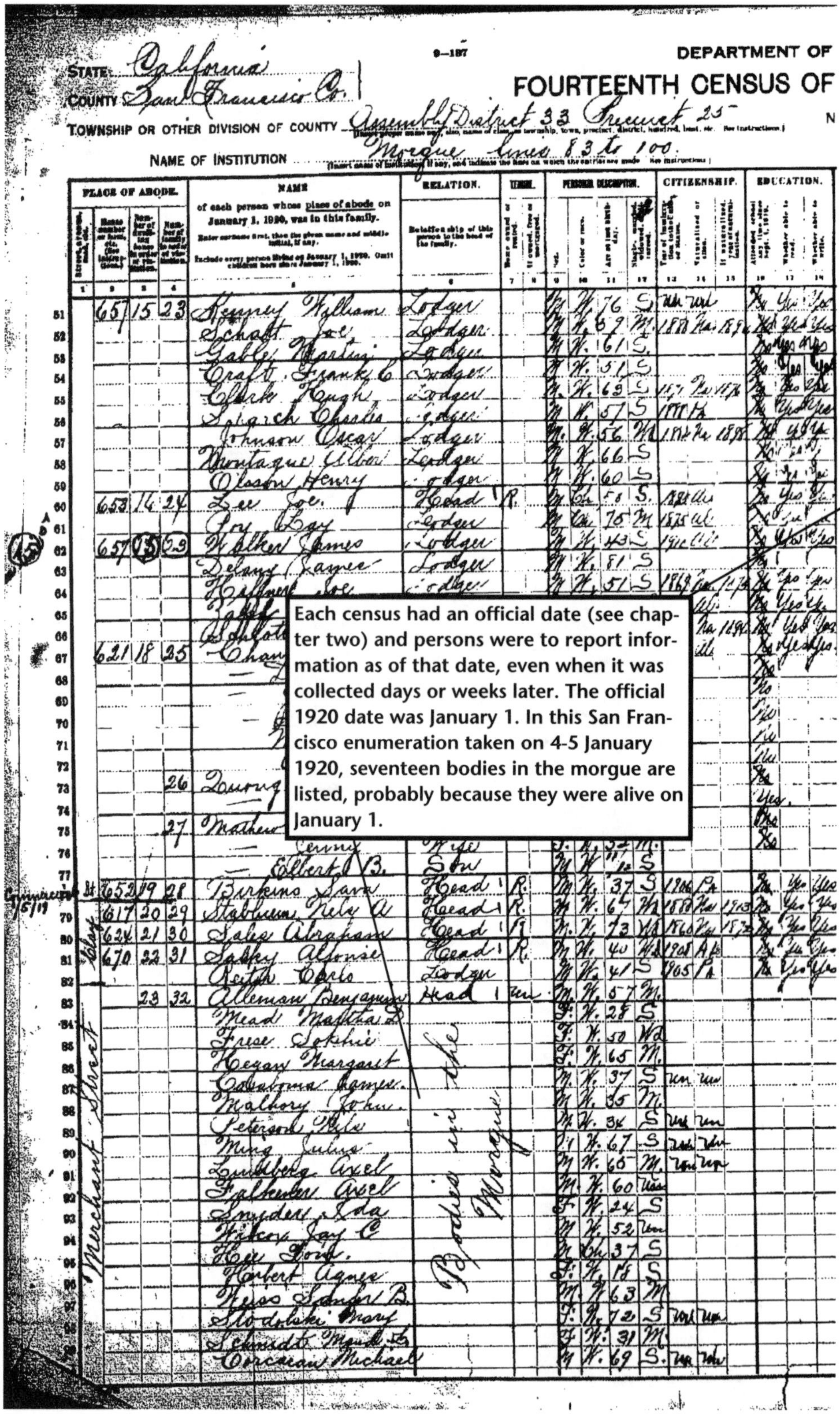
STATE: California
COUNTY San Francisco Co.
TOWNSHIP OR OTHER DIVISION OF COUNTY Assembly District 33 Precinct 25
NAME OF INSTITUTION Morgue Lines 83 to 100.

DEPARTMENT OF
FOURTEENTH CENSUS OF

PLACE OF ABODE. | NAME | RELATION. | TENURE. | PERSONAL DESCRIPTION. | CITIZENSHIP. | EDUCATION.

Each census had an official date (see chapter two) and persons were to report information as of that date, even when it was collected days or weeks later. The official 1920 date was January 1. In this San Francisco enumeration taken on 4-5 January 1920, seventeen bodies in the morgue are listed, probably because they were alive on January 1.

**Figure 3-17**
1920 U.S. census, San Francisco County, California, population schedule, San Francisco, Assembly District 33, Precinct 25, supervisor's district [S.D.] 4, enumerator district [E.D.] 258, sheet 2B; National Archives micropublication T625, roll 140.

COMMERCE—BUREAU OF THE CENSUS    [D1-578]

THE UNITED STATES: 1920—POPULATION

ME OF INCORPORATED PLACE *San Francisco*

ENUMERATED BY ME ON THE ~~7~~ 5 day of *January* 1920   *Josephine M. Ertola* ENUMERATOR

SUPERVISOR'S DISTRICT NO. *4*   SHEET NO.

ENUMERATION DISTRICT NO. *258*   *2* B

WARD OF CITY   124/50 0650

| Place of birth | Mother tongue | Place of birth | Mother tongue | Place of birth | Mother tongue | | Trade, profession, or particular kind of work done | Industry, business, or establishment in which at work | | No. of farm sched. |
|---|---|---|---|---|---|---|---|---|---|---|
| Ireland | English | Ireland | English | Ireland | English | | Retired | Railroadman | | 51 |
| Switzerland | German | Switzerland | German | Switzerland | German | | Woodsman | Lumber Camp | W | 52 058 |
| New York | | Germany | German | Germany | German | | ? | Grocer | W | 53 196 |
| Missouri | | France | French | ? | French | | ? | General | W | 54 176 |
| Ireland | English | Ireland | English | Ireland | English | | ? | Logging Camp | W | 55 058 |
| ? | German | Austria | French | Switzerland | German | Yes | Cook | Restaurant | W | 56 954 |
| Sweden | Swedish | Sweden | Swedish | Sweden | Swedish | Yes | ? | House | W | 57 148 |
| ? | | ? | | ? | | | Cook | Hotel | W | 58 ?54 |
| Maine | | Denmark | Danish | Denmark | Danish | | Soldier | Army | W | 59 822 |
| China | Chinese | China | Chinese | China | Chinese | Yes | Fisherman | ? | OA | 60 080 |
| China | Chinese | China | Chinese | China | Chinese | | ? | | | 61 |
| England | English | England | English | England | English | | Helper | Carpenter | W | 62 252 |
| Maine | | England | English | Maine | | | Packer | Flint | W | 63 796 |
| Germany | German | Germany | German | Germany | German | Yes | ? | Ranch | W | 64 016 |
| ? | German | Germany | German | Germany | German | Yes | ? | Farm | W | 65 012 |
| Yokohama | French | Honolulu | German | Honolulu | ? | Yes | ? | General | W | 66 196 |
| China | Chinese | China | Chinese | China | Chinese | Yes | Salesman | Jewelry | W | 67 791 |
| ? | | China | Chinese | China | Chinese | | None | | | 68 |
| California | | China | Chinese | ? | | | ? | | | 69 |
| California | | China | Chinese | ? | | | ? | | | 70 |
| California | | China | Chinese | ? | | | ? | | | 71 |
| California | | China | Chinese | ? | | | ? | | | 72 |
| California | | China | Chinese | ? | Chinese | | Merchant | Wholesale Store | OA | 73 782 |
| California | | China | Chinese | California | | | None | | | 74 |
| Texas | | Tennessee | | Alabama | | | Keeper | Restaurant | OA | 75 944 |
| ? | | Texas | | ? | | | None | | | 76 |
| California | | Texas | | Texas | | | | | | 77 |
| Servia | German | Servia | German | Servia | German | Yes | Keeper | Cafe | OA | 78 944 |
| Norway | Norwegian | Norway | Norwegian | Norway | Norwegian | Yes | Janitor | Office Bldg | W | 79 918 |
| West Russia | Jewish | West Russia | Jewish | West Russia | Jewish | Yes | Merchant | Merchandise | OA | 80 786 |
| Russia | Polish | Poland | Polish | Poland | Polish | Yes | Merchant | House Furnishing | OA | 81 750 |
| Russia | Polish | Russia | Polish | Russia | Polish | Yes | Blacksmith | General | W | 82 362 |
| Utah | | U.S. | | U.S. | | | Clerk | Telephone | W | 83 136 |
| Illinois | | U.S. | | U.S. | | | None | | | 84 994 |
| California | | U.S. | | U.S. | | | Retired | | | 85 — |
| Massachusetts | Italian | Italy | Italian | Italy | Italian | | ? | | | 86 — |
| ? | Italian | Italy | Italian | Italy | Italian | | Clerk | Store | | 87 196 |
| California | | U.S. | | U.S. | | | Janitor | ? | | 88 707 |
| Sweden | Swedish | Sweden | Swedish | Sweden | Swedish | | Keeper | Saloon | | 89 918 |
| Switzerland | German | Switzerland | German | Switzerland | German | | Not Known | | | 90 974 |
| Sweden | Swedish | Sweden | Swedish | Sweden | | | Not Known | | | 91 |
| Not Known | | U.S. | | U.S. | | | None | | | 92 — |
| California | | U.S. | | U.S. | | | Officer | Special | | 93 |
| Not Known | | U.S. | | U.S. | | | Laborer | | | 94 820 |
| California | | U.S. | | U.S. | | | Stenographer | | | 95 196 |
| California | | U.S. | | U.S. | | | Carpenter | | | 96 999 |
| Pennsylvania | | U.S. | | U.S. | | | ? | | | 97 148 |
| Germany | German | Germany | German | Germany | German | | Retired | | | 98 |
| ? | | U.S. | | U.S. | | | None | | | 99 |
| England | English | England | English | England | English | | Fireman | Marine | | 100 176 |

63

- Time Allotted: one month
- Population: 106 million.
- This is the only census to request the year in which a person was naturalized.

## The Census of 1930
### The Fifteenth Census of the United States
- Census Day: 1 April 1930; 1 October 1929 in Alaska.
- Time Allotted: one month.
- Population: 123.2 million.

**Quotes**

---

**DO YOU OWN A RADIO SET?**

Several enumerators reported there seemed to be a general reluctance to admit possession of radios. Repeated questions as to the reason for the lack of desire to answer this question disclosed that a belief was prevalent that the government was going to tax all radios. One woman admitted that music from an adjoining room was coming from a radio, but denied she was the owner. The enumerator put her down as an owner.

—*New York Times*, April 9, 1930, 29:6

# AVAILABILITY OF FEDERAL CENSUS SCHEDULES FOR 1940 THROUGH 2000

In accordance with privacy laws, census schedules remain confidential for seventy-two years, which is why the 1930 census was not released for public inspection until April 2002. The 1940 enumeration will be released in 2012; the 1950 census will not be public until the year 2022.

Special procedures allow you to obtain some information from census records collected from 1940 through 2000. The Census Bureau provides an age search service for the public <www.census.gov/genealogy/www/agesearch.html>. The service is called Age Search because it was developed to assist individuals trying to prove their age in order to receive retirement benefits, apply for a passport, or resolve other age-related issues.

The Census Bureau will search the census and issue an official transcript of the results, but the information will be released *only* to the named person, heirs of the named person, or that person's legal representative. Here is a summary of the process:

- An application for Search of Census Records, Form BC-600, must be completed. To obtain the form, write to the U.S. Department of Commerce, P.O. Box 1545, Jefferson, Indiana 47131, or look online at <www.census.gov/genealogy/www/agesearch.html>.

- If the named person is deceased, a copy of the death certificate must be provided. Immediate family members (parent, child, sibling, grandparent), the surviving spouse, the administrator or executor of an estate, or the beneficiary by will or insurance can apply, and the relationship must be stated on the application. A legal representative must furnish a copy of the court order so naming him, and a beneficiary must furnish legal evidence of that status.

- The official transcript lists the person's name, relationship to household head, age, and state/country of birth. Citizenship is provided for a foreign-born person. The search fee is currently forty dollars for one census for one person, plus an additional ten dollars for a full schedule. Information on other family members costs another forty to fifty dollars each. Full schedules are not available for 1970 through 2000. Personal checks and money orders are accepted, but not credit cards. Processing time is three to four weeks.

| FEDERAL CENSUS DATA 1940 THROUGH 2000 | | | | | | | |
|---|---|---|---|---|---|---|---|
| | 1940 | 1950 | 1960 | 1970 | 1980 | 1990* | 2000** |
| Address | x | x | x | x | x | x | |
| Home Owned or Rented | x | | | | | | |
| Name | x | x | x | x | x | x | x |
| Relationship to Head | x | x | x | x | x | x | x |
| Age | x | x | | x | x | x | x |
| Date of Birth | | | year and quarter | month and year | month and year | year | day, month, and year |
| Race | x | x | x | x | x | x | x |
| Marital Status | x | x | x | x | x | x | |
| State/Country of Birth | x | x | | | | | |
| Citizenship Status | x | x | | | | | |
| Occupation | x | x | | | | | |
| Location of Residence Five Years Ago | x | | | | | | |

*In 1990 a long form with additional questions was sent to 17 percent of all housing units. Additional questions included place of birth, citizenship status, year of immigration, place of residence five years ago, veteran status, and occupation.

**In 2000 a long form with additional questions was sent to 17 percent of all housing units. Additional questions included marital status, place of birth, citizenship status, year of immigration, whether enrolled in school or level of education, ancestry, residence five years ago, language spoken at home, veteran status, disability, grandparents as caregivers, current labor force status, place of work and journey to work, work status last year, industry/occupation/class of worker, previous year's income, number of units in housing structure, number of rooms, number of bedrooms, plumbing and kitchen facilities, year structure built, year moved into unit, house heating fuel, number of telephones, vehicles available, whether farm residence, value of home, monthly rent, and shelter costs (selected monthly owner costs).

FOUR

# Non-Population Schedules

For some census years, additional details about some segments of the population such as farmers, business owners, prisoners, homeless children, paupers, and veterans appear in non-population schedules. The term *non-population* is misleading because it implies that the census information is not personal or genealogically important. Nothing could be further from the truth.

These non-population schedules include names of individuals and information not found in most other records. For example, agriculture schedules report the specific details about farmers' crop production, and mortality schedules give causes of death.

Some non-population schedules have been destroyed or lost, so they are not available for all areas or time periods. Specific details are provided within the discussion of each type, but the following schedules are generally available:

- Agriculture: 1850 through 1885
- Defective, Dependent, Delinquent Classes: 1880
- Industry and Manufacturing: 1810, 1820, 1850 through 1885
- Mortality: 1850 through 1885, 1900 (Minnesota only)
- Social Statistics: 1850, 1860, 1870
- Veterans: 1890

## AGRICULTURE SCHEDULES

Agriculture schedules help the genealogist reconstruct an ancestor's financial and social role in the farming community. These schedules can supplement land and tax research and document expansion or sale of a farm. If you find schedules for both 1860 and 1870 you can compare the data to see effects of the Civil War on your family.

The 1850 and 1860 agriculture schedules were completed for farms and plantations with an annual produce value of at least one hundred dollars. In

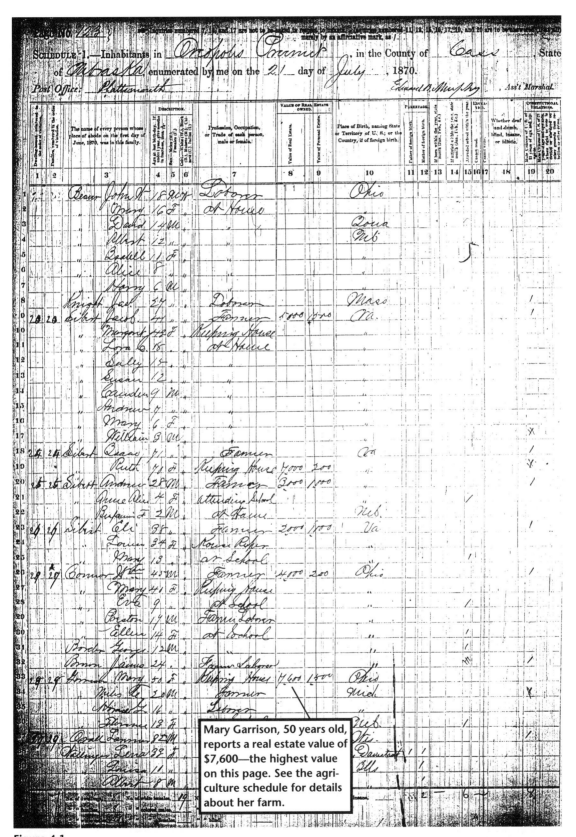

**Figure 4-1**

1870 U.S. census, Cass County, Nebraska, population schedule, Plattsmouth, Oreopolis Precinct, page 123; National Archives micropublication M593, roll 828.

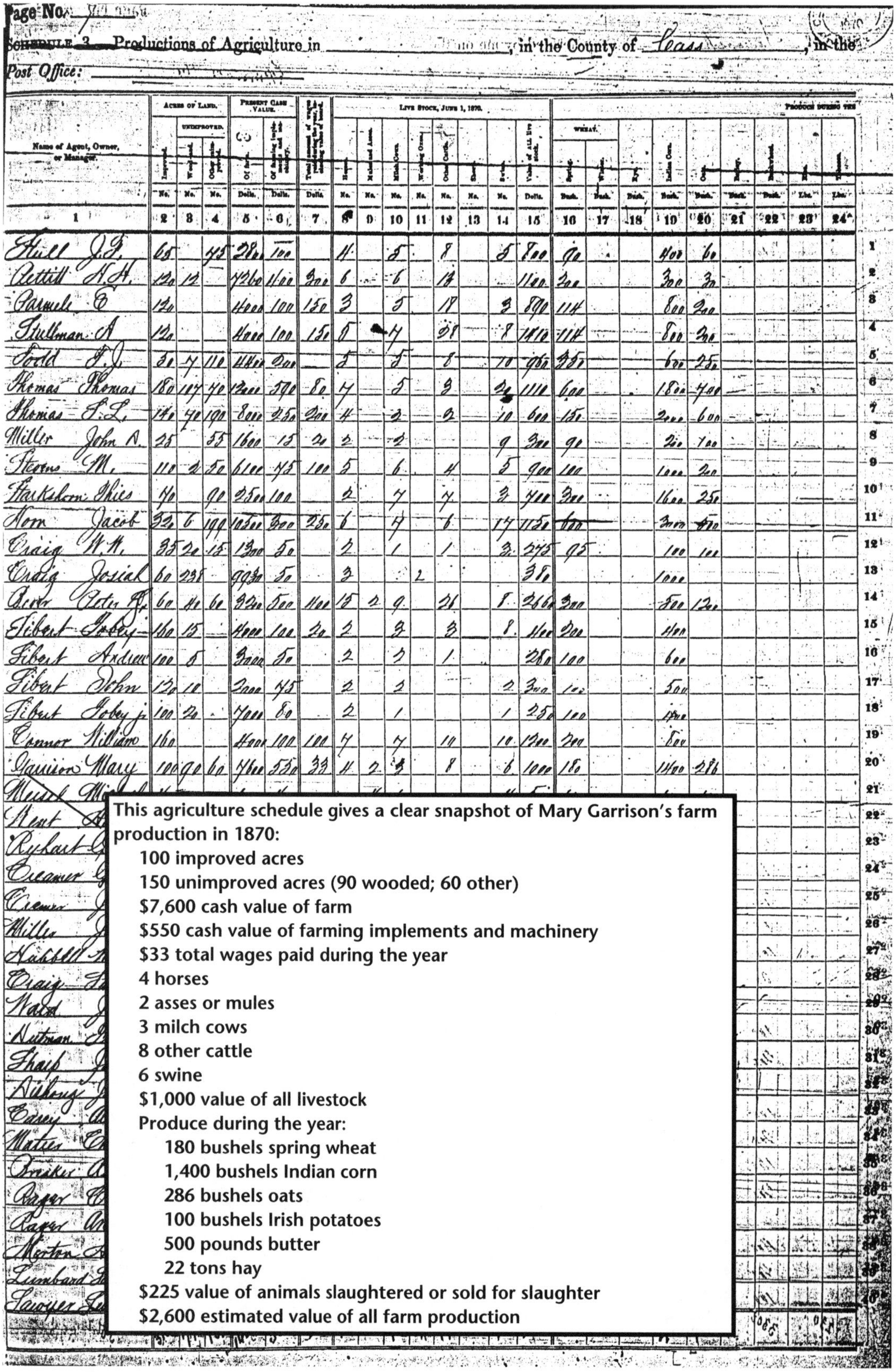
Schedule 3.—Productions of Agriculture in
in the County of Cass
Post Office:
This agriculture schedule gives a clear snapshot of Mary Garrison's farm production in 1870:
100 improved acres
150 unimproved acres (90 wooded; 60 other)
$7,600 cash value of farm
$550 cash value of farming implements and machinery
$33 total wages paid during the year
4 horses
2 asses or mules
3 milch cows
8 other cattle
6 swine
$1,000 value of all livestock
Produce during the year:
180 bushels spring wheat
1,400 bushels Indian corn
286 bushels oats
100 bushels Irish potatoes
500 pounds butter
22 tons hay
$225 value of animals slaughtered or sold for slaughter
$2,600 estimated value of all farm production

**Figure 4-2**
1870 U.S. census, Cass County, Nebraska, agriculture schedule, pages 7–8; National Archives micropublication T1128, roll 1.

Page No. _____

State of _Nebraska_ _____ enumerated by me on the _____ day of _____, 1870.

_Edmund B. Murphy_ , Ass't Marshal.

| 25 | 26 | 27 | 28 | 29 | 30 | 31 | 32 | 33 | 34 | 35 | 36 | 37 | 38 | 39 | 40 | 41 | 42 | 43 | 44 | 45 | 46 | 47 | 48 | 49 | 50 | 51 | 52 |
|---|---|---|---|---|---|---|---|---|---|---|---|---|---|---|---|---|---|---|---|---|---|---|---|---|---|---|---|
| | | | 100 | | | | | 600 | | | 30 | | | | | | | | | | | | | | | 205 | 1460 |
| | | | 100 | | | | | 700 | | | 40 | | | | | | | | | | | | | | | 90 | 1850 |
| | | | | | | | | 400 | | | 40 | | | | | | | | | | | | | | | 30 | 1760 |
| | | | 50 | | | | | 300 | | | 44 | | | | | | | | | | | | | | | 300 | 2451 |
| | 300 | | 100 | | | | | 400 | | | 5 | | | | | | | | | | 10 | 10 | | | | 295 | 2025 |
| | 30 | | | | | | | 350 | | | 30 | | | | | | | | | | 30 | 30 | | | | 377 | 3332 |
| | | | | | | | | 500 | | | 30 | | | | | | | | | | | | | | | 94 | 2380 |
| | | 25 | | | | | | 300 | | | 8 | | | | | | | | | | | | | | | | 600 |
| | | 70 | | | | | | 250 | | | 30 | | | | | | | | | | | | | | | 140 | 1850 |
| | | 25 | | | | | | 100 | | | 13 | | | | | | | | | | | | | | | 60 | 900 |
| | | | 100 | | | | | 500 | | | 30 | | | | | | | | | | 31 | 30 | | | | 430 | 4175 |
| | | | 300 | | | | | 175 | | | 5 | | | | | | | | | | | | | | | 160 | 650 |
| | | | | | | | | 100 | | | | | | | | | | | | | | | | | | 160 | 1060 |
| | | | | | | | | 500 | | | 30 | | | | | | | | | | | | | | | 300 | 1310 |
| | | | 30 | | | | | 200 | | | 8 | | | | | | | | | | | | | | | 96 | 900 |
| | | | 40 | | | | | 100 | | | 8 | | | | | | | | | | | | | | | 40 | 640 |
| | | | 40 | | | | | 150 | | | 4 | | | | | | | | | | | | | | | 140 | 440 |
| | | | 30 | | | | | 30 | | | 6 | | | | | | | | | | | | | | | 80 | 580 |
| | | | 50 | | | | | 500 | | | 13 | | | | | | | | | | 40 | | | | | 80 | 2000 |
| | | | 100 | | | | | 500 | | | 22 | | | | | | | | | | | | | | | 235 | 2600 |
| | | | | | | | | 350 | | | 10 | | | | | | | | | | | | | | | 80 | 1300 |
| | | | | | | | | 100 | | | 10 | | | | | | | | | | | | | | | 300 | 1770 |
| | | | 100 | | | | | 500 | | | 40 | | | | | | | | | 30 | | | | | | 300 | 3100 |
| | | | 80 | | | | | 150 | | | 13 | | | | | | | | | | | | | | | 100 | 1800 |
| | | | 75 | | | | | 300 | | | 20 | | | | | | | | | | | | | | | 175 | 1775 |
| | | | 80 | | | | | 100 | | | 10 | | | | | | | | | | 10 | | | | | 80 | 980 |
| | | | 100 | | | | | 150 | | | 18 | | | | | | | | | | | | | | | 300 | 1130 |
| | | | 50 | | | | | 600 | | | 15 | | | | | | | | | | | | | | | 80 | 1525 |
| | | | | | | | | | | | 4 | | | | | | | | | | | | | | | | 400 |
| | | | 100 | | | | | 300 | | | 5 | | | | | | | | | | | | | | | 40 | 900 |
| | | | 200 | | | | | 100 | | | 10 | | | | | | | | | | | | | | | 100 | 400 |
| | | | | | | | | | | | | | | | | | | | | | | | | | | | 300 |
| | | | 100 | | | | | 300 | | | 10 | | | | | | | | | | | | | | | 100 | 450 |
| | | | 300 | | | | | | | | 30 | | | | | | | | | | | | | | | | 400 |
| | | | 150 | | | | | 150 | | | 5 | | | | | | | | | | | | | | | 75 | 600 |
| | | | 300 | | | | | 100 | | | 10 | | | | | | | | | | | | | | | 100 | 1450 |
| | | | | | | | | | | | | | | | | | | | | | | | | | | | 400 |
| | | | 400 | | | | | 300 | | | 30 | | | | | | | | | | | | | | | 300 | 1300 |
| | | | 300 | | | | | 300 | | | 4 | | | | | | | | | | | | | | | 100 | 400 |
| | | | 100 | | | | | 100 | | | | | | | | | | | | | 180 | | | | | 100 | 1200 |
| 50 | | | 5995 | | | 224 | | 10515 | 618 | 2004 | 695 | | | | | | 111 | | | 60 | 521 | 70 | | | | 5362 | 59842 |

* This will include only such cheese as is made upon the farm. Milk sent to cheese factories will be regarded as milk sold off the farm.

69

1870 and 1880, farms of less than three acres were not reported unless five hundred dollars' worth of produce had been sold during the year. Nurseries and orchards were included as farms, but family vegetable gardens and cabbage and potato patches were not. Farms were enumerated regardless of whether the occupant owned or leased the land. Owners, tenants, and sharecroppers were not distinguished from one another in the schedules until 1880. Enumerators were expected to report information as accurately as possible, but unless the farmers kept precise records, the quantities and values were estimated.

In 1918 Congress authorized the disposal of supplemental schedules in order to conserve space and reduce fire hazards. Fortunately, the Census Bureau offered state archives, historical societies, and universities the opportunity to acquire some of these records, which is why some are available today. All 1900 and 1910 agriculture schedules were destroyed.

*The Guide to Federal Records in the National Archives of the United States* (U.S. Government Printing Office, 1995) reports that a few 1920 farm schedules are located at the National Archives, Washington, DC, in Record Group 29, Miscellaneous non-population schedules and supplementary records as follows:

- McLean County, Illinois
- Jackson County, Michigan
- Carbon County, Montana
- Santa Fe County, New Mexico
- Wilson County, Tennessee

Some agriculture schedules have been microfilmed and are available at the National Archives. Very few have been indexed. The records are neither complete for all states nor available in one central location.

- The Perkins Library at Duke University in Durham, North Carolina, houses non-population schedules for Colorado, the District of Columbia, Georgia, Kentucky, Louisiana, Nevada, Tennessee, Virginia, and Wyoming. Details on the collection are at <www.lib.duke.edu/access/news/census.htm>.
- The University of North Carolina in Chapel Hill sells microfilm copies of the 1850 through 1880 agriculture schedules for Alabama, Florida, Georgia, Kentucky, Louisiana, Maryland, Mississippi, North Carolina, Tennessee, Texas, Virginia, and West Virginia. Details appear at <www.lib.unc.edu/ncc/phs/census.html>.
- The Georgia, Nebraska, Pennsylvania, and Utah non-population schedules are available on microfilm at the Family History Library in Salt Lake City, Utah.
- For other states, check with the state historical society, state archives, or local library collections, as well as the National Archives microfilm locator at <www.nara.gov>.

The agriculture schedules for 1850 through 1870 recorded
- name of owner, agent, or manager of farm
- improved acres of land

**Tip**

**TIPS FOR SEARCHING SUPPLEMENTAL SCHEDULES**

Examine the full population schedule for clues suggesting follow-up research in supplemental schedules. For example: When value of real estate is reported, more details may be found in the agricultural and slave schedules.

For a family member who was deaf, blind, or idiotic in 1880, the defective, dependent, and delinquent schedules provide more specific information.

If a family member is missing from any of the 1850 through 1880 population schedules, check the corresponding mortality schedules. People who died within the year preceding a census should appear on the mortality schedule.

| AGRICULTURE CENSUS SCHEDULES: 1850 THROUGH 1885 | | | | | |
|---|---|---|---|---|---|
| State | 1850 | 1860 | 1870 | 1880 | 1885 |
| Alabama | x | x | x | x | |
| Arkansas | x | x | x | x | |
| California | x | x | x | x | |
| Colorado | | | x | x | x |
| Connecticut | x | x | x | x | |
| Dakota Territory | | | | x | x |
| Delaware | x | x | x | x | |
| District of Columbia | x | x | x | x | |
| Florida | x | x | x | x | x |
| Georgia | x | x | x | x | |
| Idaho | | | x | x | |
| Illinois | x | x | x | x | |
| Indiana★ | x | x | x | x | |
| Iowa | x | x | x | x | |
| Kansas | | x | x | x | |
| Kentucky | x | x | x | x | |
| Louisiana | x | x | x | x | |
| Maine | x | x | x | x | |
| Maryland | x | x | x | x | |
| Massachusetts | x | x | x | x | |
| Michigan | x | x | x | x | |
| Minnesota | x | x | x | x | |
| Mississippi | x | x | x | x | |
| Missouri | x | x | x | x | |
| Montana | | | x | x | |
| Nebraska | | x | x | x | x |
| Nevada | | | | x | |
| New Hampshire | x | x | x | x | |
| New Jersey | x | x | x | x | |
| New Mexico Territory | | | | | x |
| New York | x | x | x | x | |
| North Carolina | x | x | x | x | |
| Ohio (Incomplete) | x | x | x | x | |
| Oregon | x | x | x | | |
| Pennsylvania | x | x | x | x | |

| | | | | | |
|---|---|---|---|---|---|
| Rhode Island | | | x | | |
| South Carolina | x | x | x | x | |
| Tennessee | x | x | x | x | |
| Texas | x | x | x | x | |
| Utah | x | x | x | x | |
| Vermont | x | x | x | x | |
| Virginia | x | x | x | x | |
| Washington | | x | x | x | |
| West Virginia | x | x | x | x | |
| Wisconsin | x | x | x | x | |
| Wyoming | | | | x | |

★ Many rural families in Indiana were missed during the 1850 population enumeration because of poor weather and impassable trails. The agriculture schedule was taken at a different time of the year, and most of the rural residents were included in that enumeration.

- unimproved acres of land
- cash value of farm
- value of farming implements and machinery
- livestock:
  - horses
  - asses and mules
  - milch cows
  - working oxen
  - other cattle
  - sheep
  - swine
  - value of livestock
- produce during the year:
  - bushels of wheat
  - bushels of rye
  - bushels of Indian corn
  - bushels of oats
  - pounds of rice
  - pounds of tobacco
  - bales of ginned cotton, four hundred pounds each
  - pounds of wool
  - bushels of peas and beans
  - bushels of Irish potatoes
  - bushels of sweet potatoes
  - bushels of barley
  - bushels of buckwheat
  - value of orchard products in dollars
  - gallons of wine

> value of produce of market gardens
> pounds of butter
> pounds of cheese
> tons of hay
> bushels of clover seed
> bushels of grass seed
> pounds of hops
> tons of drew rotten hemp
> tons of water rotten hemp
> other prepared hemp
> pounds of flax
> bushels of flaxseed
> pounds of silk cocoons
> pounds of maple sugar
> hogsheads of one hundred pounds each of cane sugar
> gallons of molasses, and from what made
> pounds of beeswax
> pounds of honey
> value of homemade manufactures

- value of animals slaughtered

For 1880 the agriculture schedule was expanded to cover almost twice what it had in previous years and included

- name of person who conducts the farm
- occupier is the owner of the farm
- occupier rents at a fixed money rental
- occupier conducts farm for shares of products
- acres of land:
  > improved acreage:
  > > tilled, including fallow and grass in rotation whether pasture or meadow
  > > permanent meadows, pastures, orchards, vineyards
  > unimproved acreage:
  > > woodland and forest
  > > other unimproved, including "old fields" not growing wood
- farm values:
  > dollar value of farm, including land, fences, and buildings
  > dollar value of farming implements and machines
  > dollar value of livestock
- fences, cost of buildings and repairing fences in 1879
- cost of fertilizers purchased in 1879
- labor * (see note on page 76):
  > amount paid for wages for farm labor during 1879, including value of board
  > weeks of hired labor in 1879 upon farm (and dairy) excluding housework

- estimated value of all farm productions (sold, consumed, or on hand for 1879)
- grasslands:
    acreage in 1879:
        mown
        not mown
    products harvested in 1879:
        hay
        clover seed
        grass seed
- horses of all ages on hand 1 June 1880
- mules and asses of all ages on hand 1 June 1880
- meat cattle and their products:
    working oxen on hand 1 June 1880
    milch cows on hand 1 June 1880
    other cattle on hand 1 June 1880
    calves dropped in 1879
    movement in 1879 for cattle of all ages:
        purchased
        sold living
        slaughtered
        died, strayed, and not recovered
    gallons of milk sold or sent to butter and cheese factories in 1879
    pounds of butter made on the farm in 1879
    pounds of cheese made on the farm in 1879
- sheep:
    number on hand 1 June 1880
    number of lambs dropped
    sheep and lambs
        purchased
        sold living
        slaughtered
        killed by dogs
        died of disease
        died of stress of weather
    clip, spring, 1880, shorn and to be shorn:
        fleeces
        weight in pounds
- swine on hand 1 June 1880
- poultry on hand 1 June 1880, exclusive of spring hatching:
    barnyard
    other
- dozens of eggs produced in 1879
- cereal production in 1879 (acres planted and bushels yielded):
    barley
    buckwheat

       Indian corn

       oats

       rye

       wheat

- pulse:

       Canada peas (dry) in bushels in 1879

       beans, dry bushels in 1879

- fiber:

       flax area given in acres, 1879

       bushels of flaxseed, 1879

       tons of flax straw, 1879

       pounds of flax fiber, 1879

       acres of hemp

       tons of hemp

- sugar:

       sorghum area given in acres, 1879

       pounds of sorghum sugar, 1879

       gallons of sorghum molasses, 1879

       pounds of maple sugar, 1879

       gallons of maple molasses, 1879

- broomcorn, 1879:

       acres

       pounds harvested

- hops, 1879:

       acres

       pounds harvested

- potatoes (Irish), 1879:

       acres planted

       bushels harvested

- potatoes (sweet), 1879:

       acres planted

       Bushels harvested

- tobacco, 1879:

       acres planted

       pounds harvested

- orchards, 1879:

       apple production:

          acres

          number of bearing trees

          bushels harvested, 1879

       peach production:

          acres

          number of bearing trees

          bushels harvested, 1879

       total value of orchard products of all kinds sold or consumed

- nurseries:

acres

dollar value of produce sold in 1879

- vineyards:

  acres

  pounds of grapes sold in 1879

  gallons of wine made in 1879

- market gardens, value of produce sold, 1879
- bees, 1879:

  pounds of honey

  pounds of beeswax

- forest products:

  cords of wood cut in 1879

*Note: A slightly modified schedule that distinguished between white and black labor was used in the South. It also added inquiries on rice, cotton, and cane and omitted questions on broomcorn and hops.

## DEFECTIVE, DEPENDENT, DELINQUENT CLASSES

The DDD schedules, officially termed Supplemental Schedules 1–7: Defective, Dependent, and Delinquent Classes, were used only in 1880. The purpose of the DDD schedules was to collect statistics to aid the government in budgeting the building and maintenance of institutions and prisons and providing financial aid for the disabled. **For the genealogist, the resulting data can be significant in compiling health histories and studying genetic diseases.**

**Idea Generator**

These unusually detailed census schedules can provide information about your ancestors that is not available in the regular returns and probably not in any other source. For example, Donna Rachal Mills, author of *Florida Unfortunates. The 1880 Federal Census: Defective, Dependent, and Delinquent Classes* (Mills Historical Press: Tuscaloosa, Ala., and Orlando, Fla., 1993) tells about John M. Lee, who was serving a prison term in Brevard County, Florida, for changing election returns; Charles Alexander and George McElroy were awaiting trial for shooting a dog and wounding a cow, respectively. Within the same Florida return is William A. McClaming, of Sumter County, whose cause of idiocy was an overdose of quinine at age two. The circumference of his head was two feet, five inches.

Each person reported in the DDD schedules was first entered on the population schedule. The page and line of the population schedule was then entered on the supplemental schedule, thereby making it possible to correlate the dependent person with the rest of his family or the institution where he resided. The Census Bureau expected parents to conceal or deny the existence of some afflictions, so the enumerators were instructed to rely on their own observation. They were instructed to verify information with physicians and to quiz neighbors when necessary in order to report all defective, dependent, and delinquent individuals. The city, county, and state of residence that were reported in these

# 1880 DDD SCHEDULES—NEW CASTLE COUNTY, DELAWARE

The original Delaware 1880 Supplemental Schedules 1–7: Defective, Dependent, and Delinquent Classes (DDD schedules) are located at the Delaware State Archives in Dover, Delaware. A microfilm copy is available at the Family History Library in Salt Lake City (film number 1,421,306; item 3). Persons who were insane, homeless (children only), idiots, paupers, blind, or prisoners and enumerated in Wilmington, New Castle County, E.D. 20, pages 17–21 in the population schedule can be found in these DDD schedules. Examples of unusual data within these schedules follow.

## Supplemental Schedule 1: Insane Inhabitants

Forty-four insane persons, ranging from age twenty to fifty-five, are named. Seven required the use of handcuffs, three needed leg irons, and four required both.

## Supplemental Schedule 2: Idiots

All but one of the forty-one persons listed had been idiots since they were babies. Fifty percent had large heads. Ages are not reported on this schedule, therefore a comparison with the population schedule would help determine if the persons named were adults in 1880.

## Supplemental Schedule 3: Deaf-Mutes

No deaf-mutes were reported as residing in New Castle County in 1880.

## Supplemental Schedule 4: Blind Inhabitants

Of the nine blind persons named, four were partly blind. A twenty-five-year-old woman reported the cause of blindness as disease, whereas a sixty-seven-year-old man attributed his blindness to old age. A sixty-five-year-old woman claimed abuse as the cause, and a forty-five-year-old reported "blowed up," suggesting an accident. The others did not know the cause.

## Supplemental Schedule 5: Homeless Children (in Institutions)

The ages of the twenty-five children are not reported; however, that information can be obtained from the population schedule. All of the children had at least one living parent, although ten had been abandoned by their parent(s). Fifty percent of the parents had surrendered control of their children. A surprising statistic is that fifteen of the twenty-five children were born in the institution; that may explain why twenty-one of the twenty-five children were illegitimate. Only five children are reported as having had respectable origins, and one had been prosecuted as a criminal. Four children were also idiots with additional information reported in Supplemental Schedule 2.

continued

> **Supplemental Schedule 6: Inhabitants in Prison (See Figure 4-3)**
>
> The alleged offenses of fifty prisoners in the New Castle County Jail include murder, assault and battery, manslaughter, rape, larceny, receiving stolen goods, and vagrancy. Sentences ranged from three months to life, and one rapist was condemned to hang.
>
> **Supplemental Schedule 7: Pauper and Indigent Inhabitants**
>
> Nearly half of the twenty-one persons who were paupers or indigents residing in institutions, poorhouses or asylums were also insane. Only two were considered able-bodied, and none of them had a relative residing with them.

schedules were supposed to be the individuals' residences when at home rather than the locations of institutions, hospitals, poorhouses, or prison.

## Supplemental Schedule 1: Insane Inhabitants

Insane persons were described as suffering from mania (delirium), melancholia (depression), paresis (general paralysis), dementia, epilepsy, or dipsomania (uncontrollable desire for spirituous liquors). Instructions to the enumerators distinguished between the deteriorated minds of the insane and the retarded mentality of idiots.

- Number of page and line from population schedule
- Name of insane person
- City or town of residence
- County (if in same state as guardian or legal agent) or state (if in some other state)
- Whether an inmate of an institution and whether a pay patient
- Form of illness
- Duration of present attack
- Total number of attacks
- Age at first attack
- Whether person required to be kept in a cell by day or night
- Whether person required restraint by mechanical appliance
- Whether person had ever been an inmate of any hospital or asylum, and if so the name of the hospital or asylum
- Total length of time in asylums
- Date (year only) of discharge
- Whether person was epileptic
- Whether person was suicidal
- Whether person was homicidal

## Supplemental Schedule 2: Idiots

An idiot was defined as a person with extreme mental deficiency in infancy or childhood. Causes of idiocy could include scarlet fever, measles, meningitis, a

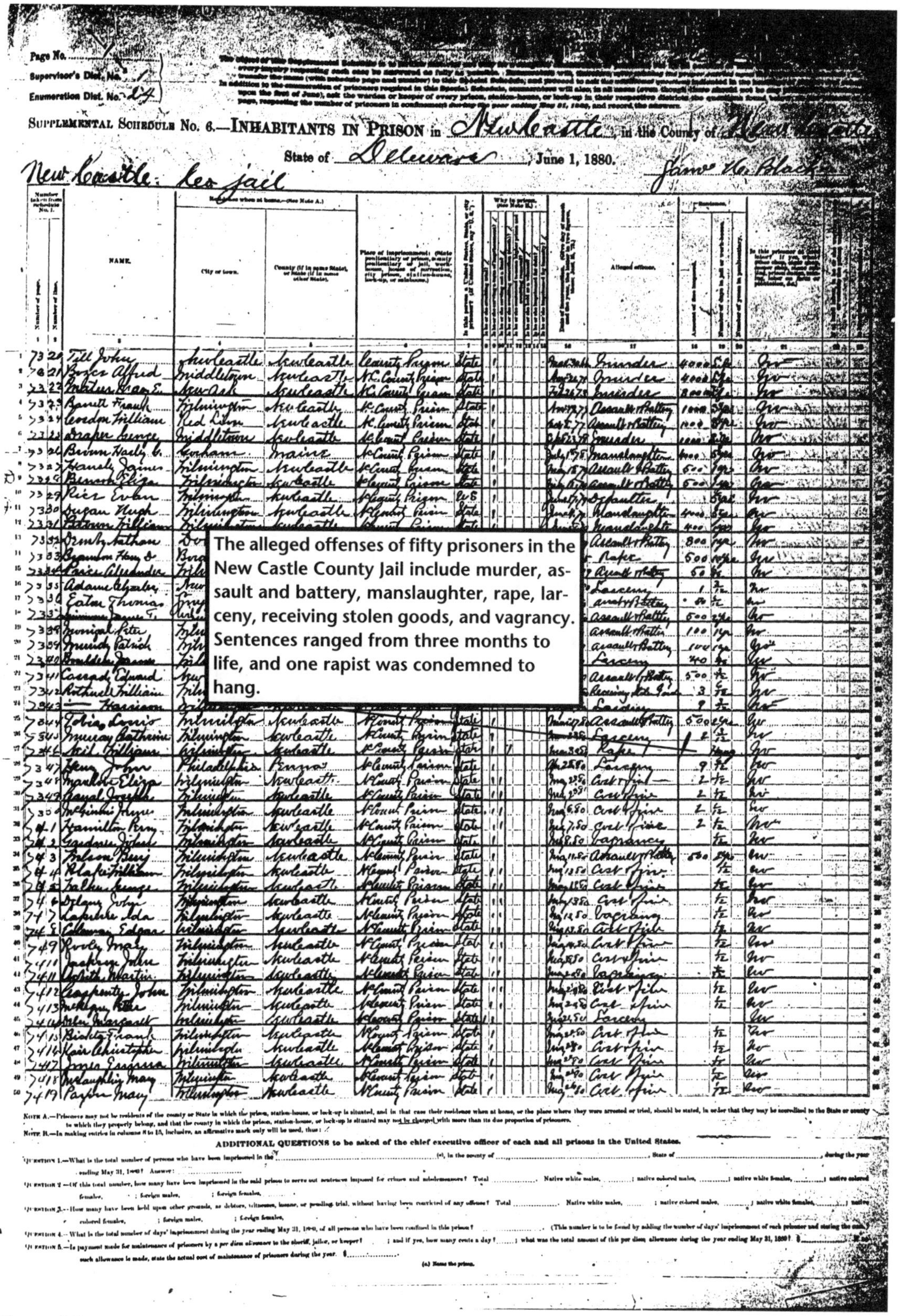

**Figure 4-3**

1880 U.S. census, New Castle County, Delaware, Supplemental Schedule Number 6 for the Defective, Dependent and Delinquent Classes, Inhabitants in Prison, New Castle County Jail, supervisor's district [S.D.] 1, enumeration district [E.D.] 24, page 1. Originals at Delaware State Archives. Family History Library film number 1,421,306; item 3.

blow to the head, a fall, or a fright. Demented persons were to be classified as insane.

- Number of page and line from population schedule
- Name of idiot
- City or town of residence
- County (if in same state) or state (if in some other state)
- Whether person was self-supporting or partly so
- Age at which idiocy occurred
- Cause of idiocy
- Size of head: large, small, or natural
- Whether person had been an inmate of a training school for idiots, and if so, the name of the training school
- Total length of time spent during life in training school or schools
- Date (year only) of discharge
- Whether person was also insane
- Whether person was also blind
- Whether person was also deaf
- Whether person was also an epileptic
- Whether person was paralyzed, and if so, which side

## Supplemental Schedule 3: Deaf-Mutes

A deaf-mute was defined as a person who could not speak because he could not hear sufficiently enough to learn to speak. Enumerators were instructed to be careful to exclude persons who were only deaf or hard of hearing or only dumb (tongue-tied).

A semi-mute was a deaf-mute who had lost his hearing after acquiring partial knowledge of the spoken language. Some semi-mutes retained the ability to speak imperfectly, while others lost speech entirely. If a deaf-mute had learned to speak, she was considered a semi-mute unless she was taught to speak in an institution for deaf-mutes.

The enumerators were encouraged to seek information on deaf-mutes from physicians and schoolteachers. But enumerators were also advised to query the deaf-mutes about other deaf-mutes in the region since the deaf-mutes sought one another's companionship to alleviate their sense of isolation.

- Number of page and line from population schedule
- Name of deaf-mute
- City or town of residence
- County (if in same state) or state (if in some other state)
- Whether person was self-supporting or partly so
- Age at which deafness occurred
- Supposed cause of deafness, if known
- Whether person is semi-mute
- Whether person is semi-deaf
- Whether person had ever been an inmate in an institution for deaf-mutes, and if so, the name of the institution
- Total length of time spent during life in any institution

- Date (year only) of discharge
- Whether person was also insane
- Whether person was idiotic
- Whether person was blind

## Supplemental Schedule 4: Blind

This enumeration included the totally blind and the semi-blind. A person was totally blind if he was unable to distinguish forms or colors; a semi-blind person could distinguish forms or colors but could not see well enough to read. Enumerators were instructed to make a special effort to indicate whether blindness occurred at birth.

- Number of page and line from population schedule
- Name of blind person
- City or town of residence
- County (if in same state) or state (if in some other state)
- Whether person was self-supporting, or partly so
- Age at which blindness occurred
- Form of blindness
- Supposed cause of blindness, if known
- Whether person was totally blind
- Whether person was semi-blind
- Whether person had ever been an inmate of an institution for the blind, and if so, the name of the institution
- Total length of time spent in any institution
- Date (year only) of discharge
- Whether person was also insane
- Whether person was idiotic
- Whether person was also a deaf-mute

## Supplemental Schedule 5: Homeless Children

Special attention was given to the arrest records of children in orphanages to determine those from "respectable" as opposed to "vicious" backgrounds.

- Number of page and line from population schedule
- Name of homeless child
- City or town of residence
- County (if in same state) or state (if in some other state)
- Whether child's father was deceased
- Whether child's mother was deceased
- Whether child had been abandoned by the parents
- Whether the child's parents had surrendered control to the institution
- Whether the child was born in this institution, and if not, the year when admitted
- Whether child was illegitimate
- Whether child was separated from living mother
- Whether child had ever been arrested, and if so, for what alleged offense
- Whether child had ever been convicted or sentenced

- Whether origin of child was respectable
- Whether child had been rescued from criminal surroundings
- Whether child was blind
- Whether child was a deaf-mute
- Whether child was an idiot

## Supplemental Schedule 6: Inhabitants in Prison

The enumerators were instructed to direct the questions to the warden or keeper of the prison rather than to the prisoner.

- Number of page and line from population schedule
- Name of prisoner
- City or town of residence
- County (if in same state) or state (if in some other state)
- Place of imprisonment (e.g., state penitentiary or prison, county penitentiary or jail, workhouse, house of correction, city prison, stationhouse, lockup or calaboose
- Whether prisoner of United States, a state, or a city
- Whether prisoner was awaiting trial
- Whether prisoner was serving a term of imprisonment
- Whether prisoner was serving out a fine
- Whether prisoner was awaiting execution
- Whether prisoner was sentenced to a higher prison and awaiting removal
- Whether prisoner was being held as a witness
- Whether imprisoned for debt
- Whether imprisoned for insanity
- Date of incarceration
- Alleged offense
- Amount of time imposed
- Number of days in jail or workhouse
- Number of years in penitentiary
- Whether prisoner at hard labor, and if so, what type (shoe shop, cigar shop, cooper shop, stonecutting, prison duties, mining, labor on farm or plantation, etc.)
- If at hard labor, whether working inside or outside prison walls
- Whether prisoner's labor was contracted out

## Supplemental Schedule 7: Pauper and Indigent

This schedule was designed for inhabitants in institutions, poorhouses, or asylums and those boarded at public expense in private houses. If any person enumerated in this schedule was also blind, deaf and dumb, insane, or idiotic, the other appropriate schedule was to also be completed by the enumerator.

- Number of page and line from population schedule
- Name of resident
- City or town of residence
- County (if in same state) or state (if in some other state)
- Whether supported at cost to city or town

- Whether supported at cost to county
- Name of county or state that provided support
- Whether supported at cost to institution
- Whether person was able bodied
- Whether person was habitually intemperate
- Whether an epileptic
- Whether ever convicted of a crime
- If disabled, form of disability (crippled, consumption, dropsy, old age, lying-in, etc.)
- Whether person was born in this establishment
- Date of admission
- Whether other members of the family of this person were in this establishment:
    husband
    wife
    mother
    father
    sons (how many)
    daughters (how many)
    brothers (how many)
    sisters (how many)
- Whether person was also blind
- Whether person was deaf and dumb
- Whether person was insane
- Whether person was idiotic

# PRODUCTS OF INDUSTRY AND MANUFACTURER SCHEDULES
## 1810 and 1820 Manufacturers Schedules

The first census of the manufacturing industry was taken in 1810 and included only three questions—the kind, quantity, and value of goods produced. The census was designed to "show the practical foundation, actual progress, condition, and establishment of the American arts and manufactures and their connection with the wealth and strength of the United States." This census was considered to be extremely inaccurate since data was not collected from many cities or counties. Most of the schedules, except for a few that are bound with the population schedules, have been lost. See pages 90–92 for an inventory that includes page numbers in the appropriate census microfilm.

The 1820 manufacturing census was expanded and included the following data:

- owner's name
- location of establishment
- number of employees
- kind and quantity of machinery
- capital invested

| LOCATION OF ORIGINAL DDD SCHEDULES | |
|---|---|
| Alabama | Alabama Department of Archives and History, Montgomery, Alabama |
| Arkansas | University of Arkansas, Fayetteville, Arkansas |
| California | California State Library, Sacramento, California |
| Colorado | Duke University, Durham, North Carolina |
| Connecticut | Connecticut State Library, Hartford, Connecticut |
| Dakota Territory | South Dakota State Historical Society, Pierre, South Dakota |
| Delaware | Delaware Public Archives, Hall of Records, Dover, Delaware |
| District of Columbia * | Duke University, Durham, North Carolina |
| Florida | Florida State University, Tallahassee, Florida |
| Georgia * | Duke University, Durham, North Carolina |
| Idaho | Idaho Historical Society, Boise, Idaho |
| Illinois | Illinois State Library, Springfield, Illinois |
| Indiana | Indiana State Library, Indianapolis, Indiana |
| Iowa | State Historical Society of Iowa, Des Moines, Iowa |
| Kansas * | Kansas State Historical Society, Topeka, Kansas |
| Kentucky * | Duke University, Durham, North Carolina |
| Louisiana * | Duke University, Durham, North Carolina |
| Maine | Maine State Archives, Augusta, Maine |
| Massachusetts * | State Library of Massachusetts, Boston, Massachusetts |
| Michigan | Michigan State Archives, Lansing, Michigan |
| Minnesota | Minnesota State Historical Society, St. Paul, Minnesota |
| Mississippi | Mississippi Department of Archives and History, Jackson, Mississippi |
| Missouri | Missouri Historical Society, St. Louis, Missouri |
| Montana * | Montana Historical Society, Helena, Montana |
| Nebraska * | Nebraska State Historical Society, Lincoln, Nebraska |
| Nevada | Nevada Historical Society, Reno, Nevada |
| New Hampshire | New Hampshire State Library, Concord, New Hampshire |
| New Jersey | New Jersey State Library, Trenton, New Jersey |
| New York | New York State Library, Albany, New York |
| North Carolina | North Carolina State Archives, Raleigh, North Carolina |
| Ohio * | State Library of Ohio, Columbus, Ohio |
| Oregon | Oregon State Library, Salem, Oregon |
| Pennsylvania * | National Archives and Records Administration, Washington, DC |

| South Carolina | South Carolina Department of Archives and History, Columbia, South Carolina |
|---|---|
| Tennessee * | Duke University, Durham, North Carolina |
| Texas * | Texas State Library, Austin, Texas |
| Vermont | Vermont Department of Libraries, Montpelier, Vermont |
| Virginia * | Virginia State Library, Richmond, Virginia |
| Washington * | Washington State Library, Olympia, Washington |
| West Virginia | West Virginia Archives and History Library, Charleston, West Virginia |
| Wisconsin | Wisconsin Historical Society, Madison, Wisconsin |

\* Microfilmed copies are available at the National Archives and Records Administration, Washington, DC, in Record Group 29:

| | |
|---|---|
| District of Columbia | M1795 (one roll) |
| Georgia | T1137 (one roll) |
| Kansas | T1130 (four rolls) |
| Kentucky | M1528 (two rolls) |
| Louisiana | T1136 (one roll) |
| Massachusetts | T1204 (four rolls) |
| Montana | M1806 (one roll) |
| Nebraska | T1128 (one roll) |
| Ohio | T1159 (three rolls) |
| Pennsylvania | M597 (fourteen rolls) |
| Tennessee | T1135 (two rolls) |
| Texas | T1134 (five rolls) |
| Virginia | T1132 (two rolls) |
| Washington | A1154 (one roll) |

- articles manufactured
- annual production
- general remarks on business and demand for products

The original 1820 manufacturing schedules are located at the National Archives in Washington, DC (Record Group 29). They have been microfilmed (M279, twenty-seven rolls) and are available for purchase from the National Archives, Scholarly Resources, or Heritage Quest.

## 1850 Through 1870 Industry Schedules

**Since the 1810 and 1820 manufacturing schedules were incomplete and filled with errors,** the government did not collect this type of data in 1830 and 1840. From 1850 to 1870, the manufacturers schedule was termed the Industry Schedule, and it included the same questions in all three census years. The annual production needed to exceed five hundred dollars in order for the business to be included.

**Warning**

- Census (population schedule) page number and location
- Name of company, corporation, or individual who owned the business
- Name of individual business owner

*Report of William Leavenworth Jun' of the City of Albany Manufacturer of wooden Clocks*

| | | |
|---|---|---|
| **RAW MATERIALS EMPLOYED.** | { | 1. The kind ?<br>2. The quantity annually consumed ?<br>3. The cost of the annual consumption ? |
| **NUMBER OF PERSONS EMPLOYED.** | { | 4. Men ?<br>5. Women ?<br>6. Boys and Girls ? |
| **MACHINERY.** | { | 7. Whole quantity and kind of Machinery ?<br>8. Quantity of Machinery in operation ? |
| **EXPENDITURES.** | { | 9. Amount of capital invested ?<br>10. Amount paid annually for wages ?<br>11. Amount of Contingent Expenses ? |
| **PRODUCTION.** | { | 12. The nature and names of Articles manufactured ?<br>13. Market value of the Articles which are annually manufactured ? |

14. General Remarks concerning the establishment, as to its actual and past condition, the demand for, and sale of, its Manufactures.

Answers to the above Questions—

No. 1. wood
2. not able to ascertain
3. do.
4. 5 men
5. 3 women
6. 1 Boy
7. 4 Turning Lathes & 2 cutting engines going by water
8. all in use
9. about 2000
10. about 1500
11. not known
12. wooden Clocks
13. about 17,200 dol on
14. Mr Leavenworth's father is the original Patentee for making wooden Clocks and on account of the failure of Mr Wm Leavenworth Senr the present Proprietor has undertaken the business formerly they made and sold 4 times the quantity of the present Their sales are confined exclusively to the State of New York —

> Genealogical gems such as this one can be hidden in a seemingly boring business record: "Mr. Leavenworth's father is the original Patentee for making wooden clocks and on account of the failure of Mr. Wm. Leavenworth Sen'. the present proprietor has undertaken the business. Formerly they made and sold 4 times the quantity of the present. Their sales are confined exclusively to the State of New York."

**Figure 4-4**
Report of William Leavenworth Jun', 1820 U.S. census, Albany County, New York, manufacturing schedule, Albany, Albany County, New York, page 5; National Archives micropublication M279, roll 5.

---

## 1860 INDUSTRY SCHEDULE
## FREDERICKSBURG, SPOTSYLVANIA COUNTY, VIRGINIA

The 1860 Industry Schedule for Fredericksburg, Spotsylvania County, Virginia, has been transcribed and is available on the Internet at <http://departments.mwc.edu/hipr/www/fbg60man.htm>. Types of businesses and occupations listed include

| | |
|---|---|
| coopering | undertaker |
| wheat machinery | bookbindery |
| house and sign painter | tin and sheet iron factory |
| tallow chandlery | confectionery |
| shoemaker | saddler |
| tanner and currier | brick maker |
| tailor | carriage maker |
| millenary | iron factory |
| house carpenter | blacksmith and wheelwright |
| tinner and plumber | tobacconist |
| bookmaker | wheat fan maker |
| cabinetmaker | |

---

- Name of business, manufacture, or product
- Capital invested in real and personal estate for the business
- Quantities, kinds, and values of raw materials
- Kind of motive power, machinery, structure, or resource
- Average number of male and female hands
- Average male or female monthly wage
- Quantities, kinds, and values of annual products

## 1880 Manufacturers Schedule

The manufacturers schedule, reinstated in 1880, collected data on the twelve industries listed below. The questions about materials, labor, machinery, and products were similar to those from 1850 through 1870.

- Agricultural implements
- Paper mills
- Boots and shoes
- Leather and tanning/curing
- Flourmills and gristmills
- Cheese, butter, and condensed milk factories
- Slaughtering and meatpacking
- Salt
- Lumber mills and sawmills
- Brickyards and tile works
- Coal mines
- Quarries

Special agents were appointed to collect information on the manufacture of cotton, wool and worsted goods, and silk and silk goods; the manufacture of iron and steel; the coke industry; the glass industry; the mining of metals, coal, and petroleum; distilleries and breweries; shipbuilding; and fisheries.

None of the schedules prepared by these special agents exist today, but the schedules prepared by regular enumerators for the first twelve industries named above do survive for some states. The industry and manufacturing schedules are scattered in various repositories:

- The Perkins Library at Duke University in Durham, North Carolina, houses the schedules for Colorado, District of Columbia, Georgia, Kentucky, Louisiana, Tennessee, and Virginia. Details appear online at <www.lib.duke.edu/access/news/census.htm>.
- The University of North Carolina in Chapel Hill, North Carolina, sells microfilm copies of the manufacturing schedules of 1850 through 1880 for Alabama, Arkansas, Florida, Georgia, Kentucky, Louisiana, Maryland, Mississippi, North Carolina, Tennessee, Texas, Virginia, and West Virginia. Details are online at <www.lib.unc.edu/ncc/phs/census.html>.
- For other states, check with the state historical society, archives, or library, and consult the Family History Library catalog.

## 1885 Products of Industry

The special census of 1885 was taken only for the states of Colorado, Florida, and Nebraska, and the territories of Dakota and New Mexico. Schedule Number 3, Products of Industry, listed name of the owning corporation or individual, name of the business or products, amount of capital invested, number of employees, wages and hours, number of months in operation during the year, value of materials used, value of products, and amount and type of power used.

The originals are located at the National Archives in Washington, DC; schedules of many counties are missing. This census has been microfilmed and is available for purchase or examination at the Family History Library in Salt Lake City and at the Family History Centers.

## MORTALITY SCHEDULES

The mortality schedules (1850 through 1885 and 1900 [Minnesota only]) reported the names of persons who died during the twelve months preceding June 1 of the census year. In other words, persons who died 1 June 1849 through 31 May 1850 are listed in the 1850 mortality schedules. **Deaths that occurred after the census date were not supposed to be reported, although enumerators sometimes made such errors which benefit genealogists.**

**Reminder**

Since death certificates were not generally created until around the turn of the twentieth century, these one-year death registers created every ten years provide an invaluable amount of data for historians and genealogists.

Mortality schedules are available for examination at the National Archives and the Family History Library and can be purchased from Heritage Quest. The records have been indexed and are described in Thomas Jay Kemp's *The*

| INDUSTRY AND MANUFACTURING SCHEDULES: 1810, 1820, and 1850 THROUGH 1885 | 1810 | 1820 | 1830 | 1840 | 1850 | 1860 | 1870 | 1880 | 1885 |
|---|---|---|---|---|---|---|---|---|---|
| Alabama | | x | | | x | x | x | x | |
| Arkansas | | x | | | | | | x | |
| California | | | | | x | x | x | x | |
| Colorado | | | | | | | x | x | x |
| Connecticut | | x | | | x | x | x | x | |
| Dakota Territory | | | | | | | | x | x |
| Delaware | * | x | | | x | x | x | x | |
| District of Columbia | | x | | | x | x | x | x | |
| Florida | | | | | x | x | x | x | x |
| Georgia | | x | | | x | x | x | x | |
| Idaho | | | | | | | x | x | |
| Illinois | | x | | | | x | x | x | |
| Indiana | | x | | | x | x | x | x | |
| Iowa | | | | | x | x | x | x | |
| Kansas | | | | | | x | x | x | |
| Kentucky | | x | | | x | x | x | x | |
| Louisiana | * | x | | | | | | x | |
| Maine | * | x | | | x | x | x | | |
| Maryland (1860: Baltimore city, county only) | * | x | | | x | x | | x | |
| Massachusetts | * | | | | x | x | x | x | |
| Michigan | | | | | x | x | x | x | |
| Minnesota | | | | | x | x | x | x | |
| Mississippi | | | | | x | x | x | x | |
| Missouri | | | | | x | x | x | x | |
| Montana | | | | | | | x | x | |
| Nebraska | | | | | | x | x | x | x |
| Nevada | | | | | | | | x | |
| New Hampshire | * | x | | | x | x | x | | |
| New Jersey | | x | | | x | x | x | x | |
| New Mexico | | | | | | | | | x |
| New York | * | x | | | x | x | x | x | |
| North Carolina | * | x | | | x | x | x | x | |
| Ohio | * | x | | | x | x | x | x | |
| Oregon | | | | | x | x | x | x | |

| Pennsylvania | * | x | | | x | x | x | x | |
|---|---|---|---|---|---|---|---|---|---|
| Rhode Island | * | x | | | x | x | x | | x |
| South Carolina | * | x | | | x | x | x | x | |
| Tennessee | | x | | | x | x | x | x | |
| Texas | | | | | x | x | x | x | |
| Utah | | | | | x | x | x | x | |
| Vermont | * | x | | | x | x | x | x | |
| Virginia | * | x | | | x | x | x | x | |
| Washington | | | | | | x | x | x | |
| West Virginia | | | | | | | x | x | |
| Wisconsin | | | | | x | x | x | x | |

*Manufacturing schedules are bound with the population schedules and do not include all counties. The following inventory is adapted from *Preliminary Inventory No. 161, Records of the Bureau of the Census* (Washington, D.C.: National Archives and Records Administration, 1964).

## 1810 MANUFACTURING SCHEDULES MICROFILMED WITH POPULATION SCHEDULES NARA MICROPUBLICATION M252

| State | Roll Number | County or Parish | Page Numbers |
|---|---|---|---|
| Delaware | 4 | Sussex | 476–481 |
| Louisiana | 10 | Attakapas (St. Martin)<br>Avoyelles<br>Lafourche<br>Opelousas (St. Landry)<br>Ouachita<br>Pointe Coupee | 43<br>115<br>187–204<br>334<br>347<br>384 |
| Maine | 11 | Cumberland<br>Hancock<br>Kennebec | 412<br>720<br>943 |
| Maine | 12 | Oxford | 398 |
| Maryland | 13 | Baltimore (city)<br>Baltimore County | 344<br>491 |
| Maryland | 14 | Talbot | 443 |
| Maryland | 16 | Somerset | 318 |
| Massachusetts | 17 | Berkshire | 129, 130, 183, 185, 206, 215 |
| Massachusetts | 18 | Essex<br>Norfolk | 113–118<br>354–492 |
| Massachusetts | 19 | Hampshire | 207, 217, 219, 220–237 |
| Massachusetts | 20 | Middlesex | 318–323, 357x, 357y |

| New Hampshire | 23 | Cheshire | 9, 17, 27, 43, 49, 57, 67, 73, 81, 89, 95, 101, 109, 119, 127, 130 |
|---|---|---|---|
| New Hampshire | 25 | Strafford | 621–624 |
| New York | 26 | Broome<br>Chenango | 208–217<br>366 |
| New York | 27 | Essex<br>Genesee | 1–68<br>150, 151 |
| New York | 29 | Niagara<br>Orange | 250–276<br>1072–1074 |
| New York | 30 | Clinton<br>Dutchess | 25–38<br>43–167 |
| New York | 31 | Cayuga | 1280 |
| New York | 34 | Queens | 338 |
| North Carolina | 38 | Brunswick<br>Caswell<br>Halifax<br>Person<br>Richmond<br>Robeson | 35–44<br>46–75<br>95–124<br>126–153<br>214<br>245 |
| North Carolina | 39 | Burke<br>Cabarrus<br>Camden<br>Carteret | 360, 361<br>389<br>419<br>455 |
| North Carolina | 40 | Franklin<br>Granville<br>Guilford<br>Haywood<br>Hyde<br>Johnston<br>Jones<br>Lincoln | 101<br>118–149<br>190<br>203<br>234<br>278<br>306<br>325–342 |
| North Carolina | 42 | Bladen<br>Columbus<br>Mecklenburg<br>Northampton<br>Rutherford<br>Sampson<br>Warren | 2–14<br>16–20<br>23–57<br>60–82<br>84–147<br>151–164<br>167–185 |
| North Carolina | 43 | Stokes<br>Surry<br>Tyrrell | 91–118<br>198<br>213–215 |
| Ohio | N/A | National Archives micropublication M1803 (one roll). Original manuscript schedules are in the Marietta College Library in Marietta, Ohio. | N/A |

| Pennsylvania | 45 | Berks | 58–84 (totals on page 79) |
|---|---|---|---|
| Pennsylvania | 46 | Centre | 193–195 |
| Pennsylvania | 47 | Clearfield | 390 |
| Pennsylvania | 49 | Luzerne | 86–102, 124, 125, 127, 147, 171–197 |
| Pennsylvania | 51 | Mifflin<br>Northampton<br>Tioga<br>Westmoreland | 35–54<br>55–64<br>485, 487<br>862 |
| Pennsylvania | 53 | Somerset | 475–477 |
| Rhode Island | 59 | Kent | 124, 125 |
| South Carolina | 60 | Barnwell<br>Beaufort | 194<br>270 |
| South Carolina | 61 | Lancaster<br>Marion<br>Lexington<br>Orangeburg<br>Sumter<br>Union | 9<br>40<br>63a<br>137<br>465, 488<br>519–556 |
| South Carolina | 62 | Greenville<br>Kershaw<br>Georgetown | 135, 136<br>176, 177<br>222–227 |
| Vermont | 64 | Bennington<br>Franklin<br>Orange | 76–141<br>249–334<br>361, 364, 366–402, 437–442 |
| Vermont | 65 | Rutland<br><br>Windham | 220–279, 319–332, 351<br>120, 132–136, 142–188, 204, 205–250, 257–279 |
| Virginia | 66 | Brooke (now West Virginia) | 357, 358 |
| Virginia | 70 | Monroe (now West Virginia)<br>Northumberland | 602<br>969–980 |
| Undetermined | 65 | At the end of Windham County, Vermont, is an inventory of manufacturers from an undetermined area. | |

*American Census Handbook* (Wilmington, Del.: Scholarly Resources, Inc., 2001).

Mortality schedules recorded

- name of deceased
- age

---

**1880 MORTALITY SCHEDULE**
**NEW CASTLE COUNTY, DELAWARE**

The 1880 mortality schedule (see Figure 4-5) for Wilmington, New Castle County, Delaware, includes additional remarks for some deaths:

Family 47: Emma Dolbow died in Pensgrove, New Jersey. Mother married Edward Shoemaker.

Family 99: Henry Gebert was an 8 month child [meaning he was born during the eighth month of pregnancy]. Lived 2 hours.

Family 106: Anderson Parks run over by wagon. Deaf. Died in Alms House. Brought from North Carolina by Lewis Fox.

Family 113: Francis Bailey died October 1879 in Pensgrove, New Jersey.

Family 170: William Wagner committed suicide, overdose of laudanum. Temporary insanity. Cause strong drink.

Family 214: Elijah Maxwell had room at Stephen Pratt's house, No. 337 East Lowell St.

Family 282: William Lynch demented mind. Wandered from house. Died in Media Hospital, Delaware County, Pennsylvania.

---

- sex
- color (white, black, mulatto)
- free or slave [recorded in 1850 and 1860 only]
- married or widowed
- place of birth (state, territory, or country)
- month of death
- occupation
- disease or cause of death
- number of days ill
- whether father or mother were of foreign birth [added in 1870]
- birthplace of parents [added in 1880]
- place where disease was contracted [added in 1880]
- how long the deceased person had been a citizen or resident of the area [added in 1880]
- page number and family number from population schedule [added in 1880]

## 1900 Mortality Schedule

Mortality schedules were compiled in 1900 for all states except Connecticut, Massachusetts, New Hampshire, and Rhode Island, and they were not made for some counties and cities in New Jersey and New York. (These states and

| MORTALITY SCHEDULES: 1850 THROUGH 1900 | | | | | | |
|---|---|---|---|---|---|---|
| | 1850 | 1860 | 1870 | 1880 | 1885 | 1900 |
| Alabama | x | x | x | x | | |
| Arizona | | | x | x | | |
| Arkansas | x | x | x | x | | |
| California | x | x | x | x | | |
| Colorado | | | x | x | x | |
| Connecticut | x | x | x | x | | |
| Dakota Territory | | x | | x | x | |
| Delaware | x | x | x | x | | |
| District of Columbia | x | x | x | x | | |
| Florida | x | x | x | x | x | |
| Georgia | x | x | x | x | | |
| Idaho | | | x | x | | |
| Illinois | x | x | x | x | | |
| Indiana | x | x | x | x | | |
| Iowa | x | x | x | x | | |
| Kansas | | x | x | x | | |
| Kentucky | x | x | x | x | | |
| Louisiana | x | x | x | x | | |
| Maine | x | x | x | x | | |
| Maryland | x | x | x | x | | |
| Massachusetts | x | x | x | x | | |
| Michigan | x | x | x | x | | |
| Minnesota | x | x | x | x | | x |
| Mississippi | x | x | x | x | | |
| Missouri | x | x | x | x | | |
| Montana | | | x | x | | |
| Nebraska | | x | x | x | x | |
| Nevada | | | | x | | |
| New Hampshire | x | x | x | x | | |
| New Jersey | x | x | x | x | | |
| New Mexico | | | | | x | |
| New York | x | x | x | x | | |
| North Carolina | x | x | x | x | | |
| Ohio (incomplete for 1850, 1870, and 1880) | x | x | x | x | | |

| | | | | | |
|---|---|---|---|---|---|
| Oregon | x | x | x | x | | |
| Pennsylvania | x | x | x | x | | |
| Rhode Island | | | x | | | |
| South Carolina | x | x | x | x | | |
| Tennessee | x | x | | x | | |
| Texas | x | x | x | x | | |
| Utah | | x | x | x | | |
| Vermont | x | x | x | x | | |
| Virginia | x | x | x | x | | |
| Washington | | x | x | x | | |
| West Virginia | x | x | x | x | | |
| Wisconsin | x | x | x | x | | |

counties were exempted because they had already established death registration and could provide to the government statistics on causes of death.) Unfortunately, these mortality schedules were destroyed by order of Congress once the statistics had been compiled.

When Minnesota officials compared the deaths per the mortality schedules with the official death registers, they discovered that over three thousand deaths listed on the enumerators' schedules had not been recorded with the state. Partial transcripts of the information about these individuals were copied from the original schedules to another set of mortality schedule forms and retained by the Minnesota State Board of Health. A few years ago this extra set of schedules was discovered at the Minnesota Historical Society. James W. Warren transcribed these records and published *Minnesota 1900 Census Mortality Schedule* (Warren Research & Marketing Publication: St. Paul, Minn., 1991). **This 120-page compilation, which includes Indian reservations, represents the only known surviving 1900 mortality schedule for any state.**

## SOCIAL STATISTICS SCHEDULES

The 1850 through 1870 and 1885 social statistics schedules were created to gather statistics on wealth, public debt, taxes, schools, libraries, newspapers, churches, wages, paupers, and criminals. The enumerators obtained the information from official records, printed reports, and archives of schools, asylums, and courts.

The genealogical value of these schedules lies in the detailed information on cemeteries, fraternal organizations, churches, and newspapers; such information can assist researchers in locating and using these record types. For example, knowing that there were only two churches in a community in 1850 or that there was a German newspaper published in a county may be helpful. If your ancestor had a personal library of more than one thousand volumes, this was reported in the social statistics.

**Important**

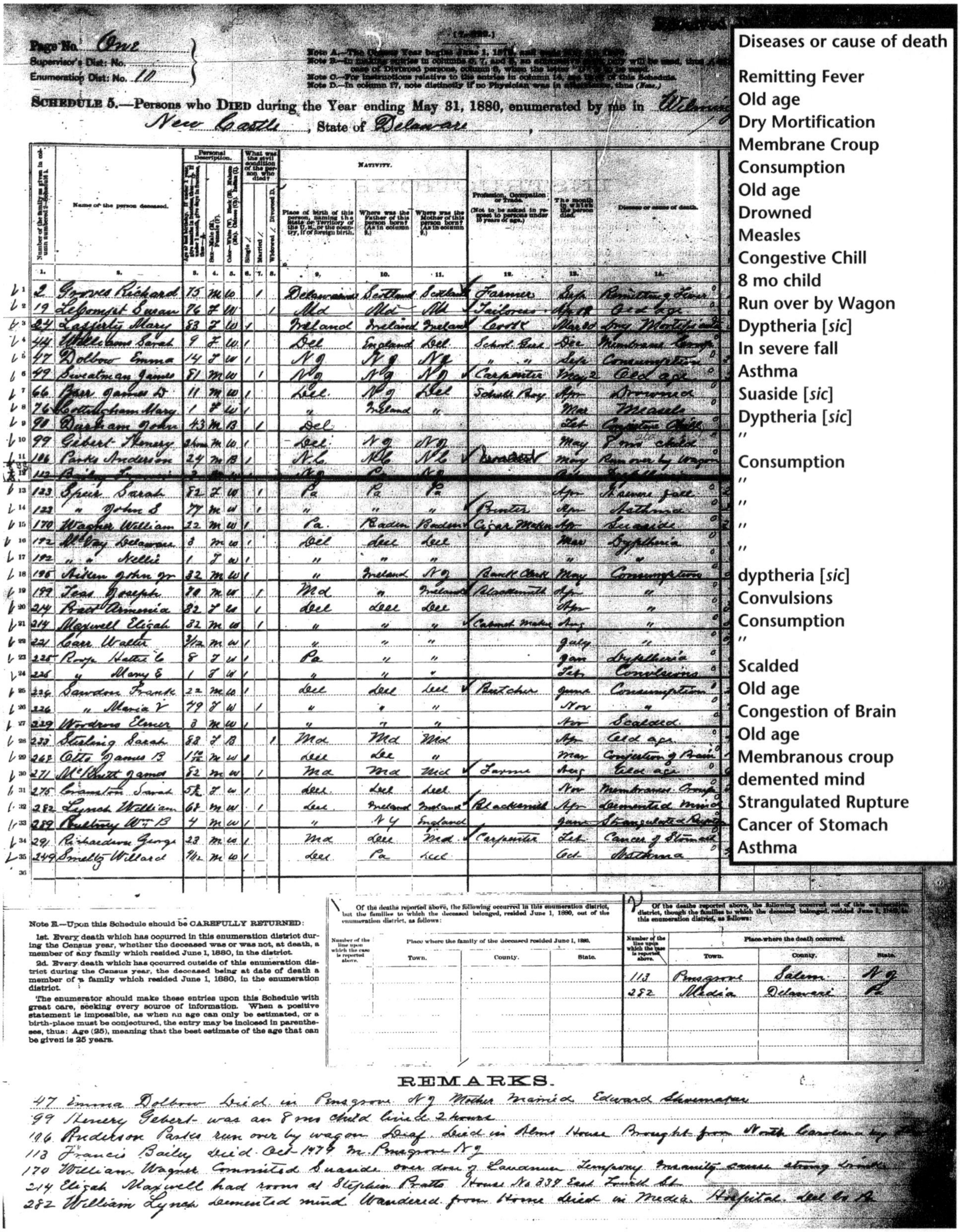

**SCHEDULE 5.—Persons who DIED during the Year ending May 31, 1880, enumerated by me in** *Wilmington* *New Castle*, **State of** *Delaware*,

**Diseases or cause of death**

Remitting Fever
Old age
Dry Mortification
Membrane Croup
Consumption
Old age
Drowned
Measles
Congestive Chill
8 mo child
Run over by Wagon
Dyptheria [sic]
In severe fall
Asthma
Suaside [sic]
Dyptheria [sic]
"
Consumption
"
"
"
dyptheria [sic]
Convulsions
Consumption
"
Scalded
Old age
Congestion of Brain
Old age
Membranous croup
demented mind
Strangulated Rupture
Cancer of Stomach
Asthma

**REMARKS.**

47 Emma Dollow died in Pensgrove N J Mother married Edward Shumaker
99 Henery Gebert was an 8 mo child lived 2 hours
106 Anderson Parks run over by wagon Deaf died in Alms House Brought from North Carolina
113 Francis Baily died Oct 1879 in Pensgrove N J
170 William Wagner Committed Suaside over dose of Laudanum Temporay insanity cause strong drink
214 Elizah Maxwell had rooms at Stephin Pratts House No 339 East Fourth St.
282 William Lynch demented mind Wandered from home died in Media Hospital. Del Co Pa

## Figure 4-5

1880 U.S. census, New Castle County, Delaware, mortality schedule, Wilmington, enumeration district [E.D.] 10, page 1; Hall of Records, Dover, Delaware. *United States Census of Delaware; Persons Who Died During the [Census] Year, 1850–1880;* Family History Library, Salt Lake City, Utah; film number 1,421,306; item 1.

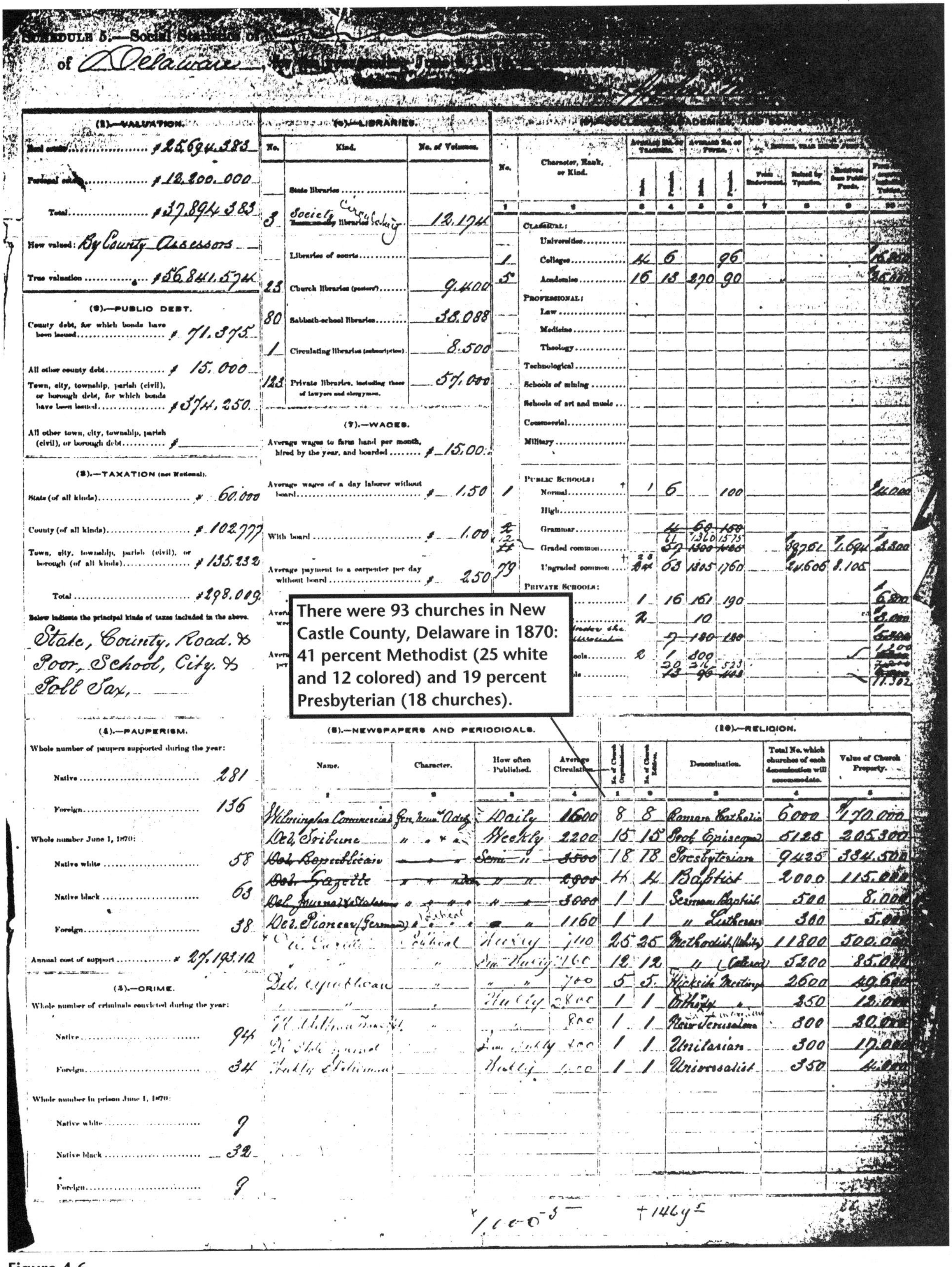

SCHEDULE 5.—Social Statistics of

of *Delaware*

**(1)—VALUATION.**

Real estate.......... $25,694,383

Personal estate.......... $12,200,000

Total.......... $37,894,383

How valued: By County Assessors

True valuation.......... $56,841,574

**(2)—PUBLIC DEBT.**

County debt, for which bonds have been issued.......... $71,375

All other county debt.......... $15,000

Town, city, township, parish (civil), or borough debt, for which bonds have been issued.......... $374,250

All other town, city, township, parish (civil), or borough debt.......... $

**(3)—TAXATION (not National).**

State (of all kinds).......... $60,000

County (of all kinds).......... $102,777

Town, city, township, parish (civil), or borough (of all kinds).......... $135,232

Total.......... $298,009

Below indicate the principal kinds of taxes included in the above.

*State, County, Road & Poor, School, City & Poll Tax,*

**(4)—PAUPERISM.**

Whole number of paupers supported during the year:

Native.......... 281

Foreign.......... 136

Whole number June 1, 1870:

Native white.......... 58

Native black.......... 63

Foreign.......... 38

Annual cost of support.......... $27,193.12

**(5)—CRIME.**

Whole number of criminals convicted during the year:

Native.......... 94

Foreign.......... 34

Whole number in prison June 1, 1870:

Native white.......... 9

Native black.......... 32

Foreign.......... 9

**(6)—LIBRARIES.**

| No. | Kind. | No. of Volumes. |
|---|---|---|
| 3 | State libraries | |
| | Society libraries (circulating) | 12,194 |
| 1 | Libraries of courts | |
| 23 | Church libraries (pastors') | 9,400 |
| 80 | Sabbath-school libraries | 38,088 |
| 1 | Circulating libraries (subscription) | 8,500 |
| 123 | Private libraries, including those of lawyers and clergymen | 57,000 |

**(7)—WAGES.**

Average wages to farm hand per month, hired by the year, and boarded.......... $15.00

Average wages of a day laborer without board.......... $1.50

With board.......... $1.00

Average payment to a carpenter per day without board.......... $2.50

[Callout box:] There were 93 churches in New Castle County, Delaware in 1870: 41 percent Methodist (25 white and 12 colored) and 19 percent Presbyterian (18 churches).

**(8)—SCHOOLS AND EDUCATION.**

(table partially legible)

| No. | Character, Rank, or Kind. | | | | | | |
|---|---|---|---|---|---|---|---|
| | CLASSICAL: | | | | | | |
| | Universities | | | | | | |
| 1 | Colleges | 4 | 6 | 96 | | | |
| 5 | Academies | 16 | 13 | 270 | 90 | | |
| | PROFESSIONAL: | | | | | | |
| | Law | | | | | | |
| | Medicine | | | | | | |
| | Theology | | | | | | |
| | Technological | | | | | | |
| | Schools of mining | | | | | | |
| | Schools of art and music | | | | | | |
| | Commercial | | | | | | |
| | Military | | | | | | |
| | PUBLIC SCHOOLS: | | | | | | |
| 1 | Normal | 1 | 6 | 100 | | | |
| | High | | | | | | |
| | Grammar | | | | | | |
| | Graded common | | | | | | |
| | Ungraded common | | | | | | |
| | PRIVATE SCHOOLS: | | | | | | |

**(9)—NEWSPAPERS AND PERIODICALS.**

| Name. | Character. | How often Published. | Average Circulation | | | Denomination. | Total No. which churches of each denomination will accommodate. | Value of Church Property. |
|---|---|---|---|---|---|---|---|---|
| Wilmington Commercial | Gen. news, adv. | Daily | 1600 | 8 | 8 | Roman Catholic | 6000 | $170,000 |
| Del. Tribune | " " | Weekly | 2200 | 15 | 15 | Prot. Episcopal | 5125 | 205,300 |
| Del. Republican | | Semi " | 5000 | 18 | 18 | Presbyterian | 9425 | 334,500 |
| Del. Gazette | | " " | 5900 | 4 | 4 | Baptist | 2000 | 115,000 |
| Del. Journal & States | | " | 3000 | 1 | 1 | German Baptist | 500 | 8,000 |
| Del. Pioneer (German) | | " | 1160 | 1 | 1 | " Lutheran | 300 | 5,000 |
| | political | Daily | | 25 | 25 | Methodist (white) | 11800 | 500,000 |
| | | Semi-weekly | 360 | 12 | 12 | " (colored) | 5200 | 85,000 |
| Del. Republican | | " | 700 | 5 | 5 | Hicksite Meeting | 2600 | 49,000 |
| | | Weekly | 2800 | 1 | 1 | Orthodox | 250 | 12,000 |
| | | | 800 | 1 | 1 | New Jerusalem | 800 | 30,000 |
| | | Semi-weekly | 800 | 1 | 1 | Unitarian | 300 | 17,000 |
| | | Weekly | | 1 | 1 | Universalist | 350 | |

**Figure 4-6**

1870 U.S. census, New Castle County, Delaware, social statistics schedule, Hall of Records, Dover, Delaware. *United States Census of Delaware; Social Statistics Schedules, 1850–1870*; Family History Library, Salt Lake City, Utah; film number 1,421,306; item 2.

---

## DISEASES AND MEDICAL TERMS

Remember that causes of death in mortality schedules were based on medical knowledge at the time of compilation. For example, young children were often reported as dying from "teething." It is more likely that the cause of death was an infection the baby contracted after being weaned from mother's milk.

Cyndi's List, <www.cyndislist.com/medical.htm>, provides links to several Web sites that define diseases and medical terms found in the mortality schedules. For more information, you can also refer to medical dictionaries published near the time of the census.

*Your Guide to Cemetery Research,* by Sharon DeBartolo Carmack (Cincinnati: Betterway Books, 2002) has a comprehensive glossary of nineteenth-century causes of death, as well as a discussion on diagnoses found in early death records and on mortality schedules.

---

The Perkins Library at Duke University in Durham, North Carolina, houses the social statistics schedules for Colorado, District of Columbia, Georgia, Kentucky, Louisiana, and Tennessee. Details are online at <www.lib.duke.edu/access/news/census.htm>.

For other states, check with the state historical society, archives, or library, and consult the Family History Library catalog.

# VETERANS SCHEDULE
## Union Veterans and Widows of Union Veterans

The act of 1 March 1889 establishing a census office in the Department of the Interior specified that in coordination with the 1890 population census a special enumeration of Union veterans and widows be taken. Anyone who had served in the Army, Navy, or Marine Corps of the United States in the war of the rebellion (Civil War) or was a survivor of such a veteran was to be enumerated. The act also provided that in preparation of the census, a list of the names, organizations, and length of service of surviving soldiers, sailors, and marines and a list of veterans' widows be compiled.

The census office consequently prepared a list of 458,677 names of surviving veterans from records of the pension office, rosters of Grand Army of the Republic posts, and adjutant general reports.

For one year after the census enumeration (from 1 August 1890 through 30 June 1891) the census office examined the special schedules for accuracy and completeness. Thousands of letters were written to veterans to obtain information not reported by the enumerators. Notices were published in about five hundred newspapers throughout the country to encourage a higher response rate from the veterans. The new data was added to the schedules by the census

| SOCIAL STATISTICS SCHEDULES: 1850 THROUGH 1870 AND 1885 | | | | |
|---|---|---|---|---|
| | 1850 | 1860 | 1870 | 1885 |
| California | x | x | x | |
| Colorado | | | x | x |
| Dakota Territory | | | x | x |
| Delaware | x | x | | |
| District of Columbia | x | x | x | |
| Florida | x | x | x | x |
| Georgia | x | x | x | |
| Illinois | x | x | x | |
| Indiana | x | x | x | |
| Kansas | x | x | x | |
| Kentucky | x | x | x | |
| Louisiana | x | x | x | |
| Maine | x | x | x | |
| Maryland | x | x | | |
| Massachusetts | x | x | x | |
| Michigan | x | x | x | x |
| Minnesota | x | x | x | |
| Mississippi | x | x | x | |
| Missouri | x | x | x | |
| Montana | | | x | |
| Nebraska | | x | x | |
| New Hampshire | x | x | x | |
| New Jersey | x | x | x | |
| New York | x | x | x | |
| North Carolina | x | x | x | |
| Oregon | x | x | x | |
| Pennsylvania | x | x | x | |
| Rhode Island | x | x | x | |
| South Carolina | x | x | x | |
| Tennessee | x | x | x | |
| Texas | x | x | x | |
| Vermont | x | x | x | |
| Virginia | x | x | x | |
| Washington | | x | x | |
| Wisconsin | x | x | x | |

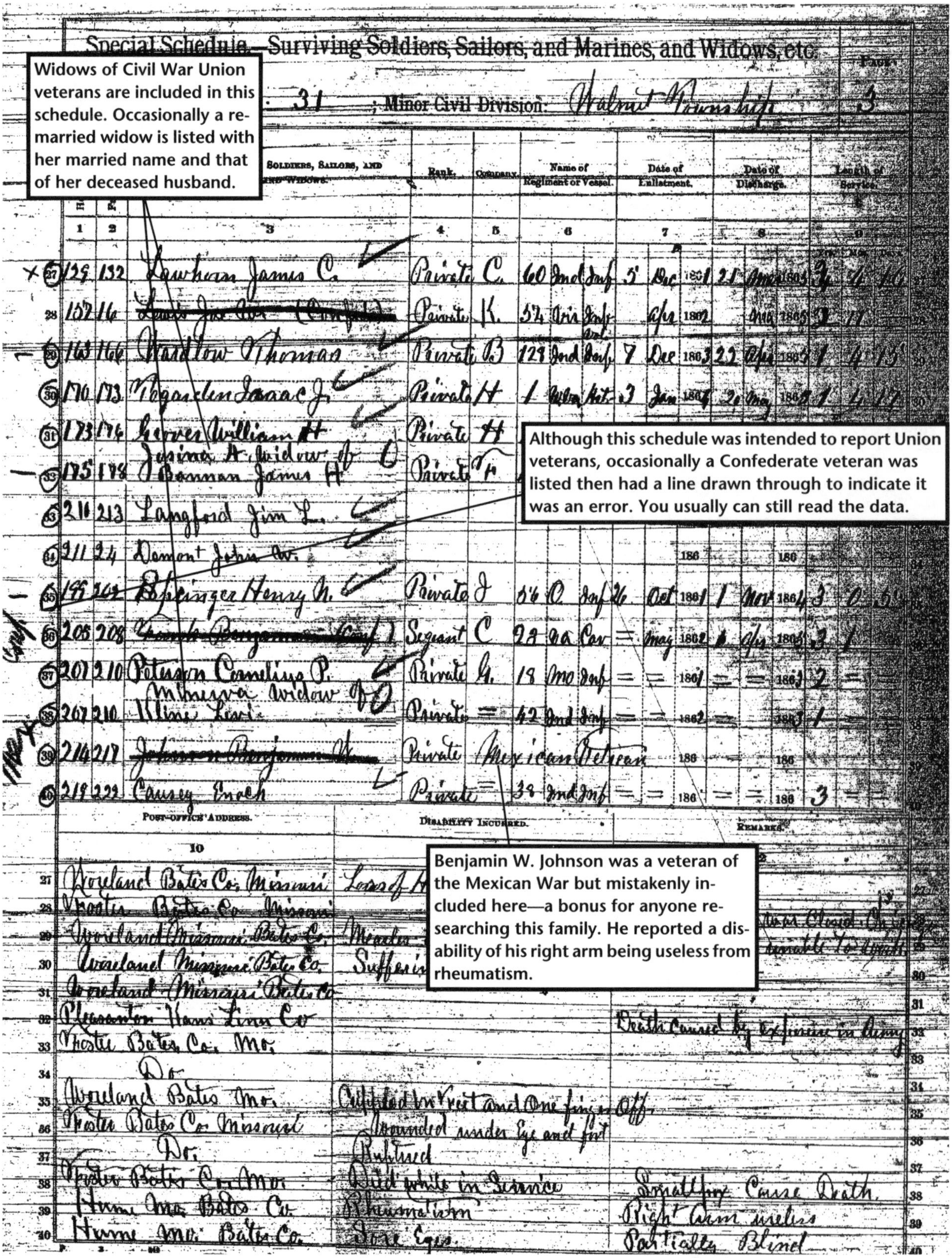

**Figure 4-7**
1890 U.S. census, Bates County, Missouri, Union Veterans and Widows of Union Veterans of the Civil War, Walnut Township, supervisor's district [S.D.] 6, enumeration district [E.D.] 31, page 3; National Archives micropublication M123, roll 32.

office, and incorrect items, such as names of Confederate veterans, were crossed out. You can see these corrections on the microfilmed copies.

Most of the 1890 population schedule (see chapter three) was destroyed in a fire in 1921. It is often reported that the veterans schedules survived the fire, but administrative records do not support this conclusion. According to the introduction with each roll of the veterans schedules microfilm, the schedules were transferred to the Commissioner of Pensions in April 1894, and in 1930 transferred to the Veterans Administration, where they remained until being transferred to the National Archives on 24 March 1943. If this is the case, **the veterans schedules were not stored with the population census at the time of the fire in 1921.**

The schedules were put into bundles and arranged alphabetically by the name of the state or territory. Bundles 1 through 53, containing nearly all the schedules for Alabama through Kansas and approximately half of Kentucky, were apparently misplaced or destroyed prior to the transfer to the National Archives in 1943.

**Notes**

National Archives Microfilm Publication M123 (118 rolls) is part of Records of the Veterans Administration (RG 15) and contains the special schedules for Kentucky through Wyoming. Roll number 118 titled "Washington, DC, and Miscellaneous" contains fragments from states alphabetically before Kentucky:

- California (Alcatraz)
- Connecticut (Fort Trumbull, Hartford County Hospital, and U.S. Naval Station)
- Delaware (Delaware State Hospital for the Insane)
- Florida (Fort Barrancas and St. Francis Barracks)
- Idaho (Boise Barracks and Fort Sherman)
- Illinois (Cook County and Henderson County)
- Indiana (Warrick County and White County)
- Kansas (Barton County)

While this schedule never intended to count Confederate veterans or veterans from other wars, many were included on the schedules. Some veterans of the War of 1812 appear, and there are numerous entries for veterans of the Mexican War. Confederates are often named and have a line drawn through to indicate the error, but the data is usually readable. For this reason, do not consider the 1890 veterans schedules as a source for only Union families.

Content of the 1890 Union veterans schedule is

- name of the soldier, sailor, marine, or veteran's widow
- veteran's rank
- name of company
- regiment or vessel
- dates of enlistment and discharge
- length of service in years, months, and days
- post office address
- nature of disability, if any
- remarks

## CIVIL WAR VETERANS' DISABILITIES

Disabilities and wounds commonly named in the 1890 Union veterans schedule include

| | |
|---|---|
| chronic diarrhea | stiffness of hips |
| rheumatism | deafness |
| consumption | loss of teeth |
| bone scurvy | gunshot wound in thigh |
| kidney trouble | gunshot wound through lungs |
| ruptured bowels | leg amputated |
| piles | loss of eye |
| heart disease | shot through foot |

A good source for information on medical terms used during the Civil War is Robert Hooper's *Lexicon Medicum or Medical Dictionary* (1843, reprint Westminster, Md.: Willow Bend Books, 2000).

To date no comprehensive index to all of the 1890 veterans schedules exists, but some transcriptions and indexes appear on the Internet. The following list of Web pages includes those with full transcriptions only; sites that have only an index are not included. Should you find an ancestor in any of these transcriptions, follow up your research by obtaining a microfilm copy and comparing the data. It is easy for a transcriber to misinterpret handwriting or inadvertently miss some data.

## 1890 Veterans Schedule Transcriptions on the Internet
### Kentucky
Carter County: www.rootsweb.com/~kycarter/census/1890c.htm
Casey County: www.rootsweb.org/~usgenweb/ky/casey/casey.html
Elliott County: http://ram.ramlink.net/~cbarker/ell1890.htm
Harlan County: www.rootsweb.com/~kyharlan/data/1890harl.html
Johnson County: www.bright.net/~kat/1890vet.htm
Letcher County: ftp://ftp.rootsweb.com/pub/usgenweb/ky/letcher/census/
1890spe.txt
Pulaski County (includes links to full images): www.rootsweb.com/~usgen
web/ky/pulaski/census/1890/

### Louisiana
Caldwell County: ftp://ftp.rootsweb.com/pub/usgenweb/la/caldwell/
military/unio1890.txt
Winn County: ftp://ftp.rootsweb.com/pub/usgenweb/la/winn/military/union
cen.txt

## Massachusetts

Dukes County (Tisbury): www.vineyard.net/vineyard/history/dukes/soldiers
.htm#1890

Essex County (Marblehead): www.bridgemedia.net/genweb/specens.asp

## Michigan

Isabella County: www.rootsweb.com/~usgenweb/mi/isabella/3701cen.htm

Menominee County: www.geocities.com/Heartland/Cabin/2842/1890
cen.htm

## Minnesota

Becker County: www.rootsweb.com/~mnbecker/1890.htm

Beltrami County: ftp://ftp.us-census.org/pub/usgenweb/census/mn/beltrami/
1890/pg0029.txt

## Missouri

Bollinger County: ftp://ftp.rootsweb.com/pub/usgenweb/mo/bollinger/cen
sus/1890boll.txt

Butler County: ftp://ftp.rootsweb.com/pub/usgenweb/mo/butler/census/
1890butl.txt

Cape Girardeau County: ftp://ftp.rootsweb.com/pub/usgenweb/mo/capegira
rdeau/census/1890cape.txt

Carter County: ftp://ftp.rootsweb.com/pub/usgenweb/mo/carter/census/
1890cart.txt

Chariton County: www.geocities.com/Heartland/Plains/5982/javamenu
.htm

Cooper County: www.rootsweb.com/~mocooper/Census/1890_Cooper_
Census.html

Dunklin County: ftp://ftp.rootsweb.com/pub/usgenweb/mo/dunklin/census/
1890dunk.txt

Iron County: ftp://ftp.rootsweb.com/pub/usgenweb/mo/iron/census/1890
iron.txt

Linn County: www.geocities.com/Heartland/Plains/5982/javamenu.htm

Macon County: www.geocities.com/Heartland/Plains/5982/javamenu.htm

Mississippi County: ftp://ftp.rootsweb.com/pub/usgenweb/mo/mississippi/ce
nsus/1890miss.txt

New Madrid County: ftp://ftp.rootsweb.com/pub/usgenweb/mo/newmad
rid/census/1890/1890madr.txt

Oregon County: ftp://ftp.rootsweb.com/pub/usgenweb/mo/oregon/census/
1890/1890oreg.txt

Perry County: ftp://ftp.rootsweb.com/pub/usgenweb/mo/perry/census/1890/
1890perr.txt

Pemiscot County: ftp://ftp.rootsweb.com/pub/usgenweb/mo/pemiscot2/cen
sus/1890/1890pemi.txt

Randolph County: http://freepages.genealogy.rootsweb.com/~randolphro
ots/Randolph/

Reynolds County: ftp://ftp.rootsweb.com/pub/usgenweb/mo/reynolds/census/1890reyn.txt

Ripley County: ftp://ftp.rootsweb.com/pub/usgenweb/mo/ripley/census/1890/1890ripl.txt

Scott County: ftp://ftp.rootsweb.com/pub/usgenweb/mo/scott/census/1890/1890scot.txt

Scotland County: www.geocities.com/Heartland/Hollow/3184/scotland.html

Shannon County: ftp://ftp.rootsweb.com/pub/usgenweb/mo/shannon/census/1890shan.txt

St. Francois County: ftp://ftp.rootsweb.com/pub/usgenweb/mo/stfrancois/census/1890stfr.txt

Stoddard County: ftp://ftp.rootsweb.com/pub/usgenweb/mo/stoddard2/census/1890stod.txt

Stone County: www.rootsweb.com/~mostone/census/1890special.htm

Washington County: ftp://ftp.rootsweb.com/pub/usgenweb/mo/washington/census/1890wash.txt

Wayne County: ftp://ftp.rootsweb.com/pub/usgenweb/mo/wayne/census/1890wayn.txt

## Nebraska

Colfax County: www.rootsweb.com/~necolfax/1890census.html

Cuming County: ftp://ftp.rootsweb.com/pub/usgenweb/ne/cuming/census/1890/veterans.txt

Dodge County: www.rootsweb.com/~nedodge/census/dodgev1890.txt

Frontier County: ftp://ftp.rootsweb.com/pub/usgenweb/ne/cuming/census/1890/veterans.txt

Gosper County: www.rootsweb.com/~negosper/war.htm

Hayes County: www.rootsweb.com/~nehayes/olr/cwvets.htm

Keith County: www.rootsweb.com/~nekeith/keithvet.htm

Merrick County: ftp://ftp.rootsweb.com/pub/usgenweb/ne/merrick/vetcen.txt

Nance County: www.rootsweb.com/~nenance/olres/1890vets.html

Platte County: www.rootsweb.com/~neplatte/1890/veterans.html

Perkins County: www.rootsweb.com/~neperkin/perkvet.html

## Nevada

Lander County: ftp://ftp.us-census.org/pub/usgenweb/census/nv/lander/1890/

Lincoln County: ftp://ftp.us-census.org/pub/usgenweb/census/nv/lincoln/1890/

Lyon County: ftp://ftp.us-census.org/pub/usgenweb/census/nv/lyon/1890/

Nye County: ftp://ftp.us-census.org/pub/usgenweb/census/nv/nye/1890/

Ormsby County: ftp://ftp.us-census.org/pub/usgenweb/census/nv/ormsby/1890/

Storey County: ftp://ftp.us-census.org/pub/usgenweb/census/nv/storey/1890/

## New Mexico

Dona Ana County: http://nmgs.org/art1890cen.htm

**New York**

Franklin County: www.rootsweb.com/~nyfrankl/civilwar/1890.html

Herkimer County: www.rootsweb.com/~nyherkim/index.html

Lewis County (Highmarket): www.rootsweb.com/~nylewis/1890high market.html

Montgomery County: www.rootsweb.com/~nyherkim/index.html

Richmond County: www.rootsweb.com/~nyrichmo/1890_census.shtml

**North Carolina**

Cherokee County: www.goldenbranches.com/nc-state/cherokee/data.html

Hyde County: www.rootsweb.com/~nchyde/HYDE1890.HTM

Tyrell County: ftp://ftp.rootsweb.com/pub/usgenweb/nc/tyrrell/military/ 1890vet.txt

**North Dakota**

Pembina County: ftp://ftp.rootsweb.com/pub/usgenweb/nd/pembina/census/ pemcw90.txt

**Ohio**

Erie County: ftp://ftp.rootsweb.com/pub/usgenweb/oh/erie/census/Flo 1890V.txt

Knox County: http://hometown.aol.com/Shortyhack/1890for142nd.html

Lawrence County: www.wwd.net/user/historical/civilwar/cwindex.html

Marion County: www.genealogy.org/~smoore/marion/1890BI.htm

**Oregon**

Coos County: www.rootsweb.com/~orcoos/1890cnss.htm

**Pennsylvania**

Blair County: ftp://ftp.us-census.org/pub/usgenweb/census/pa/blair/1890/

Cambria County: ftp://ftp.us-census.org/pub/usgenweb/census/pa/cambria/ 1890/

Schuylkill County: www.geocities.com/Heartland/Prairie/4280/index.html

Somerset County: ftp://ftp.us-census.org/pub/usgenweb/census/pa/somerset/ 1890/

**South Carolina**

York County: http://freepages.genealogy.rootsweb.com/~york/Pension/1890 .htm

**South Dakota**

Aurora County: www.rootsweb.com/~sdaurora/cwvets.htm

**Tennessee**

Bledsoe County: www.tngenweb.org/bledsoe/1890bvc.htm

Campbell County: http://minder.netmind.com/go/10001/24224224/8952
548/141/census/census/cbresch.html

Clay County: www.rootsweb.com/~tnfentre/civil.htm

Fentress County: www.rootsweb.com/~tnfentre/civil.htm

Greene County: www.rootsweb.com/~tngreene/census/index

Hancock County: www.rootsweb.com/~tnhawkin/1890vethan.html

Jackson County: ftp://ftp.rootsweb.com/pub/usgenweb/tn/jackson/census/
1890/jckson90.txt

Loudon County: www.rootsweb.com/~tnloudon/census/1890v1.html

Pickett County: www.rootsweb.com/~tnfentre/civil.htm

Sequatchie County: www.tngenweb.org/sequatchie/1890vc.htm

Sumner County: www.tngenweb.org/sequatchie/1890vc.htm

Roane County: http://roanetnheritage.com/research/census/1890/01.htm

## Texas

Burnet County: www.rootsweb.com/~txburnet/cwarvets.html

Rusk County: www.rootsweb.com/~txrusk/yankee.html

## Vermont

Addison County: http://store.yahoo.com/vtfamilyhistory/18vetcen.html

## Virginia

Augusta County: http://jefferson.village.virginia.edu/vshadow2/au1890veter
ans.html

Buchanan County: http://members.aol.com/jweaver300/grayson/buch
1890.htm

Culpeper County: www.rootsweb.com/~takelley/c1890.htm

Rappahannock County: www.rootsweb.com/~takelley/r1890.htm

Russell County: www.rhobard.com/census/1890census.html

## Virginia (southwestern counties)

Bath, Buchanan, Carroll, Craig, Dickenson, Floyd, Grayson, Henry, Highland, Lee, Montgomery, Nelson, Patrick, Pittsylvania, Pulaski, Roanoke,
Russell, Scott, Smyth, Tazewell, Washington, Wise, and Wythe counties:
www.ls.net/~newriver/va/1890swva.htm

## West Virginia

Calhoun County: www.rootsweb.com/~wvcalhou/90cen.htm

Grant County: www.rootsweb.com/usgenweb/wv/grant.htm

Greenbrier County: ftp://ftp.rootsweb.com/pub/usgenweb/wv/greenbrier/
census/1890/1890vet.txt

Hampshire County: www.rootsweb.com/usgenweb/wv/hampshir.htm

Hardy County: ftp://ftp.rootsweb.com/pub/usgenweb/wv/hardy/census/
1890/sspg0001.txt

Mineral County: www.rootsweb.com/~wvminera/1890census.html

Marshall County: www.rootsweb.com/~wvmarsha/1890cen.htm

Ohio County: www.rootsweb.com/~wvwags/1890.txt

Pleasants County: www.rootsweb.com/~wvpleasa/90cen.htm

## Wisconsin

Ashland County: www.wlhn.org/census/ashland1890.html

Jackson County: ftp://ftp.rootsweb.com/pub/usgenweb/wi/jackson/census/

Lincoln County: ftp://ftp.rootsweb.com/pub/usgenweb/census/wi/lincoln/
1890/pg00001.txt

Marathon County: http://lonestar.texas.net/~gdalum/marathon/marathon_
cw.html

Marinette County: ftp://ftp.rootsweb.com/pub/usgenweb/wi/marinette/cen
sus/1890/marint.txt

Shawano County: http://lonestar.texas.net/~gdalum/shawano/1890
cens3.html

This list will undoubtedly grow as individuals or societies transcribe and publish census records. To locate online transcriptions, use the phrase "1890 Veteran" plus the name of the state in search engines. Cyndi's List <www.cyndis list.com> and RootsWeb <www.rootsweb.com> also provide links to transcriptions as they are posted.

**FIVE**

# Census Media: Handwritten to Electronic

ith the abundance of census records throughout the genealogical community, we can lose sight of the fact that federal census records come in several varieties:

- original manuscripts
- handwritten copies, made at the time of a census, of the originals
- microfilmed copies of the originals or surviving copies
- digitally enhanced images of the microfilmed versions

Unfortunately, not all census enumerations still survive. Most early records were eventually deposited with the federal government, but the procedures and requirements for this transfer varied greatly, resulting in an incomplete collection.

## TRUE ORIGINALS OR COPIES?

\di'fin\ *vb*

**Definitions**

**The *original manuscript* is the one the census marshal carried when he questioned local residents.** He traveled from household to household and completed the form. Depending on the law at the time, handwritten copies of these manuscripts were made prior to their distribution to government officials. Unfortunately, it is nearly impossible to know whether records we examine today are the true original or a copied version.

### 1790 Through 1820

Total of Three Manuscripts—Original and Two Handwritten Copies
  One sent to clerk of federal district court
  Two posted for public viewing

The laws from 1790 through 1820 required the census marshal to make two handwritten copies of the original. The copies were supposed to be posted in two public places so citizens could examine them for accuracy. The assistants turned over their work to the U.S. marshals, who were to file the returns with the clerks of the federal district courts. The marshals tallied the totals and reported the aggregate amounts to the president in 1790 and to the secretary of state in 1800 through 1840.

The handwritten copies were bound to contain transcription errors. Some marshals also took it upon themselves not only to copy the record, but to rearrange the entries in alphabetical order—sometimes by first letter of the surname and sometimes by first letter of given name. In most cases, the filmed version is not the true original but rather a second or third copy made after corrections were made by the citizens. See the 1810 census (figure 3-3) in chapter three for an example of an alphabetical schedule.

## 1830 and 1840

Total of Two Manuscripts—Original and a Handwritten Copy

> One sent to clerk of district court
> One sent to U.S. secretary of state

The process changed somewhat in 1830 in that copies were not posted for public review. Congress passed a law in 1830 requiring the states to submit the 1790 through 1820 original full census schedules. Only the states of Connecticut, Maryland, New Hampshire, New York, North Carolina, Pennsylvania, Vermont, Rhode Island, South Carolina, and the two districts of present-day Maine and Massachusetts complied with the law. See "Missing or Lost Schedules" on page 112 of this chapter for more details.

## 1850 Through 1870

Total of Three Manuscripts—Original and Two Handwritten Copies

> One sent to the federal census office
> One sent to secretary of the state or territory
> One sent to clerk of county court

### 1870 MINNESOTA CENSUS

A large portion of the federal copy of the 1870 Minnesota census was destroyed by a fire in 1896. Records survived for only thirteen counties—Stearns, Steele, Stevens, St. Louis, Todd, Wabasha, Wadena, Waseca, Washington, Watonwan, Wilkin, Winona, and Wright.

The Minnesota Historical Society's copy of the 1870 census was microfilmed in its entirety by the National Archives to replace the burned schedules. Consequently two filmings exist for the surviving thirteen counties, i.e., micropublication M593 (the federal copy), and T132 (the state copy). If you research these counties, check both versions as there may be slight differences. The state copy also has some mortality schedules interfiled with the population schedules.

Instructions changed slightly from 1850 through 1870. The procedure was to display the original census at the county courthouse rather than at other public places such as a church or saloon. Census marshals were instructed to mail one set of the returns to the census office as soon as possible following completion of the enumeration. A handwritten copy was made for the secretary of the state or territory, and one copy remained with the clerk of the county court.

A few state or county copies of the federal census records have been located in state archives and other record repositories, and a few are available at the Family History Library. Unfortunately, a specific inventory has not yet been compiled or published. It is worth some time and effort to locate other copies of a census record because they are rarely identical:

| EXAMPLES OF DIFFERENCES BETWEEN STATE AND FEDERAL COPIES | | |
| --- | --- | --- |
| Census | State Copy | Federal Copy |
| 1850 Annsville, Oneida County, New York | Begins with family #11 | Begins with family #68 |
| 1850 Oxford County, Maine | Some communities report town of birth. (Microfilm copy is available only at the Maine State Archives.) | Does not give town of birth. |
| 1850 Perquimans County, North Carolina | Easy to use. Satisfactory arrangement of pages. County of birth given for persons born in North Carolina. | Difficult to use. Pages out of order; some missing. |
| 1860 East Feliciana Parish, Louisiana | Parish copy gives full name. | Gives initials of given name rather than full name. |

To determine if a state copy exists for your area of interest, check the Family History Library catalog and the holdings of the state and county archives or historical societies. State copies of the federal census are cataloged under the state and the sub-category of census at the Family History Library rather than by county and state as is normal for the federal census. The state census microfilms are also filed differently, i.e., they are not in the census microfilm file cabinets dedicated to the National Archives census microfilm, but instead intermingled with other microfilm for the state.

## 1880

### Total of Two Manuscripts—Original and Abbreviated Copy
### Original (full schedule) sent to superintendent of the census
### Abbreviated copy retained locally

The Census Act of 1880 stipulated that each enumerator make a list of the names, ages, sex, and color of all persons in the district and post the list in a public place. The abbreviated list was created alphabetically by the first letter of the surname of each person, thereby destroying family groupings from neighborhood settings and including different surnames. No inventory exists of these "short forms," so it is not known how many survive.

The original, full manuscript (corrected or not) was sent to the superintendent of the census in Washington, DC. No full copies were made at the direction of the Census Bureau.

## 1890 Through 1930
### Original Manuscript Only

Beginning in 1890, copies of census records were not made at the time of the census. The original manuscripts were submitted to the government for processing and tabulation. A municipality could request a short form similar to those created in the 1880 procedure, but this was rarely done. No inventory of 1890 short forms exists.

---

**CENSUS TRIVIA**

The 1890 census was not completely destroyed in the 1921 fire. The surviving fragments from eleven states (Alabama, District of Columbia, Georgia, Illinois, Minnesota, New Jersey, New York, North Carolina, Ohio, South Dakota, and Texas) give details on 6,160 individuals. See page 50 in chapter three for specifics on each state.

---

## Handwritten Copies Made in 1921?

The *New York Times* reported in 1921 (Jan. 12, 27:2) following the disastrous fire, that at least one-third of the census records from 1790 through 1910 would have to be copied due to water damage. The Census Bureau estimated that this would take two or three years and cost approximately two million dollars. According to Kellee Blake's article "First in the Path of the Firemen: The Fate of the 1890 Population Census" (*Prologue* [Quarterly of the National Archives and Records Administration], Spring 1996, vol. 27, no. 1; <www.nara.gov/publications/prologue/1890cen1.html>) this estimate was later changed to about 10 percent of the following water-damaged schedules:

> 1830: six states
> 1840: seven states
> 1880: twenty states
> 1900: forty-eight states and Indian Territory
> 1910: forty-eight states and District of Columbia

It is unclear whether the government followed through with the plan to copy the water-damaged schedules, as nothing definitive has been published on this matter.

At the time of the fire, the schedules for 1790 through 1820 and 1850 through 1870 were stored on a different floor of the Commerce Building and consequently not damaged, and the 1920 census was temporarily in a different building.

## MISSING OR LOST SCHEDULES

There is conflicting information regarding the loss of 1790 schedules for Delaware, Georgia, Kentucky, New Jersey, Tennessee, and Virginia. Most genealogical reference books report that these schedules were destroyed when the British burned the Capitol during the War of 1812. This is disputed in the 1909 publication *A Century of Population Growth From the First Census of the United States to the Twelfth 1790–1900* (page 49):

> There is a record that the 1790 returns for Virginia were destroyed when the British burned the Capitol at Washington during the War of 1812. But it is a question whether anything more than the marshal's summary was burned; if the First Census law was complied with, the original returns must have been in the custody of the clerk of the district court of Virginia.

If this was true for Virginia, it was most likely the same for the other five states. Missing or lost census schedules include the following:

| | |
|---|---|
| Alabama | 1820 |

The *Alabama Historical Quarterly*, vol. 6 (Fall 1944) published the 1820 territorial census (not a federal census, although content is similar) for Baldwin, Conecuh, Dallas, Franklin, Limestone, St. Clair, Shelby, and Wilcox counties. The Lawrence County schedule was later found and published as *1820 State Census of Lawrence County, Alabama: A Special Edition of Valley Leaves* (Huntsville, Ala.: Tennessee Valley Genealogical Society, 1977).

| | |
|---|---|
| Alaska | 1870, 1880 |
| Arkansas | 1820 |
| California | 1850 (Contra Costa, San Francisco, and Santa Clara counties only) |
| Delaware | 1790 |
| District of Columbia | 1810 |
| Florida | 1860 (Hernando County only) |
| Georgia | 1790, 1800 (except Oglethorpe County), 1810, 1820 (Franklin, Rabun, and Twiggs counties only) |
| Illinois | 1810 |
| Indiana | 1800, 1810, 1820 (Daviess County only), 1830 (Wabash County only) |

The 1807 Indiana Territorial census, compiled by Rebah Fraustein, was published by the Indiana Historical Society in 1980. The index is also available through the AIS indexes at <www.ancestry.com> (see chapter seven for explanation of AIS indexes).

| | |
|---|---|
| Kentucky | 1790, 1800 |
| Louisiana | 1860 (Bienville County only) |
| Maine | 1800 (part of York County only), 1810 (half of Oxford County), 1820 (Houlton Plantation in Washington County only) |

## COMPARING PUBLISHED CENSUS RECORDS

The 1820 state census for Lawrence County, Alabama, is published in two places:

1. on the Internet at <http://members.aol.com/rpennin975/1820lcce.html> and

2. in a special publication of the Tennessee Valley Genealogical Society, Mrs. Walter H. Johnson, ed., *1820 State Census of Lawrence County, Alabama: A Special Edition of Valley Leaves* (Huntsville, Ala.: TVGS, 1977).

Comparing these two publications reveals how important it can be to seek the original record rather than relying upon an abstract or index.

The Internet version is arranged in alphabetical order and includes the statistics for each family. Neighborhood reconstruction is virtually impossible with this style. This abstract also failed to include page numbers from the original schedule.

The Tennessee Valley Genealogical Society published photocopies of the original census, and the publication includes the following entry:

Robt Madra for Saunders 1,0,0,0,1,0,10,11

The Internet transcription of this entry is listed alphabetically under S as

Saunders, Robt. Madra for 1,0,0,0,1,0,10,11

If a descendant of the Madra family searched the Internet version of this census, he would not find the listing easily because the indexer misinterpreted the entry, created a new person named Robert Saunders, and placed the entry in the S portion of the index.

Errors such as this are common. Be certain you research beyond an index or abstract in order to be accurate in your genealogical conclusions.

| | |
|---|---|
| Maryland | 1790 (Allegheny, Calvert, Somerset and part of Dorchester counties only), 1800 (Baltimore County outside of city of Baltimore only), 1830 (Montgomery, Prince George, Queen Anne's, St. Mary's, and Somerset counties only) |
| Massachusetts | 1800 (Boston and part of Suffolk County only), 1890 veterans (Worcester County only) |
| Michigan | 1810 |
| Mississippi | 1830 (Pike County only), 1860 (Hancock, Sunflower, and Washington counties only) |
| Missouri | 1810, 1820 |
| New Hampshire | 1800 (parts of Rockingham and Strafford |

| | |
|---|---|
| | counties only), 1820 (Grafton County and parts of Rockingham and Strafford counties only) |
| New Jersey | 1790 through 1820 (except 1800 Cumberland County) |
| New York | 1810 (Cortland and part of Broome counties only) |
| North Carolina | 1790 (Caswell, Granville, and Orange counties only), 1810 (Craven, Greene, New Hanover, and Wake counties only), 1820 (Currituck, Franklin, Martin, Montgomery, Randolph, and Wake counties only) |
| Ohio | 1800 and 1810 (except Washington County), 1820 (Franklin and Wood counties only) |
| Pennsylvania | 1800 (part of Westmoreland County only), 1810 (parts of Bedford, Cumerland, and Philadelphia counties only), 1820 (parts of Lancaster and Luzerne counties only), 1870 (Philadelphia City, wards 27 only) |
| South Carolina | 1800 (Richland District only), 1820 through 1850 (Clarendon County only) |
| Tennessee | 1790, 1800, 1810 (except Grainger and Rutherford counties), 1820 (Anderson, Bledsoe, Blount, Campbell, Carter, Claiborne, Cocke, Grainger, Greene, Hamilton, Hawkins, Jefferson, Knox, McMinn, Marion, Monroe, Morgan, Rhea, Roane, Servier, Sullivan, and Washington counties only) |
| Texas | 1860 (Tarrant County only) |
| Virginia | 1790, 1800 (except Accomack and Louisa counties), 1810 (Alexandria, Cabell, Grayson, Greenbrier, Halifax, Hardy, Henry, James City, King William, Lee, Louisa, Mecklenburg, Middlesex, Nansemond, Northampton, Orange, Patrick, Pittsylvania, Russell, and Tazwell counties only) |
| Washington | 1860 (Benton, Columbia, San Juan, Snohomish, and Stevens counties only), 1870 (Benton and Columbia counties only) |

## STORAGE OF ORIGINAL SCHEDULES

The census marshals were instructed in 1790 through 1820 to deposit the census returns with the clerks of the district courts within their districts. Congress passed a law in 1830 requiring the states to return the original 1790 through 1820 census schedules. Only the states of Connecticut, Maryland, New Hampshire, New York, North Carolina, Pennsylvania, Rhode Island, South Carolina, Vermont, and the two districts of present-day Maine and Massachusetts complied with the law.

All census manuscripts were in the custody of the secretary of state until 1849, when they were transferred to the secretary of the interior. They were stored in a fireproof vault in the Patent Office until June 1904, when they were transferred to the Census Bureau.

When fire destroyed most of the 1890 census in 1921, the records had been scattered within the Commerce Building. The 1790 through 1820 and 1850 through 1870 schedules had been on the fifth floor; the 1830, 1840, 1880, 1900, and 1910 schedules had been in the basement vault; and the 1890 census had been piled in the corridors of the basement. *The New York Times* editorial of 12 January, 1921 charged that Congress had ignored warnings of a fire hazard and pleas to appropriate funds for proper storage facilities.

By 1930 a new fireproof vault had been completed for storage of all census records at the Census Bureau. See chapter two, page 27 for a *New York Times* article about the new vault.

**Notes**

**CENSUS TRIVIA**

California's first census participation was 1850, a year after the state's admission to the Union, and 93,000 persons were tallied in the state. San Francisco's census records for that year were later destroyed by fire.

## MICROFILMING AND DISTRIBUTION OF ORIGINALS

The National Archives microfilmed all census manuscripts in their possession in the 1940s. In 1956, the National Archives offered the fragile 1880 population schedules to various state and university libraries and state archives. The Daughters of the American Revolution (DAR) accepted the original schedules for the states of Arizona, Connecticut, Idaho, Iowa, Kansas, Mississippi, Missouri, New Hampshire, Nebraska, New Mexico, Rhode Island, and Utah. The DAR library had possession of these schedules from 1956 until 1980, when repositories in each state accepted the deteriorating volumes. The present locations of the original 1880 population schedules are as follows:

| | |
|---|---|
| Alabama | Department of Archives and History, Montgomery, Alabama. |
| Arizona | Arizona Department of Library, Archives and Public Records, Phoenix, Arizona. |
| Arkansas | Arkansas History Commission, Little Rock, Arkansas. |
| California | California State Archives, Sacramento, California. |
| Colorado | Colorado State Archives, Denver, Colorado. |
| Connecticut | Connecticut State Library, State Archives, Hartford, Connecticut. |
| Delaware | Delaware Public Archives, Hall of Records, Dover, Delaware. |
| District of Columbia | Historical Society of Washington, Washington, DC. |

| | |
|---|---|
| Florida | Florida State University, Tallahassee, Florida. |
| Georgia | Georgia Department of Archives and History, Atlanta, Georgia. |
| Idaho | Idaho State Historical Society, Boise, Idaho. |
| Illinois | Illinois State Archives, Springfield, Illinois. |
| Indiana | Indiana State Library, Indianapolis, Indiana. |
| Iowa | State Historical Society of Iowa, Des Moines, Iowa. |
| Kansas | Kansas DAR Library, Dodge City, Kansas. |
| Kentucky | Kentucky Department of Libraries and Archives, Frankfort, Kentucky. |
| Louisiana | Louisiana State University, Baton Rouge, Louisiana. |
| Maine | Maine Division of Vital Statistics, Augusta, Maine. |
| Maryland | Maryland State Archives, Annapolis, Maryland. |
| Massachusetts | Archives of the Commonwealth, Boston, Massachusetts. |
| Michigan | Michigan Department of State, Lansing, Michigan. |
| Minnesota | Minnesota Historical Society, St. Paul, Minnesota. |
| Mississippi | Location unknown. The Mississippi Department of Archives and History reports that it does not have the schedules. |
| Missouri | Missouri State Archives, Jefferson City, Missouri. |
| Montana | Montana Historical Society, Helena, Montana. |
| Nebraska | Edith Abbott Memorial Library, Grand Island, Nebraska. |
| Nevada | Nevada State Museum, Carson City, Nevada. |
| New Hampshire | New Hampshire Division of Records Management and Archives, Concord, New Hampshire. |
| New Jersey | Rutgers University, New Brunswick, New Jersey. |
| New Mexico | Location unknown. The New Mexico Records Center and Archives reports that it does not have these schedules. |
| New York | New York State Library, Albany, New York. |
| North Carolina | North Carolina State Archives, Raleigh, North Carolina. |
| North Dakota | State Historical Society of North Dakota, Bismarck, North Dakota. |
| Ohio | Ohio State Museum, Columbus, Ohio. |

| | |
|---|---|
| Oregon | Oregon State Library, Salem, Oregon. |
| Pennsylvania | University of Pittsburgh, Pittsburgh, Pennsylvania. |
| Rhode Island | Rhode Island Historical Society, Providence, Rhode Island. |
| South Carolina | South Carolina Department of Archives and History, Columbia, South Carolina. |
| South Dakota | South Dakota Historical Society, Pierre, South Dakota. |
| Tennessee | Tennessee State Library and Archives, Nashville, Tennessee. |
| Texas | Texas State Library, Austin, Texas. |
| Utah | Utah State Archives and Records Services, Salt Lake City, Utah. |
| Vermont | Vermont State Library, Montpelier, Vermont. |
| Virginia | Virginia State Library, Richmond, Virginia. |
| Washington | Washington State Library, Olympia, Washington. |
| West Virginia | West Virginia Historical Society, Charleston, West Virginia. |
| Wisconsin | Wisconsin Historical Society, Madison, Wisconsin. |
| Wyoming | Wyoming State Archives, Cheyenne, Wyoming. |

For the locations of the original 1880 non-population schedules, see chapter four.

## DESTRUCTION OF SCHEDULES FOR 1900 THROUGH 1940

In 1956, Congress authorized the destruction of the original 1900 through 1940 schedules in order to save space.

The National Archives acquired the master negative microfilm from the Census Bureau but could not correct some of the poor-quality filming. The 1910 microfilm copies are especially poor, with thousands of pages illegible. Unfortunately those censuses cannot be remicrofilmed since the originals were destroyed.

## SUMMARY OF DISPOSITION OF CENSUS RECORDS

| | |
|---|---|
| 1790–1870 | Surviving official copy (not always the original) located at National Archives. Some copies exist for some areas and are scattered in county and state archives or libraries. These hand-copied documents are not likely to be exact duplicates of the originals. |

| | |
|---|---|
| 1880 | Originals have been distributed to various state or university libraries. Abbreviated copies can be found in some local repositories. |
| 1890 | Nearly all records destroyed in 1921 fire. |
| 1900–1940 | Originals intentionally destroyed after microfilming. |

A few exceptions involve surviving agriculture or farm schedules. See "Summary of Population and Non-population Schedules" in chapter four for details.

## SECOND MICROFILMING

The 1850, 1860, and 1870 censuses were microfilmed twice. The Family History Library, in Salt Lake City, has microfilmings for both 1860 and 1870, and each box of microfilm is clearly labeled accordingly. The National Archives and its branches have the second microfilming only. **The first microfilm shows two facing pages to a frame; the second, one page to a frame.** The first microfilm is labeled with the old NARA microfilm publication numbers T6, T7, and T8.

The second microfilm is usually easier to read, but the ink on some pages has faded. If data on the National Archives microfilm (from the second microfilming) is faded, examine a copy of the first microfilm.

### 1870 Second Enumeration
**Indianapolis, New York City, Philadelphia**
Controversy over the accuracy of the 1870 population counts for Indianapolis, New York City, and Philadelphia resulted in a second enumeration of these cities several months after the first. The National Archives microfilmed both 1870 enumerations. If you are researching these cities for 1870, be sure to examine both enumerations as the content varies.

### 1880 Second Enumeration
**St. Louis**
The city of St. Louis, Missouri, was enumerated twice in 1880, and both versions have been microfilmed by the National Archives. Examine both enumerations; you may find conflicting information.

## DIGITIZED CENSUS RECORDS

The latest innovation in census research is the creation of digitized images of census records. Major vendors, such as Ancestry.com, HeritageQuest Online, and Genealogy.com, are scanning census microfilm obtained from the National Archives and creating digitized images. HeritageQuest Online <www.heritage quest.com> sells CDs with the digitized images for 1790 through 1920. Ancestry.com, Genealogy.com, and HeritageQuest Online offer subscriptions to review the images online. The quality of the image is generally improved, although sometimes the digitized image appears fuzzy when compared to a microfilm version.

**Notes**

**For More Info**

**1870 SECOND ENUMERATION NEW YORK CITY**

The second 1870 enumeration of New York City, taken in late December, included street addresses, whereas the first enumeration did not. A street index to the seventeenth ward—the largest ward, having nearly 100,000 people—can help you find someone by narrowing the search to a specific enumeration district. See Kory L. Meyerink's article "The Second Enumeration—The 1870 New York City Census," *The New York Genealogical and Biographical Record,* October 1984, pp. 199–202, for instructions on how to use the street index.

# DECIDING WHICH MEDIUM TO USE

Original? Microfilm? CD-ROM? Internet?

These various options may be overwhelming and confusing, especially if you are just learning how to research your family history. Consider the following factors in deciding what type of census record to use in your research:

- Original. The surviving original manuscripts are not available for general research. The National Archives guards these fragile and historically valuable records. They allow supervised on-site examination when the microfilm copy is illegible or when a researcher demonstrates that pages are missing from the microfilm.

- Microfilm. Microfilm is the most available type of census record. See chapter six for a list of major libraries that hold complete collections of the census. Many other local libraries have smaller collections of census records relating to their state and/or neighboring areas.

- Another advantage of microfilm is ease of use. The entire image appears on the screen of a microfilm reader, and moving from page to page is simple and fast. Some libraries have microfilm printers that produce an 11″×17″ (28cm×43cm) photocopy—the most desirable size for viewing the image. Microfilm can be borrowed through interlibrary loan or purchased.

- CD-ROM. CD-ROM versions of census images are easy to use, although your computer screen may not provide as large an image as a microfilm reader does. Purchasing a CD-ROM for areas you will research heavily may be helpful because you can view these images in the comfort of your home.

- Internet. **The biggest drawback of viewing census images online is access time.** It takes time to load the images, so moving from page to page can be an exercise in patience. The improved image quality, however, is an important benefit as is the convenience of researching online.

When you view census records, remember that other forms of those records exist. You may find it beneficial to compare, for example, a hard-to-read microfilm copy to a digitized version.

Tip

**TIPS FOR READING MICROFILM**

Try this if you have difficulty reading a census microfilm:

- Place a piece of colored paper on the screen. Yellow, pink, and blue are the most effective.

- Be certain the room is darkened and the reader light is strong.

- Make a negative print of the page. The reverse black and white can sometimes help with deciphering the handwriting.

Warning

# PART TWO

# Finding Census Records and Indexes

# SIX

# Where to Find Federal Census Records

C ensus records are housed at the National Archives and its thirteen branches, the Family History Library in Salt Lake City and the regional Family History Centers, and hundreds of public and university libraries throughout the United States. The records appear on CD-ROM, on microfilm, and in digitized format on the Internet. They can be borrowed, purchased, viewed for free, or accessed via subscription. The following summary can help you decide how to access census records for your family history research.

## Research Facilities

### Complete Census and Soundex Collection, 1790–1930

- National Archives in Washington, DC, and the thirteen regional facilities:
    Alaska (Anchorage)
    California (Laguna Niguel)
    California (San Bruno)
    Colorado (Denver)
    Georgia (Atlanta)
    Illinois (Chicago)
    Massachusetts (Boston)
    Massachusetts (Pittsfield)
    Missouri (Kansas City)
    New York (New York City)
    Pennsylvania (Philadelphia)
    Texas (Fort Worth)
    Washington (Seattle)

Go to <www.nara.gov/nara/gotonara.html> to find research hours and directions to the facilities, or see Appendix A for a complete list of the National Archives regional facilities and their contact information and hours.

- The Family History Library, in Salt Lake City, Utah, has a complete collec-

**For More Info**

For information on using the Family History Library, the Family History Centers, or the FamilySearch Web site, see *Your Guide to the Family History Library* by Paula Stuart Warren and James W. Warren (Cincinnati: Betterway Books, 2001).

tion of the U.S. federal census and Soundex. The microfilm can also be borrowed through one of the more than 3,400 Family History Centers located throughout the world. To find a Family History Center near you, check at <www.familysearch.org>, or look in your telephone book under "Church of Jesus Christ of Latter-day Saints."

- The Allen County Public Library, Genealogy Department, 900 Webster Street, Fort Wayne, Indiana, 46801-2270.

## Research Facilities

### Complete Census Collection, 1790–1920

(Note: To determine if any of these libraries purchased the recently released 1930 census, write, telephone, or e-mail them.)

**California**

California State Library
　　Sutro Library
　　480 Winston Dr.
　　San Francisco, CA 94132
　　(415) 731-4477
　　www.onelibrary.com/Library/calslsut.htm
　　Complete Soundex for 1880 through 1920.
Los Angeles Family History Center
　　10741 Santa Monica Blvd.
　　Los Angeles, CA 90025
　　(310) 474-9990
　　Complete Soundex for 1880 through 1920.
Los Angeles Public Library
　　History & Genealogy Department
　　630 W. Fifth St.
　　Los Angeles, CA 90071
　　(213) 228-7400
　　www.lapl.org/central/history.html
　　Complete Soundex for 1880 through 1920.
San Diego Family History Center
　　4195 Camino del Rio South
　　San Diego, CA 91208
　　(619) 584-7668
　　Incomplete Soundex.

**Florida**

Indian River County Public Library
　　1600 Twenty-first St.
　　Vero Beach, FL 32960
　　(561) 770-5060
　　http://indian-river.fl.us/library/index.html
　　No Soundex.

## OTHER RESEARCH FACILITIES WITH NEARLY COMPLETE CENSUS COLLECTIONS

The following research facilities have excellent census collections that cannot be categorized as complete because of some gaps in some time periods:

Colorado

Denver Public Library

10 W. Fourteenth Ave. Pkwy.

Denver, CO 80204

(720) 865-1821

www.denver.lib.us.co

Most states through 1870. Censuses for 1900 through 1920 for Arizona, Colorado, Idaho, Kansas, Missouri, Montana, Nebraska, Nevada, New Mexico, North Dakota, Oklahoma, South Dakota, Texas (not 1920), Utah, and Wyoming.

District of Columbia

National Society, Daughters of the American Revolution

1776 D St., NW

Washington, DC 20006

(202) 628-1776

www.chesapeake.net/DAR/

Census and Soundex for 1800 through 1900.

Illinois

Newberry Library

60 W. Walton St.

Chicago, IL 60610

www.newberry.org

Complete for 1790 through 1850. Complete for all midwestern states through 1880. The 1870 holdings are complete for all southern and border states, and the 1860 and 1880 holdings for many of these states are also complete. The 1900 through 1920 collection is complete for Illinois only.

Massachusetts

Boston Public Library

Copley Square

Boston, MA 02117

(617) 536-5400

www.bpl.org/

New England states for 1790 through 1920.

New England Historic Genealogical Society

101 Newbury St.

Boston, MA 02116

(617) 536-5740

www.nehgs.org/

New England states for 1790 through 1920 (including indexes). Most states through 1850. Various states for 1850 through 1900.

Missouri

St. Louis Public Library
1301 Olive St.
St. Louis, MO 63103
(314) 241-2288
www.slpl.lib.mo.us/library.htm
A table of available census records is at www.slpl.lib.mo.us/libsrc/gene.htm.

New York

New York Public Library
Schomburg Center for Research in Black Culture
515 Malcolm X Blvd.
New York, NY 10037
(212) 491-2200
www.nypl.org/research/sc/sc.html
1790 through 1900
Incomplete Soundex.

Orlando Public Library
101 E. Central Blvd.
Orlando, FL 32801
www.rrc.usf.edu/publib/orange/main.html
No Soundex.

**Louisiana**

East Baton Rouge Library
Bluebonnet Branch
9200 Bluebonnet Blvd.
Baton Rouge, LA 70810
(225) 763-2240
www.ebr.lib.la.us/
Incomplete Soundex.

**Michigan**

Detroit Public Library
Burton Historical Collection
5201 Woodward
Detroit, MI 48202
(313) 833-1000
www.detroit.lib.mi.us/burton/
Complete collection of the population schedules for 1790 through 1920. Soundex for 1880, 1900, and 1910 (Michigan only). 1920 Soundex for

Alabama, Arkansas, Georgia, Illinois, Indiana, Kentucky, Mississippi, New York, Ohio, Pennsylvania, Tennessee, and Wisconsin.

Library of Michigan
717 W. Allegan St.
P.O. Box 30007
Lansing, MI 48909
(517) 373-1580
http://libraryofmichigan.org/
Complete Soundex for 1880 through 1920.

## Missouri

Mid-Continent Library
317 W. 24 Hwy.
Independence, MO 64050
(816) 252-7228
www.mcpl.lib.mo.us/
Complete Soundex for 1880 through 1920.

## Ohio

Public Library of Cincinnati and Hamilton County
800 Vine St.
Cincinnati, OH 45202
(513) 369-6900
www.plch.lib.oh.us/
Complete Soundex for 1880 through 1920.

Western Reserve Historical Society
10825 East Blvd.
Cleveland, OH 44106
(216) 721-5722
www.wrhs.org
Complete 1880 and 1900 Soundex indexes. 1910 Miracode for Alabama, Kentucky, Michigan, Mississippi, North Carolina, Ohio, Pennsylvania, and West Virginia. 1920 Soundex for Indiana, Kentucky, Michigan, New York, Ohio, Pennsylvania, Rhode Island, Vermont, and West Virginia.

## Texas

Clayton Library
Center for Genealogical Research
5300 Caroline
Houston, TX 77004
(713) 284-1999
www.hpl.lib.tx.us/clayton/
Complete Soundex for 1880 through 1920.

Dallas Public Library
1515 Young St.
Dallas, TX 75201

(214) 670-1400
http://dallaslibrary.org
Incomplete Soundex.

### Wisconsin

Wisconsin Historical Society
816 State St.
Madison, WI 53706
(608) 264-6535
www.shsw.wisc.edu/library/
Incomplete Soundex.

Many other public libraries and archives have incomplete census collections that usually focus on their state or region. Your local genealogical society, library, or state historical society or archives should be able to provide an inventory of locally available census records.

## INTERLIBRARY LOAN

You can borrow census microfilm through your local library's interlibrary loan program. Census indexes, however, are most often considered reference material and cannot be borrowed. Ask your librarian for assistance.

## RENTAL OR PURCHASE OF MICROFILM

The following businesses offer census microfilm for rent or purchase:

**National Archives Microfilm Rental Program**
P.O. Box 30
Annapolis Junction, MD 20701-0030
(301) 604-3699
Microfilm for rent. The National Archives Microfilm Rental Program offers microfilm of federal population schedules from 1790 through 1930, including the Soundex. For more information, write to request a free brochure.

**National Archives Trust Fund (NATF)**
P.O. Box 100793
Atlanta, GA 30384-0793
Microfilm for sale. You must provide the microfilm publication number and specific roll numbers per the National Archives Microfilm Catalogs. To order a catalog or view the online edition, go to <www.nara.gov/publications/micro.html#census>. You can also contact the National Archives Product Sales Section (NWPS), Room G7, 700 Pennsylvania Avenue NW, Washington, DC 20408; phone: (202) 501-7190 or (800) 234-8861. NWPS staff can answer any questions or help you determine what roll to order.

**Scholarly Resources, Inc.**
104 Greenhill Ave.

Wilmington, DE 19805
(302) 654-7713
www.scholarly.com
    Microfilm for sale.
**Heritage Quest**
  669 West 900 North
  North Salt Lake, UT 84054
  (800) 760-2455
  www.heritagequest.com/genealogy/microfilm/
    Microfilm for sale or rent. Rental program is available only to Heritage
Quest Club members.

## CD-ROM IMAGES AND INDEXES

Census images and indexes are published on CD-ROMs. (See chapter seven for
information on using different types of indexes.) The census CD-ROMs may
be purchased from any of the following:
  AllCensus
    P.O. Box 206
    Green Creek, NJ 08219
    www.allcensus.com/
  Blue Roses Publishing Company
    P.O. Box 60934
    San Angelo, TX 76906
    www.angelfire.com/tx/1850censusrecords/cdrom/
  Census View
    P.O. Box 39
    Ripley, OK 74062
    www.censusview.org/
  FamilySearch
    Family and Church History Department
    50 East North Temple St.
    Salt Lake City, UT 84150-3400
    (800) 346-6044
    www.familysearch.org
      Offers 1880 National Index.
  Genealogy.com
    P.O. Box 22295
    Denver, CO 80222
    (800) 548-1806
    www.genealogy.com
  Heritage Quest
    669 West 900 North
    North Salt Lake, UT 84054
    (800) 760-2455
    www.heritagequest.com

S-K Publications
  P.O. Box 8173
  Wichita, KS 67208-0173
  www.skpub.com/genie/

## DIGITAL CENSUS IMAGES ON THE INTERNET

During the summer of 2000, Ancestry.com launched a document images database called Images Online with images of Civil War pension cards. Shortly afterward they began offering digitized census records through their subscription service. By the end of 2001, they had digitized more than ten million census pages for 1790 through 1920.

The images are linked to Ancestry.com's AIS census indexes (see chapter seven for information on AIS indexes) or to the head-of-household indexes they are creating. Users can also browse page by page.

Genealogy.com digitized the 1900 federal census with a head-of-household index. The images are viewable via subscription on the Internet.

HeritageQuest Online <www.heritagequest.com> offers census images and indexes 1790 through 1930 in digital format. A subscription is required.

The Library of Michigan offers digitized images of the 1870 Michigan census at the library's Web site, <http://envoy.libofmich.lib.mi.us/1870_census/>. The Library of Michigan does not charge a subscription or search fee for access to these images.

## CENSUS TRANSCRIPTIONS ON THE INTERNET

Definitions

**A census transcription is an exact handwritten or typed replication of the information in a document.** A transcription of a census record is therefore different from an index to census records because it gives complete data such as age, place of birth, occupation, and enumeration date. The census renderings found in book form and on the Internet are not transcriptions when they do not include 100 percent of the data. Those are merely abstracts of information—useful, but incomplete. The ultimate goal is always to review the original image of the census record and not rely on abstracts or transcriptions, where human error is likely to exist.

In 1997, the USGenWeb Census Project began with a mission of transcribing all of the U.S. federal census records and making them available online—permanently and free of charge. Go to <www.rootsweb.com/~usgenweb/cen_img.htm> for state links.

The well-known Cyndi's List site, <www.cyndislist.com>, contains links to census Web sites, vendors, indexes, magazine articles, software, supplies, and transcriptions. Census Links, at <http://censuslinks.com/>, provides links to census indexes, transcriptions, and other genealogical data. Use Cyndi's List and Census Links concurrently since their links are not completely identical.

## CENSUS REFERENCE BOOKS AND CD-ROMs FOR SALE

The major book publishers and sellers who offer census indexes, CD-ROMs, and census reference books are

Ancestry
    360 West 4800 North
    Provo, UT 84604
    (800) 262-3787
    www.ancestry.com

Frontier Press
    21 Railroad Ave.
    P.O. Box 126
    Cooperstown, NY 13326
    (800) 772-7559
    www.frontierpress.com/frontier.cgi

Genealogical Publishing Company, Inc.
    Clearfield Company
    Gateway Press
    (800) 296-6687
    www.genealogical.com/

Heritage Quest
    669 West 900 North
    North Salt Lake, UT 84054
    (800) 760-2455
    www.heritagequest.com

Willow Bend Books
    65 E. Main St.
    Westminster, MD 21157-55036
    (800) 876-6103
    www.willowbendbooks.com

# SEVEN

# Census Finding Aids and Indexes

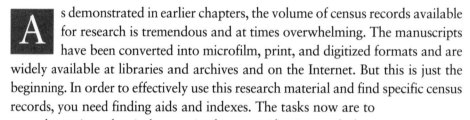A s demonstrated in earlier chapters, the volume of census records available for research is tremendous and at times overwhelming. The manuscripts have been converted into microfilm, print, and digitized formats and are widely available at libraries and archives and on the Internet. But this is just the beginning. In order to effectively use this research material and find specific census records, you need finding aids and indexes. The tasks now are to

- determine what indexes exist for a specific time and place,
- understand indexes' strengths and weaknesses,
- use the indexes at a library or on your computer.

Step By Step

## FINDING CENSUS RECORDS AND INDEXES STEP BY STEP

### Step 1: Maps

A primary step in all types of genealogical research is to find a map of the area and study the boundary changes. Understanding the development of state and county boundaries is often crucial in census research. Suggested tools:

- The Atlas of Historical County Boundaries series, edited by John Hamilton Long, is a project of the Dr. William M. Scholl Center for Family and Community History at the Newberry Library in Chicago, Illinois. These atlases are the most detailed and comprehensive references available on boundary changes. Each atlas includes a special section that lists all censuses for the state (federal, state, territorial, or colonial) and provides an outline map of the county development for each enumeration. Each state is published separately except for states too small to fill one volume (such as Delaware, Vermont, and New Hampshire) and those bound too closely together in history (such as Virginia and West Virginia). The series is projected to total forty volumes. See the bibliography on page 263 for a list of those published to date.

• Thorndale and Dollarhide's *Map Guide to the U.S. Federal Censuses, 1790-1920* (Baltimore: Genealogical Publishing Co., 1987) graphically illustrates each state's boundaries for each census year. This book includes over four hundred maps with old county lines superimposed over current boundaries.

• AniMap Plus <www.goldbug.com>, is an interactive historical atlas on CD-ROM. The program displays in color over 2,300 historical maps year by year, not just for the census years. You can view the maps as still pictures or let the program set them in motion so you can watch the boundary changes. For 1776 to the present you can view the entire United States or focus upon an exact location within a county or state. Each map includes a listing of the changes from the previous map, making it simple to keep track of parent counties. A unique "place marker" feature allows you to place up to fifty markers on a map then change the year to observe the boundary changes relative to the markers' placements. This makes it easy to determine the locations of towns that were shifted from one county to another as the boundaries changed.

• You can order reproductions of maps at the Library of Congress Map Collections 1500–1999 <http://lcweb2.loc.gov/ammem/gmdhtml/gmdhome.html>. The images were created from maps and atlases and, in general, are restricted to items that are not covered by copyright protection.

• The Perry-Castañeda Library Map Collection at the University of Texas at Austin <www.lib.utexas.edu/maps/histus.html> has maps from *The National Atlas of the United States of America* (Arch C. Gerlach, editor. Washington, D.C.: U.S. Dept. of the Interior, Geological Survey, 1970) showing territorial growth for 1775 to 1920. These maps can be viewed online. The university also provides links to several other Internet sites with historical maps.

## Step 2: Catalogs

Examine the National Archives microfilm census catalogs (see below) and record the roll number needed for your research. If you will be using microfilm from the Family History Library in Salt Lake City or at one of the Family History Centers, consult the online catalog at <www.familysearch.org>. By using these catalogs, you can learn whether or not a federal census survives for the time period and area of your interest.

National Archives Trust Fund Board. *1790–1890 Federal Population Censuses: Catalog of National Archives Microfilm*. Rev. ed. Washington, D.C.: National Archives Trust Fund Board, 1997.

————*1900 Federal Population Census: Catalog of National Archives Microfilm*. Rev. ed. Washington. D.C.: National Archives Trust Fund Board, 1996.

————*1910 Federal Population Census: Catalog of National Archives Microfilms*. Rev. ed. Washington, D.C.: National Archives Trust Fund Board, 1996.

————*1920 Federal Population Census: Catalog of National Archives Microfilms.* Rev. ed. Washington, D.C.: National Archives Trust Fund Board, 1995.

————*1930 Federal Population Census: Catalog of National Archives Microfilms.* Rev. ed. Washington, D.C.: National Archives Trust Fund Board, 2002.

These catalogs can be purchased (go to <www.nara.gov/publications/order.html> or call [800] 234-8861) or viewed online at <www.nara.gov/publications/microfilm/census/census.html>.

## Step 3: Alphabetical Index

Preparing a list of available census indexes is challenging and sometimes frustrating. It would be simple if only one official creator made all the indexes and did so perfectly. But the reality is that indexes are not perfect, and multiple indexes often exist for the same time period and place.

It is important to determine what indexes exist for your area of interest and study all of them. As shown in the 1870 Colorado Territorial Index example (see page 135), the differences among indexes can be dramatic.

Once you obtain the bibliographic information, you can purchase the index (if it is still available) or use it at a nearby library. Census indexes are rarely available through interlibrary loan as they are considered reference material. To locate census indexes, refer to the following resources:

• Family History Library Catalog <www.familysearch.org>. The Family History Library in Salt Lake City has the largest collection of census indexes created by individuals, genealogical societies, or commercial publishers.

• Thomas Jay Kemp's *American Census Handbook* is arranged alphabetically by state and county and then chronologically within the local area. More than five hundred pages list thousands of census indexes with full bibliographic citations.

• William Dollarhide's *The Census Book: A Genealogist's Guide to Federal Census Facts, Schedules and Indexes* lists countywide census extractions and indexes compiled for each state that have been published separately from statewide census indexes. Dollarhide includes the Brøderbund CD number, the Heritage Quest CD number, and the Family History Library film number or call number.

• HeritageQuest <www.heritagequest.com> sells microfilm and CD-ROM census records and indexes for all census years and locations. HeritageQuest specializes in creating unique, special order indexes, such as the 1870 index for one surname throughout the United States. See the Web site for details. HeritageQuest Online subscription service provides census images and indexes from 1790 through 1930.

• Ancestry.com has posted all census images for 1790 through 1920 online with subscription access. It is expected that the 1930 census will be added following its release in 2002. Ancestry.com's database collection includes many census indexes. Click on "Search by Locality" or "Search by Record Type" to obtain a list of the available databases. Click on the "Shop" icon to determine what census indexes are for sale.

• Genealogy.com offers online viewing of the 1900 census images via subscription and provides access to many indexes including a head-of-household index to the 1900 census. Genealogy.com also sells indexes on CD-ROM; see <www.genealogy.com>.

• The USGenWeb census project <www.rootsweb.com/~usgenweb/census/> makes census records and indexes available online free of charge. Go to the Web site for state links.

• Cyndi's List <www.cyndislist.com> is the most comprehensive genealogy portal. The census category has links, organized by census year, to online census transcriptions and indexes.

• Census Links <http://censuslinks.com> has links, organized alphabetically by state, to census indexes and transcriptions.

• Census Online <http://census-online.com> provides links, organized alphabetically by state, to over six thousand sites with census data.

• FirstSearch simultaneously researches library catalogs throughout the world by subject. It is one of the most comprehensive research tools available to you. If you are unfamiliar with this global library search, ask your librarian for assistance. FirstSearch is not available for public use in some libraries, where a librarian must execute searches for the patrons.

• Periodical Source Index (PERSI) is a subject index to more than five thousand genealogical journals and has nearly two million entries. It is available in print in many public libraries, and it can be purchased on CD-ROM. PERSI is included in the databases available via subscription from Ancestry.com. Genealogical societies often publish indexes or abstracts of census records, thus the reason to search PERSI. An online search of PERSI using the keyword "census" for the state of Nebraska resulted in 393 hits. Among these were two articles the *Rhode Island Genealogical Register* published in 1979 listing Nebraska residents in the 1880 census who had Rhode Island ancestry.

## Step 4: Transcripts With Index

Many local genealogical societies and individuals have published transcripts of census records for a county or community. Some transcripts have been posted on the Internet, but most are available in books or genealogical society journals.

**Because of their compactness and ease of use, these transcripts are excellent tools for cross-checking a newly found surname or getting an overview of a neighborhood.** They are extremely useful in tracking a family cluster in a particular area.

Check the Family History Library catalog, as well as local libraries and genealogical society publications, for these transcripts. Remember to use the transcript as a finding aid and follow up with examination of the full census schedule.

**Timesaver**

## Step 5: Soundex and Miracode (Indexes by Sound)

For the 1880, 1900, 1910, 1920, or 1930 censuses, the Soundex is available for most states. See page 138 for detailed instructions on how to use this type of index and what years and states are included.

## INDEXES ARE RARELY IDENTICAL

It is common to find more than one census index for the same place and time period. For example, the 1870 Colorado census has four indexes: three every-name indexes and one head-of-household index (see pages 135–137).

| Year Published | Type of Index | Publisher |
|---|---|---|
| 1976 | Every Name | Accelerated Indexing Systems (AIS) |
| 1977 | Every Name | Weld County Genealogical Society |
| 1995 | Every Name | Brøderbund (CD-ROM version of the AIS index) |
| 2000 | Head of Household | Heritage Quest |

Of the first fifty entries in all four indexes, only twelve entries (shaded in the table) are identical among the indexes. An additional sixteen entries are the same among the indexes only when comparing the three every-name indexes.

The lesson learned from this exercise is that you should examine every published index just in case your ancestor was misread or missed entirely by one publisher but indexed correctly by another.

## Accelerated Indexing Systems (AIS) Indexes

Genealogists often refer to a census index as an AIS index, which is an abbreviation for indexes created in the 1970s and 1980s by Ronald Vern Jackson of Accelerated Indexing Systems.

### WHICH PAGE NUMBER?

Census pages often have a stamped page number (added by the Census Bureau after the census) and a handwritten page number. Occasionally pages even have a third page number. See chapter three, page 44 for an example. This 1850 Kendall County, Illinois, census page has page numbers 449, 451, and 226 in the upper right corner.

Indexes, of course, list only one of the page numbers. But which one? Sometimes, but not always, the introduction or key to the book explains which number was used. A quick way to eliminate the frustration of figuring out which page number was used is to do some research in reverse order. Find a name on a census page and then look for that name in the index. Compare the page number in the index to those on the census page to learn which page numbers were listed in the index.

| COMPARISON OF FOUR DIFFERENT INDEXES TO THE 1870 COLORADO TERRITORY CENSUS FIRST FIFTY ENTRIES | | | |
|---|---|---|---|
| **Every-Name Index** | **Every-Name Index** | **Every-Name Index** | **Head of Household Index** |
| *1870 Colorado Territory Census Index* (Greeley, Col.: Weld County Genealogical Society, 1977) | Ronald Vern Jackson's *Colorado 1870 Census Index* (North Salt Lake City, Utah: Accelerated Indexing Systems, 1976) | *Family Tree Maker Census Index: U.S. Selected Counties/States, 1870* (CD #319. Novato, Calif.: Brøderbund Software, Inc., 1995) | Raeone Christensen Steuart's (editor) *Colorado 1870 Census Index A-Z* (Bountiful, Utah: Heritage Quest, 2000) |
| | | | ———Hannah |
| | | | ———Maria Soledad |
| | Aarington, Joshua | Aarington, Joshua | |
| | Aarrington, Albert A. | Aarrington, Albert A. | |
| | Aarrington, Mary | Aarrington, Mary | |
| | Aarrington, Thomas | Aarrington, Thomas | |
| Abair, Jose | | Abair, Jose | |
| Abair, Jose D. | | Abair, Jose D. | |
| Abair, Ma Catalina | | Abair, Ma Catalina | |
| | | | Abalton, Charles |
| Aban, Antonio | Aban, Antonio | Aban, Antonio | Aban, Antonio |
| | Aban, Felipe | Aban, Felipe | |
| | Aban, Francisco | Aban, Francisco | |
| | Aban, Jose | Aban, Jose | |
| Aban, Juan | Aban, Juan | Aban, Juan | Aban, Juan |
| | | Aban, Juan | |
| | Aban, Juana | | |
| | Aban, Juana | Aban, Juana | Aban, Juana |
| Aban, Maria | Aban, Maria | Aban, Maria | |
| | Aban, Maria S. | Aban, Maria S. | |
| | Aban, Venturo | Aban, Venturo | |
| Abane, Felipe | | Abane, Felipe | |
| Abane, Francisco | | Abane, Francisco | |
| Abane, Jose | | Abane, Jose | |
| Abane, Juana (2) | | Abane, Juana | |
| | | Abane, Maria | |
| Abane, Maria S. | | Abane, Maria S. | |
| Abane, Victoro | | | |
| | Abate, Maria T. | Abate, Maria T. | Abate, Maria T. |
| Abato, Maria | | Abato, Maria | |

| | | | |
|---|---|---|---|
| | Abatton, Charles | Abatton, Charles | |
| Abbe, William | Abbe, William | Abbe, William | Abbe, William |
| | | Abbe, William | |
| Abbott, Albert | Abbott, Albert | Abbott, Albert | |
| | | Abbott, Albert | |
| Abbott, Catherine | Abbott, Catherine | Abbott, Catherine | |
| | | Abbott, Catherine | |
| Abbott, Charles | Abbott, Charles | Abbott, Charles | Abbott, Charles |
| | | Abbott, Charles | |
| Abbott, Edward | Abbott, Edward | Abbott, Edward | Abbott, Edward |
| | | Abbott, Edward | |
| Abbott, Elizabeth | Abbott, Elizabeth | Abbott, Elizabeth | |
| | | Abbott, Elizabeth | |
| Abbott, Ellen | Abbott, Ellen | Abbott, Ellen | |
| | | Abbott, Ellen | |
| Abbott, Emily | Abbott, Emily | Abbott, Emily | |
| | | Abbott, Emily | |
| Abbott, Frank | Abbott, Frank | Abbott, Frank | |
| | | Abbott, Frank | |
| Abbott, George | Abbott, George | Abbott, George | |
| | | Abbott, George | |
| Abbott, Isabella | Abbott, Isabella | Abbott, Isabella | |
| | | Abbott, Isabella | |
| Abbott, James | Abbott, James | Abbott, James | Abbott, James |
| | | Abbott, James | |
| Abbott, John | Abbott, John | Abbott, John | Abbott, John |
| Abbott, John | | Abbott, John | |
| | Abbott, John C. | Abbott, John C. | Abbott, John C. |
| | Abbott, Litus H. | Abbott, Litus H. | Abbott, Litus H. |
| Abbott, Martha | Abbott, Martha | Abbott, Martha | |
| | | Abbott, Martha | |
| | Abbott, Mary C. | | |
| Abbott, Miles C. | Abbott, Miles C. | Abbott, Miles C. | Abbott, Miles C. |
| | | Abbott, Miles C. | |
| Abbott, Nancy | | Abbott, Nancy | |
| | Abbott, Samuel | Abbott, Samuel | Abbott, Samuel |
| Abbott, Susan | Abbott, Susan | Abbott, Susan | |

| | | Abbott, Susan | |
|---|---|---|---|
| Abbott, Titus | | Abbott, Titus | |
| Abbott, William H. | Abbott, William H. | Abbott, William H. | |
| | | Abbott, William H. | |
| Abejta, Jose Agapeto | | Abejta, Jose Agapeto | |
| Abejta, Jose Perfecto | | Abejta, Jose Perfecto | |
| Abejta, Juan Angel | | Abejta, Juan Angel | |
| Abejta, Ma Albino | | Abejta, Ma Albino | |
| Abela, Pedro | Abela, Pedro | Abela, Pedro | Abela, Pedro |
| | | Abela, Pedro | |
| | | Abene, Victoro | |
| Abernathy, Henry | | Abernathy, Henry | |
| | Abert, Eleuto | Abert, Eleuto | |
| | Abert, Francisco | Abert, Francisco | Abert, Francisco |
| | Abert, Maria Ursula | Abert, Maria Ursula | |
| | Aberworthy, Henry | Aberworthy, Henry | Aberworthy, Henry |
| | Abeshire, Francis | Abeshire, Francis | |
| Abeyta, Antonio | | | |
| Abeyta, Bentura | Abeyta, Bentura | Abeyta, Bentura | |
| Abeyta, Calnil | | | |
| Abeyta, Carmel | Abeyta, Carmel | Abeyta, Carmel | |
| | Abeyta, Epifanio | Abeyta, Epifanio | |
| Abeyta, Epifarno | | | |
| Abeyta, Esteban | Abeyta, Esteban | Abeyta, Esteban | |
| Abeyta, Fernando Ysea | Abeyta, Fernando Ysea | Abeyta, Fernando Ysea | |
| Abeyta, Francisco | Abeyta, Francisco | Abeyta, Francisco | Abeyta, Francisco |
| Abeyta, Francisco | Abeyta, Francisco | Abeyta, Francisco | |
| | Abeyta, Gabriel | Abeyta, Gabrlel | Abeyta, Gabriel |
| Abeyta, Jesus Maria (2) | Abeyta, Jesus Maria | Abeyta, Jesus Maria | Abeyta, Jesus Maria |
| | Abeyta, Jesus Maria | | |
| | Abeyta, Jose Agapito | Abeyta, Jose Agapito | Abeyta, Jose Agapito |
| Abeyta, Jose Ant. | Abeyta, Jose Antonio | Abeyta, Jose Antonio | Abeyta, Jose Ant |

AIS was the first commercial firm to mass-produce census indexes. In fact, AIS generated indexes for every extant state and territorial census from 1790 through 1860, as well as some later years. The indexes were often criticized, with some critics citing an error rate of about 20 percent. Regardless, AIS filled an urgent need to make census research on the 80 percent that was correct easier.

In 1984, AIS merged the computerized indexes into a microfiche publication called "Indexes to U.S. Censuses 1607–1906." The collection includes federal and state indexes and non-population indexes such as mortality, slave, and veterans schedules. Although the index is primarily for 1790 through 1850, it includes some later years such as 1880 for Colorado, Oregon, and Washington and 1900 and 1910 for Nevada. This master index includes approximately thirty-five million listings. For a complete inventory of contents, go to <www.ancestry.com/search/rectype/census/ais/censuslist.htm>.

The microfiche edition is divided into nine sections:

Search 1: 1607–1819, entire United States
Search 2: 1820–1829, entire United States
Search 3: 1820–1839, entire United States
Search 4: 1840–1949, entire United States
Search 5: 1850–1860, southern states
Search 6: 1850, New England and northern states
Search 7: 1850–1906, midwestern and western states
Search 8: 1850–1906, searches 5, 6, and 7 combined
Search 9: 1850–1885, United States Mortality Schedule only

This 1984 microfiche edition is available at the Family History Library in Salt Lake City, its Family History Centers, and many public libraries that purchased the index. The Family History Library's *Resource Guide: Accelerated Indexing Systems (AIS) Indexes to US. Censuses 1607–1906* gives specific instructions on using the AIS microfiche. It is available at Family History Centers and at <www.familysearch.org> under "Research Helps."

The AIS indexes are also available through Ancestry.com's subscription service. The advantage of using the computerized version is the extra search features. For example, if the head of the household for your ancestor had an unusual given name, you can search the given name field only or combine the given name with a state and/or census year.

## SOUNDEX AND MIRACODE
## 1880, 1900, 1910, 1920, 1930

**Definitions**

**The Soundex is an index based on the phonetic sounds of the consonants in a surname rather than the surname's exact spelling.** According to rules known as the Russell Soundex Coding, surnames are converted into a code of one letter and three numbers. This allows names such as Gordin, Gordon, Gardner, Graden, and Graddon to be in the same grouping then alphabetically arranged by the given name of the head of the household. Thus, George Gardner and George Graden would follow one another in the Soundex, grouped together with the Soundex code G-635. (See "Using the Soundex" on page 148 for details on coding surnames.)

When the Social Security Administration was formed in 1935, the government needed a system to verify the ages of individuals seeking old-age pensions. By using Soundex to index the census records, they could locate a person and

---

## ADVANTAGE OF SOUNDEX CARD SEARCHES

The ability to view the family cards in the Soundex allows you to use less straight-forward research techniques.

For example, imagine searching for John Butcher, who was born in 1895 in Kentucky. You do not know the names of his parents, but you do know he has an older sister named Martha. By using the Soundex and studying the names and ages of children—rather than looking for the head of the household—you may locate him. Using the more traditional head of household indexes in computerized format does not allow this flexibility.

Successful research involves a combination of using all types of indexes available, being creative with spellings, and utilizing a variety of search terms.

---

verify his age; thus an index to the 1880 and later census records was needed. The federal government commissioned the Works Progress Administration (WPA) to index the 1880 and 1900 through 1940 population schedules. The project began in 1936 and ended in 1942.

WPA workers abstracted data from the census schedules onto file cards. The cards were alphabetized by state or territory and arranged numerically by Soundex code. They were then indexed alphabetically by given name, with the N.R. category (a given name of "Not Reported") preceding the alphabet. Each card gives identifying information to locate the full census schedule: volume number, enumeration district number, and page and line numbers from the original schedules.

Three types of cards were prepared:

- Household cards (see page 140): The card lists the head of the household by name, race, age, and citizenship status. It lists each member of the household by name and relationship to the head of the household, age, birthplace, and citizenship status of foreign-born individuals. For persons living in the house who were not members of the immediate family of the head of the household, an individual card was also prepared.

- Individual cards (see page 141): Individual cards were prepared for persons living alone or with families who had different surnames. This includes persons in hotels, boarding and rooming houses, and institutions; persons on military posts and naval ships and at naval stations; and persons enumerated on U.S. flag vessels in all U.S. ports.

  These cards give the individual's name, age, birthplace, citizenship status, address, name of person or institution with whom enumerated, and relationship to that person or institution.

- Institution, military post, naval station, and U.S. flag vessel cards (see page 142): These cards list only the address of the establishment and the number of persons enumerated. Names of the individuals are not listed.

**Volume, enumeration district, sheet, and line number enable you to locate full census page in population schedule.**

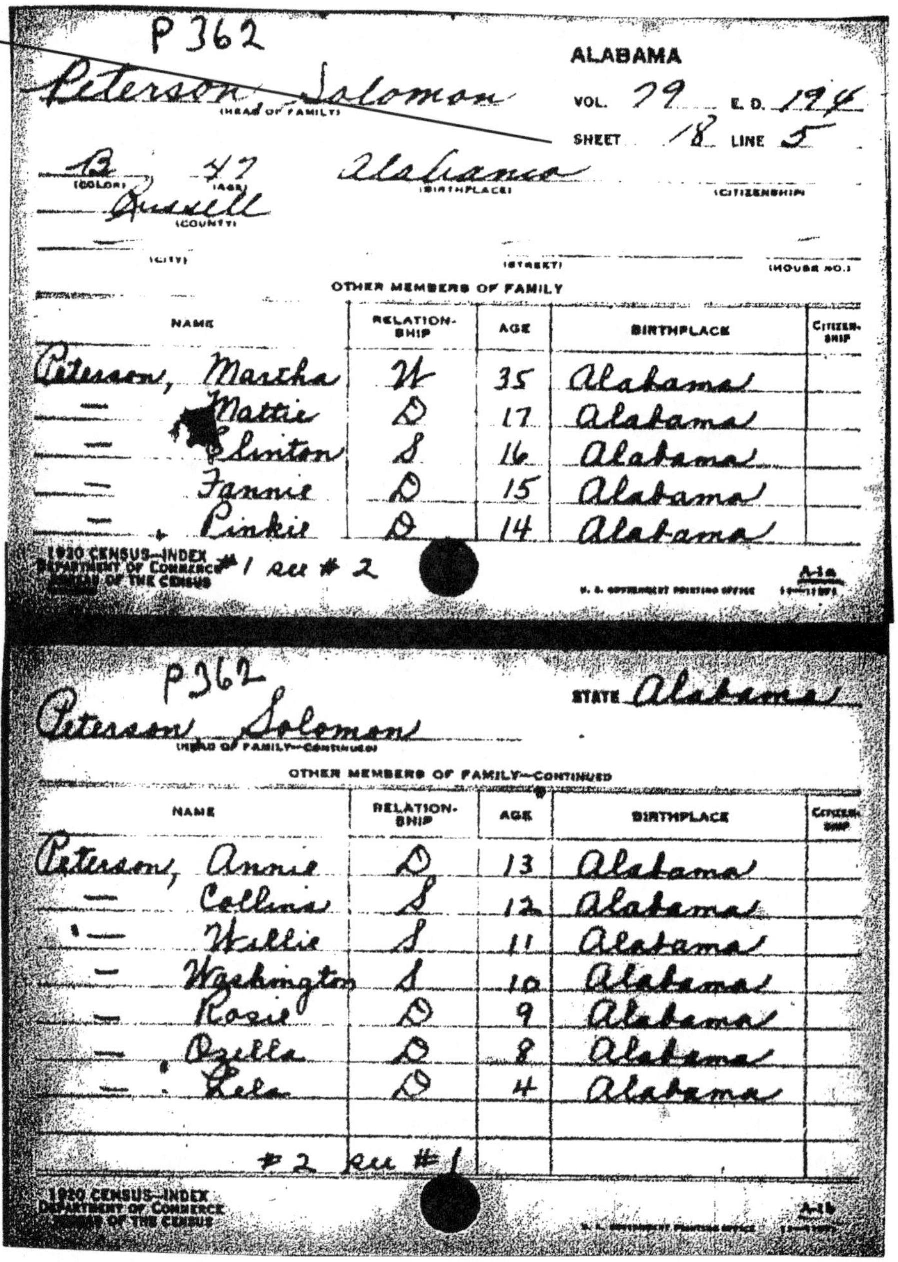
P362

ALABAMA

Peterson, Solomon (HEAD OF FAMILY) VOL. 79 E.D. 194

SHEET 18 LINE 5

B (COLOR) 47 (AGE) Alabama (BIRTHPLACE) (CITIZENSHIP)

Russell (COUNTY)

(CITY) (STREET) (HOUSE NO.)

OTHER MEMBERS OF FAMILY

| NAME | RELATIONSHIP | AGE | BIRTHPLACE | CITIZENSHIP |
|---|---|---|---|---|
| Peterson, Martha | W | 35 | Alabama | |
| — Mattie | D | 17 | Alabama | |
| — Clinton | S | 16 | Alabama | |
| — Fannie | D | 15 | Alabama | |
| — Pinkie | D | 14 | Alabama | |

1920 CENSUS—INDEX DEPARTMENT OF COMMERCE BUREAU OF THE CENSUS #1 see #2 A-1a

P362

Peterson, Solomon (HEAD OF FAMILY—CONTINUED) STATE Alabama

OTHER MEMBERS OF FAMILY—CONTINUED

| NAME | RELATIONSHIP | AGE | BIRTHPLACE | CITIZENSHIP |
|---|---|---|---|---|
| Peterson, Annie | D | 13 | Alabama | |
| — Collins | S | 12 | Alabama | |
| — Willie | S | 11 | Alabama | |
| — Washington | S | 10 | Alabama | |
| — Rosie | D | 9 | Alabama | |
| — Ozella | D | 8 | Alabama | |
| — Lela | D | 4 | Alabama | |

#2 see #1

1920 CENSUS—INDEX DEPARTMENT OF COMMERCE BUREAU OF THE CENSUS A-1b

**Figure 7-1**
1920 U.S. census, Alabama, Household Soundex card, P-362, Solomon Peterson; National Archives micropublication M1548, roll 110.

## SOUNDEX SPECIFICS BY CENSUS YEAR

### 1880 Soundex

All states were indexed; however, only households with children ten years old or younger (born 1870 or later) were included since the intent was to identify persons eligible for social security. Someone born in 1870 would have turned sixty-five years old in 1935, and those born by 1880 would have become eligible for social security by 1945.

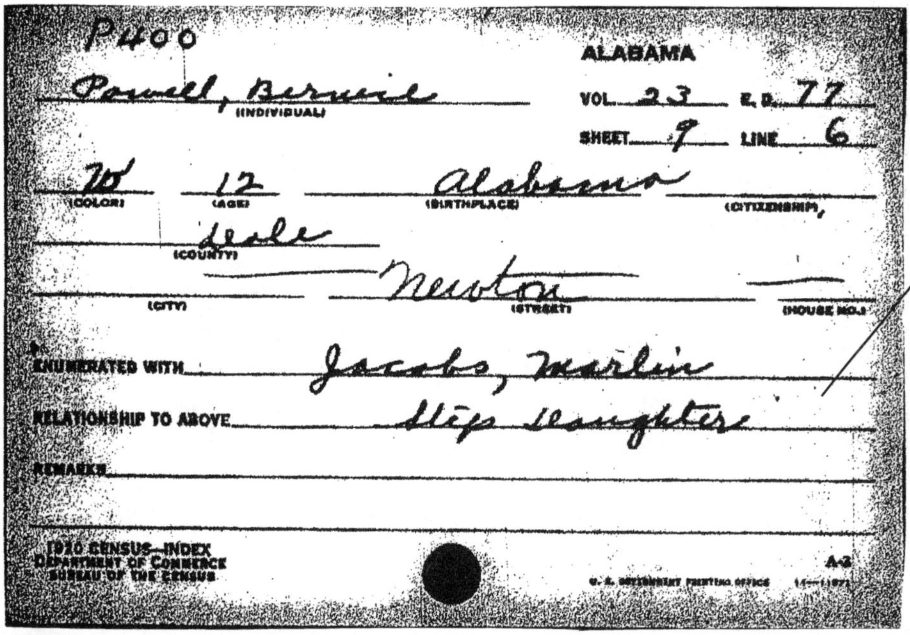
P400
ALABAMA
Powell, Bernice (INDIVIDUAL)
VOL. 23 E.D. 77
SHEET 9 LINE 6
W (COLOR) 12 (AGE) Alabama (BIRTHPLACE) (CITIZENSHIP)
Leale (COUNTY)
(CITY) Newton (STREET) (HOUSE NO.)
ENUMERATED WITH Jacobs, Marlin
RELATIONSHIP TO ABOVE Step daughter
REMARKS
1920 CENSUS—INDEX
DEPARTMENT OF COMMERCE
BUREAU OF THE CENSUS
A-2
U.S. GOVERNMENT PRINTING OFFICE

Bernice Powell is enumerated as a stepdaughter of Marlin Jacobs. A separate Soundex card was created because her surname is different than that of the head of household.

**Figure 7-2**
1920 U.S. census, Alabama, Individual Soundex card, P-400, Bernice Powell; National Archives micropublication M1548, roll 110.

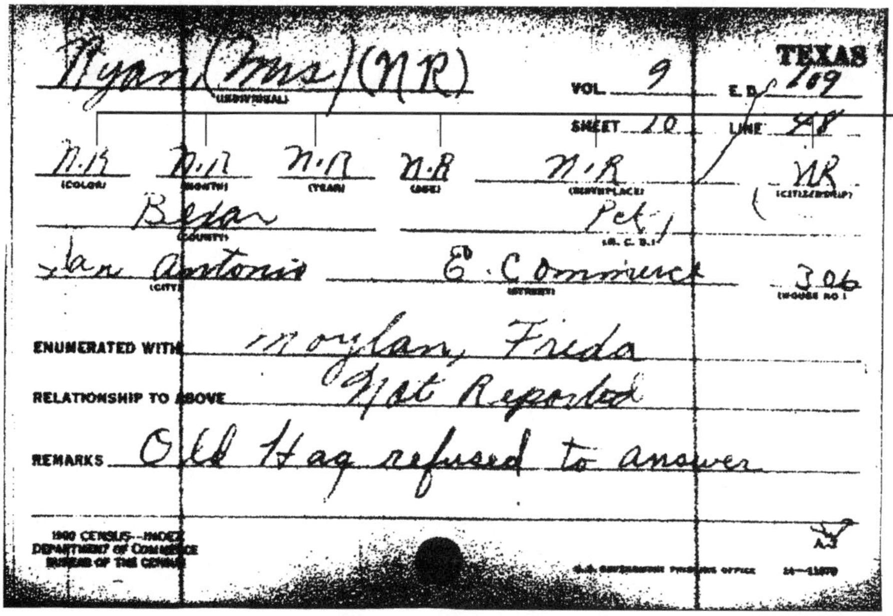
Ryan (Mrs) (NR) (INDIVIDUAL)
TEXAS
VOL. 9 E.D. 109
SHEET 10 LINE 98
N.R (COLOR) N.R (MONTH) N.R (YEAR) N.R (AGE) N.R (BIRTHPLACE) NR (CITIZENSHIP)
Bexar (COUNTY) Pct 1 (M.C.D.)
San Antonio (CITY) E. Commerce (STREET) 306 (HOUSE NO.)
ENUMERATED WITH Moylan, Frieda
RELATIONSHIP TO ABOVE Not Reported
REMARKS Old Hag refused to answer
1900 CENSUS—INDEX
DEPARTMENT OF COMMERCE
BUREAU OF THE CENSUS

"N.R." means "Not Reported." In this case, Mrs. Ryan refused to answer the enumerator's questions. Soundex cards without a given name are filed at the beginning of the Soundex code.

1900 U.S. census, Texas, Individual Soundex card, R-500, Mrs. Ryan; National Archives micropublication T1073, roll 220.

If grandparents were living alone, they do not appear in the Soundex. But if they had a grandchild or boarder under age ten residing with them, the family is included. Do not quickly disregard the 1880 Soundex as a invaluable research tool.

Institutions are filed at the end of each state's Soundex (following codes beginning with the letter *Z*).

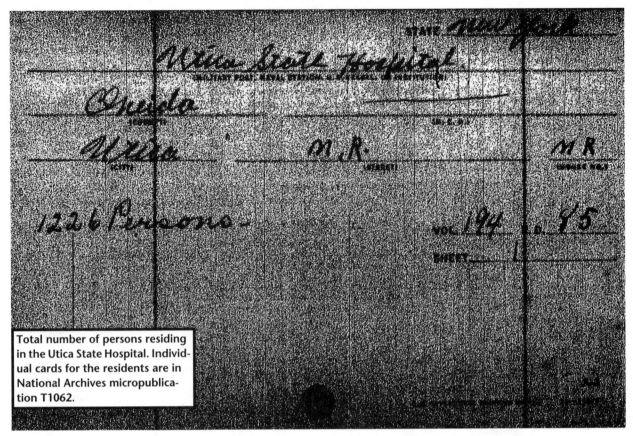

Total number of persons residing in the Utica State Hospital. Individual cards for the residents are in National Archives micropublication T1062.

**Figure 7-3**
1900 U.S. census, New York, Institution Soundex card; National Archives micropublication T1083, roll 5.

The original microfilming of the 1880 Illinois Soundex missed over one thousand cards for surnames such as O'Keefe, O'Shay, Osborne, Oswood, Ogden, Osterman, Ostrom, and Oxford—Soundex codes O-200 through O-240. Nancy Grubb Frederick published these cards in 1981 (privately printed, Evanston, Illinois). The 287-page book is at the Family History Library in Salt Lake City, and it is also available on microfiche.

## 1900 Soundex

The 1900 Soundex is complete for all states. It identifies all heads of household and any person in the home whose surname is different from that of the head of household. The military bases and naval vessels (T1081, thirty-two rolls), Indian Territory (T1082, forty-two rolls), and institutions (T1083, eight rolls) are separate from the states and territories.

## 1910 Soundex and Miracode

\di'fin\ *vb*

Definitions

Some of the states in 1910 are in Miracode (pronounced meer-a-code). This uses the same indexing principle as the Soundex; the difference lies only in how the page number, enumeration number, and family number are reported on the index card. The Miracode index was done in the 1960s with a computer; Soundex was done in the 1930s by hand.

## FAMILYSEARCH 1880 U.S. CENSUS AND NATIONAL INDEX

Volunteers of the Church of Jesus Christ of Latter-day Saints spent years transcribing and indexing approximately fifty million names in the 1880 U.S. census. The resulting collection of fifty-six CDs was released in May 2001 and can be purchased via the FamilySearch Web site at <www.familysearch.org> or by calling (800) 537-5950.

This is an every-name index, divided into seven geographical regions and accompanied by a national index. In addition to township, town, city, county, state, and page number, the index also reports

- surname, given name, and sometimes middle name or initial

- sex

- age

- race

- marital status

- occupation

- relationship to head of household

- state or country of birth

- father's and mother's state or country of birth

Search capabilities include sorting into neighborhoods and searching with limited data, such as given name combined with place of residence and/or birth.

This is an index, although it can appear to be a transcription. When viewing a neighborhood, it is not possible to determine if families resided in separate households or together. As in all census research, follow up the search results by viewing the full handwritten census schedule.

Soundex: Alabama, Georgia, Louisiana (except New Orleans and Shreveport), Mississippi, South Carolina, Tennessee, Texas

Miracode: Arkansas, California, Florida, Illinois, Kansas, Kentucky, Louisiana (New Orleans and Shreveport only), Michigan, Missouri, North Carolina, Ohio, Oklahoma, Pennsylvania, Virginia, West Virginia

The following locations are on microfilm separate from their statewide indexes:
Birmingham, Mobile, and Montgomery, Alabama
Atlanta, Augusta, Macon, and Savannah, Georgia
New Orleans and Shreveport, Louisiana
Philadelphia County, Pennsylvania
Chattanooga, Knoxville, Memphis, and Nashville, Tennessee

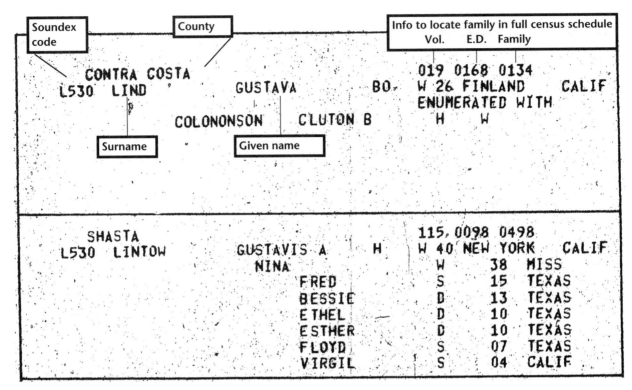

**Figure 7-4**
1910 U.S. census, California, Miracode L-530; National Archives micropublication T1261, roll 145.

**CENSUS TRIVIA**

New York City has consistently been ranked as the largest U.S. city from 1790 through 2000. The second most populous city was Philadelphia from 1790 through 1880, Chicago from 1890 through 1970, and Los Angeles since 1980.

No Soundex or Miracode exists for the remaining twenty-nine states and territories. However, the *Cross Index to Selected City Streets and Enumeration Districts, 1910 Census* (M1283, fifty fiche) converts an address into an enumeration district. Once you have the enumeration district for a specific address, your search will be limited to a few pages in the full census schedule. The selected locations are:

| | |
|---|---|
| Arizona | Phoenix |
| California | Long Beach |
| California | Los Angeles and Los Angeles County |
| California | San Diego |
| California | San Francisco |
| Colorado | Denver |
| District of Columbia | Washington |
| Florida | Tampa |
| Georgia | Atlanta |
| Illinois | Chicago |
| Illinois | Peoria |
| Indiana | Gary |
| Indiana | Indianapolis |
| Indiana | Fort Wayne |
| Indiana | South Bend |
| Kansas | Kansas City |
| Kansas | Wichita |

| Maryland | Baltimore |
| Michigan | Detroit |
| Michigan | Grand Rapids |
| Nebraska | Omaha |
| New Jersey | Elizabeth |
| New Jersey | Newark |
| New Jersey | Paterson |
| New York | New York (Manhattan, The Bronx, Brooklyn, Richmond) |
| North Carolina | Charlotte |
| Ohio | Akron |
| Ohio | Canton |
| Ohio | Cleveland |
| Ohio | Dayton |
| Ohio | Youngstown |
| Oklahoma | Oklahoma City |
| Oklahoma | Tulsa |
| Pennsylvania | Erie |
| Pennsylvania | Philadelphia |
| Pennsylvania | Reading |
| Texas | San Antonio |
| Virginia | Richmond |
| Washington | Seattle |

*Street Indexes to Unindexed Cities in the U.S. 1910 Federal Census*, compiled by Emil and Maurine Malmberg, is available through the Family History Library and Family History Centers. It provides street indexes for

| Iowa | Des Moines |
| Massachusetts | Boston |
| Minnesota | Minneapolis |
| New York | New York (Queens) |
| Utah | Salt Lake City |

## 1920 Soundex

The 1920 Soundex is complete for all states. The military bases and naval vessels and institutions were filmed separately.

## 1930 Soundex

Only ten states and portions of two others have been Soundexed:

Alabama
Arkansas
Florida
Georgia
Kentucky (Bell, Floyd, Harlan, Kenton, Muhlenberg, Perry, and Pike cos.)
Louisiana
Mississippi

| SOUNDEX/MIRACODE CHART | | | | | |
|---|---|---|---|---|---|
| **State** | **1880** | **1900** | **1910** | **1920** | **1930** |
| Alabama | | | x | | x |
| Alaska | | | | | |
| Arizona | | | Phoenix | | |
| Arkansas | | | x | | x |
| California | | | x | | |
| Colorado | | | Denver | | |
| Connecticut | | | | | |
| Delaware | | | | | |
| District of Columbia | | | Washington | | |
| Florida | | | x | | x |
| Georgia | | | x | | x |
| Hawaii | | | | | |
| Idaho | | | | | |
| Illinois | | | x | | |
| Indiana | All states and territories (households with children ten years old or younger only) | All states (all households) | Gary, Indianapolis, Fort Wayne, South Bend | All states (all households) | |
| Iowa | | | Des Moines | | |
| Kansas | | | x | | |
| Kentucky | | | x | | x Bell, Floyd, Harlan, Kenton, Muhlenberg, Perry, and Pike counties only |
| Louisiana | | | x | | x |
| Maine | | | | | |
| Maryland | | | Baltimore | | |
| Massachusetts | | | Boston | | |
| Michigan | | | x | | |
| Minnesota | | | Minneapolis | | |
| Mississippi | | | x | | x |
| Missouri | | | x | | |
| Montana | | | | | |
| Nebraska | | | Omaha | | |
| Nevada | | | | | |

This chart summarizes the availability of Soundex and Miracode, including cities with street indexes for states without a Soundex.

| | | | | | |
|---|---|---|---|---|---|
| New Hampshire | | | | | |
| New Jersey | | | Elizabeth, Newark, Paterson | | |
| New Mexico | | | | | |
| New York | | | Manhattan, Bronx, Brooklyn, Richmond | | |
| North Carolina | | | x | | x |
| North Dakota | | | | | |
| Ohio | | | x | | |
| Oklahoma | | | x | | |
| Oregon | | | | | |
| Pennsylvania | | | x | | |
| Rhode Island | | | | | |
| South Carolina | | | x | | x |
| South Dakota | | | | | |
| Tennessee | | | x | | x |
| Texas | | | x | | |
| Utah | | | Salt Lake City | | |
| Vermont | | | | | |
| Virginia | | | x | | x |
| Washington | | | Seattle | | |
| West Virginia | | | x | | x Fayette, Harrison, Kanawha, Logan, McDowell, Mercer, and Raleigh counties only |
| Wisconsin | | | | | |
| Wyoming | | | | | |

Statewide 1910 indexes for Connecticut, Delaware, District of Columbia, Idaho, Indiana, Nevada, New York (all counties except Kings, Nassau, New York, Queens, Richmond, and Suffolk), Nevada, Wyoming and the 1910 U.S. military Naval Roll, are available from Heritage Quest. Those for Rhode Island, New Hampshire, and Vermont can be purchased from Census4All. Indexes for other states will be published in the future.

North Carolina
South Carolina
Tennessee
Virginia
West Virginia (Fayette, Harrison, Kanawha, Logan, McDowell, Mercer, and
    Raleigh counties only)

**Step By Step**

## USING THE SOUNDEX

**The first step to finding someone in the Soundex or Miracode is to code the surname.**
Since the Soundex is published by state, you must also know the state of residence in order to search for someone.

Every Soundex code consists of a letter and three numbers. The letter is always the first letter of the surname, and the three numbers are assigned according to the Soundex coding chart. If fewer than three letters of the surname can be used to code the numbers, the remaining numbers become zero.

**Soundex/Miracode Coding Chart**

| Number | Represents Letters |
| --- | --- |
| 1 | B, F, P, V |
| 2 | C, G, J, K, Q, S, X, Z |
| 3 | D, T |
| 4 | L |
| 5 | M, N |
| 6 | R |

Disregard the letters A, E, I, O, U, H, W, and Y

Soundex codes can be generated with the aid of a computer. Some libraries have such a program available at a research station. The Internet sites that have coding programs include

- National Archives: www.nara.gov/genealogy/soundex/soundex.html
- Family Tree Magazine: www.familytreemagazine.com/soundex.html
- RootsWeb: http://searches.rootsweb.com/cgi-bin/Genea/soundex.sh
- JewishGen: www.jewishgen.org/jos/

Although computerized Soundex coding is quick and easy, it is important to understand the principles of Soundex and be able to do it by hand—just as we must be able to add, subtract, multiply, and divide without the aid of a calculator.

## Soundex Rules

1. The first letter of a name is never coded or eliminated. This letter of the alphabet is used as the first digit of the code.
2. Disregard the consonants *W*, *H*, and *Y* and the vowels *A*, *E*, *I*, *O*, and *U*.

## USE MULTIPLE SOUNDEX CODES

When you do not locate your family in the expected Soundex, search the codes numerically before and after you code in case the card was misfiled. Also, be aware that the WPA workers sometimes coded incorrectly; those cards are filed with an incorrect code.

Misspell the surname in as many ways as you can imagine and create corresponding Soundex codes. You might also try a different yet similar first letter for the surname. For example, the letter *H* was sometimes misread as a *C*, and the letters *S* and *L* could have been interpreted incorrectly. And, of course, *C* and *K* are interchangeable.

Keep in mind that alternate spellings of the same name can give drastically different Soundex Codes. Rogers codes to R-262, while the variation Rodgers yields R-326.

3. A Soundex code is never more than three digits after the surname letter. If you have fewer than three digits to code after the first letter, add zeros to make three numeric digits.

**Examples:**

| | |
|---|---|
| Powell | = P-400 Coded letter *l* |
| Perry | = P-600 Coded letter *r* |

4. When the surname has double letters, they should be treated s one letter.

**Examples:**

| | |
|---|---|
| Hubbard | = H-163 Coded letters *b, r, d* |
| Morrell | = M-640 Coded letters *r, l* |

5. When the second letter of a surname has the same coding value as the first letter, the second letter is disregarded in coding.

**Examples:**

| | |
|---|---|
| Schneider | = S-536 Coded letters *n, d, r* |
| Lloyd | = L-300 Coded letter *d* |

6. When adjacent letters have the same value, the second letter is disregarded in coding.

**Examples:**

| | |
|---|---|
| Hinckley | = H-524 Coded letters *n, c, l* |
| Fischer | = F-260 Coded letters *s, r* |

7. When repeated key letters or equivalent letters are separated by a vowel, the key letters are considered separately.

**Examples:**

| | |
|---|---|
| Kresek | = K-622 Coded letters *r, s, k* |
| Hessek | = H-220 Coded letters *s, k* |

8. When repeated or equivalent key letters are separated by *H* or *W*, they are coded as one key letter. This is the opposite of the above rule for letters separated by a vowel.

**Examples:**

| | |
|---|---|
| Ashcroft | = A-261 Coded letters *s, r, f* |

This surname is incorrectly coded as A226 in computerized systems.

| | |
|---|---|
| Bachs | = B-200 Coded letter *c* |

This surname is incorrectly coded B-220 in computerized systems.

9. Some names do not contain any key letters, i.e., they have only vowels and/or consonants that get eliminated. The numeric part of the code is therefore 000.

**Examples:**

| | |
|---|---|
| Lee | = L-000 Coded only the initial *L* |
| Howe | = H-000 Coded only the initial *H* |

10. Surnames with a prefix such as Con, D, De, Di, du, La, Le, van, or von should be coded with and without the prefix because they may be listed under either code.

**Examples:**

| | |
|---|---|
| De Alvarez | = D-416 Coded letters *l, v, r* |
| | A-416 Coded letters *l, v, r* |
| Von Feldt | = V-514 Coded letters *n, f, l* |
| | F-430 Coded letters *l, d* |

11. Mc and Mac are not considered to be prefixes and should be coded in the surname.

**Examples:**

| | |
|---|---|
| McDonald | = M-235 Coded letters *c, d, n* |
| MacBird | = M-216 Coded letters *c, b, r* |

## Hyphenated Surnames

Hyphenated surnames are common in modern records, but surprisingly they may also occur in historical research. Karen V. Sipe's article "Hyphenated

Names: A Modern Problem in Historic Records," published in the *NGS Newsmagazine*, January/February 2001, pp. 50–53, presents a case study of Leighton Howard-Smith (1858–1934). Sipe discovered that she needed to Soundex his surname three ways: H-630 (Howard), S-530 (Smith), and H-632 (consonants *r* and *d* in Howard and *s*, the first letter of Smith). This Soundex procedure should be utilized with hyphenated surnames for thorough research.

## Mixed Codes

When the Soundex cards were organized for microfilming, occasionally some codes were filed together under the heading "Mixed Codes." This occurred when the quantity of cards for a particular code did not justify creating a separate group.

When reading cards in the mixed codes, do not be concerned with the non-consecutive Soundex codes, but instead focus upon the alphabetical arrangement of the given names.

**Printed Source**

A free brochure titled "Using the Census Soundex," General Information Leaflet 55 (Washington, D.C.: National Archives and Records Administration, 1995) can be ordered by sending an e-mail to inquire@nara.gov. Include your name and postal address, and ask for GIL 55.

# ENUMERATION DISTRICT DESCRIPTIONS AND MAPS

When you cannot find a name in the Soundex or commercial index or an index does not exist for your location and time period, consult enumeration district descriptions and maps. With the number of the enumeration district, you can narrow your research to a few pages rather than one or more microfilm rolls.

**An enumeration district (E.D.) is a geographic area assigned to each census taker.** The Census Bureau prepared maps of these districts for 1880 to 1970. Geographic descriptions of the census enumeration districts have been published by the National Archives as micropublication T1224, *Descriptions of Census Enumeration Districts, 1830–1890 and 1910–1950* (146 rolls). *Descriptions of Census Enumeration Districts, 1900* is micropublication T1210 (ten rolls).

\di'fin\ *vb*

**Definitions**

The National Archives has no pre-1880 E.D. maps, and it has descriptions only for 1830 through 1870. There are no boundary descriptions whatsoever for 1880 for Alabama, Arizona, Arkansas, California, Colorado, Connecticut, Montana, Ohio, Oregon, Pennsylvania, and Wisconsin. The only three maps for the 1880 census are for

- Washington, DC
- Rockwall County, Texas
- Atlanta, Fulton County, Georgia.

Descriptions can vary from very brief, general descriptions to detailed street boundaries. For example:

1920: Ward 2, Precinct 2, Minneapolis, Minnesota
Bounded by E. Hennepin and Great Northern R.R., 8th Avenue S.E., 5th Street S.E., and 5th Avenue S.E.

**ENUMERATION DISTRICT FINDING AIDS**

Local libraries often have finding aids to their census records:

**Illinois (Chicago)**

The staff at the Newberry Library plotted the 1870 census enumerators' routes on a city map. A specific address can be located by using the approximate enumeration date.

The Chicago Public Library, the Newberry Library, and the Great Lakes Region of the National Archives have enumeration district finding aids for 1900 for Chicago.

**New Jersey**

The Jersey City Public Library has a map of the 1910 enumeration districts for Jersey City and Hoboken (Hudson County). Copies of this map are also available at the New Jersey State Archives in Trenton, New Jersey. Both cities are mapped on a current map of the city, and the enumeration district boundaries are based on the boundary descriptions from National Archives publication T1224.

**Rhode Island**

The staff at the Rhode Island Historical Society developed an enumeration district map finding aid to the 1910 census for Providence and Newport.

1920: Part of Ward 5, Mankato, Blue Earth County, Minnesota
All that part east of following line: Beginning at the center of Front St. at the east line of Sec. 13; thence southwesterly along Front St. to center of Byron St., thence southwesterly along Byron St., to the center of Van Brunt; due south along center of Byron and along east line of Secs. 13 and 24 to City line.

The corresponding maps (almost two million) of the enumeration districts are in RG 29, M1930, and described in the *Guide to Cartographic Records in the National Archives* (Washington, D.C.: National Archives and Records Service, 1971). An inventory of these maps for 1880 through 1940, organized by state and county, is published in Preliminary Inventory No. 103, *Cartographic Records of the Bureau of the Census*, compiled by James Berton Rhoads and Charlotte M. Ashby (Washington, D.C.: National Archives and Records Service, 1958, pp. 7–108).

The Family History Library has photocopies of the full-size maps and maps on microfiche.

Photocopies of maps can be ordered through the National Archives at <www.nara.gov/research/ordering/mapordr.html>. This site refers you to

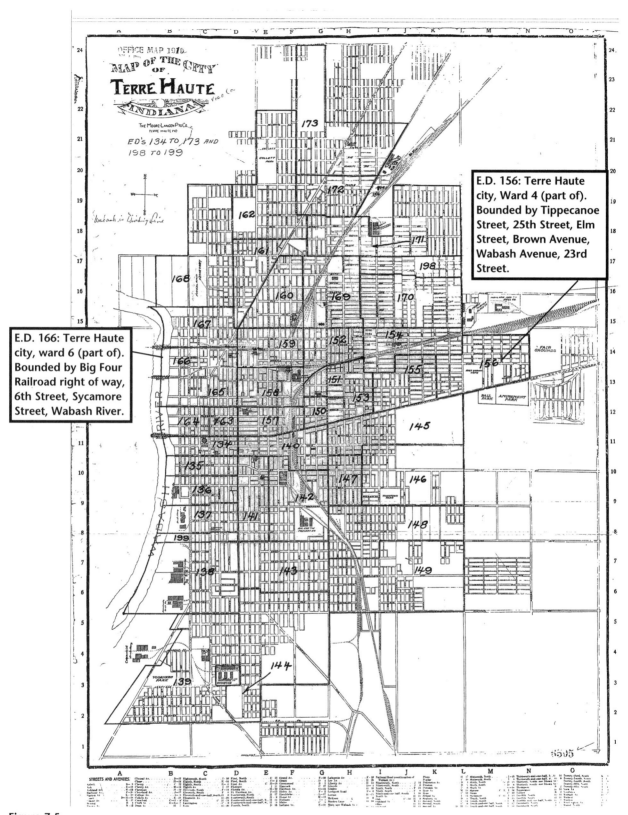

E.D. 156: Terre Haute city, Ward 4 (part of). Bounded by Tippecanoe Street, 25th Street, Elm Street, Brown Avenue, Wabash Avenue, 23rd Street.

E.D. 166: Terre Haute city, ward 6 (part of). Bounded by Big Four Railroad right of way, 6th Street, Sycamore Street, Wabash River.

**Figure 7-5**

*Map of the City of Terre Haute, Indiana* (Terre Haute, Ind.: Moore-Langen Printing, 1910). National Archives map with enumeration districts 134–173 and 198–199 for 1910 federal census handwritten on map. National Archives micropublication M1930; Family History Library microfiche number 6,049,929.

participating vendors who sell reproductions of still photographs, aerial film, maps, and drawings in the cartographic collection of the National Archives.

## FINDING ADDRESSES

In order to effectively use the enumeration district maps, you need an address for the person as close to the census year as possible. This is particularly important when searching for city residents in the unindexed 1930 census. Addresses can be found in

- birth certificates
- census records (for prior years)
- city or county directories
- court records
- death certificates
- funeral home records
- heredity and lineage applications
- land and tax records
- letters and postcards
- marriage and divorce records
- military records
- naturalization and passenger arrival records
- oral interviews
- photographs (noted on the backs)
- school records

**Case Study**

### Comparing Soundex Cards With Full Census Schedules
**Case Study: Harrison L. Thornton Jr., 1910, Abbeville County, South Carolina**
*Contributed by Nona Thornton, Watkinsville, Georgia*
The most difficult aspect of indexing, transcribing, and abstracting census records is correctly interpreting the handwriting. This example of Harrison L. Thornton Jr. in the 1910 Abbeville County, South Carolina, census demonstrates this problem, as well as other omissions and errors in family data.

The research task was to locate the family of Harrison L. Thornton Jr., Soundex code T653. It was known that Harrison was married to Pinky, but names of the children were unknown at the time the research was begun.

Upon first examination of the Soundex, the alphabetical list of given names did not include Harrison. The entire Soundex code T-653 was then studied, with attention paid to persons with the surname Thornton and a given name beginning with *H* or perhaps with Harry as a nickname. The family was still not found. A search for the wife, Pinky, as the head of household, was also negative.

The third review of the Soundex cards finally produced positive results. This time, each family card was examined for a wife named Pinky.

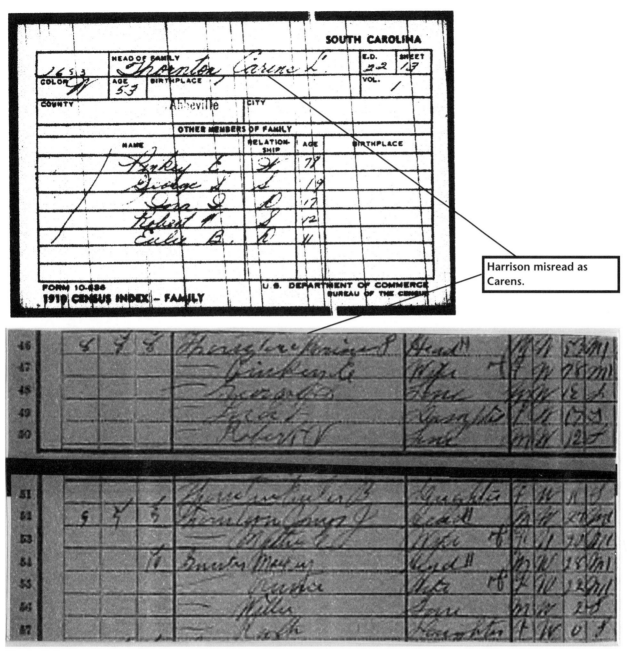

**Figure 7-6**
The poor handwriting of the enumerator made it very difficult for the individual preparing the Soundex card to correctly interpret the name Thornton Harrison.

Follow-up research with the full census schedule proved that the correct family had been located. Harrison had been misread as Carins because of poor handwriting by the enumerator. Additional errors abound in this example. The age of Pinky is reported as seventy-eight years on the Soundex card, but her correct age, reported on the full schedule, is forty-eight years—another misreading by the indexer.

**Case Study**

## RULES FOR USING CENSUS INDEXES

1. Locate all indexes for the census year and locality and check *all* of them.
2. Study the introduction and key to the index.
3. Search for all spelling variations of the surname and given name.
4. Examine all possible entries.
5. Do not give up. Even if your person is not in the index, he may be in the census.

# PART THREE

## Using the Census

# EIGHT

# Get Organized

**Step By Step**

A s much as you want to leap into actual census research, you will save time and energy if you do your homework first and stay organized. This includes gathering finding aids for the research and developing a system to manage the positive and negative results. You will appreciate being organized from the start.

## DO YOUR HOMEWORK

Before you begin census research

- Choose an individual to research.
- Summarize for that individual facts such as full name and nickname, names of siblings and other family members, approximate date of birth, and probable residences. Your data, of course, will vary in completeness for each individual.
- Locate maps of the time period and place. (See chapter seven.)
- Identify census indexes for your area of interest. When using the indexes, photocopy for future reference every page with your individual's surname. (See chapter seven for how to locate indexes.)
- Code the surname into a Soundex code. (See chapter seven for instructions.)
- Prepare a list of possible surname spelling variations and their Soundex codes.

For example, the French surname Meugniot has at least sixteen known spelling variants that result in five different Soundex codes. Organize them alphabetically and numerically, respectively, in order to be prepared for all types of indexes.

**Spelling Variants for Meugniot**

*Surname Variant Spellings*

| *Listed Alphabetically* | *Soundex Codes* |
| --- | --- |
| Maugriotte | M-263 |
| Meigniott | M-253 |
| Menginot | M-525 |
| Mengniot | M-525 |
| Menguoit | M-523 |
| Meniot | M-530 |
| Meugniot | M-253 |
| Meugnoit | M-253 |
| Meugnot | M-253 |
| Meuniot | M-530 |
| Migniot | M-253 |
| Migniott | M-253 |
| Mineout | M-530 |
| Mingnott | M-525 |
| Mugniot | M-253 |
| Muniot | M-530 |

**Soundex Codes for Meugniot Spelling Variants**

*Soundex Codes*

| *Listed Numerically* | *Surname Variants* |
| --- | --- |
| M-253 | Meigniott |
| | Meugniot |
| | Meugnoit |
| | Meugnot |
| | Migniot |
| | Migniott |
| | Mugniot |
| M-263 | Maugriotte |
| M-523 | Menguoit |
| M-525 | Menginot |
| | Mengniot |
| | Mingnott |
| M-530 | Meniot |
| | Meuniot |
| | Mineout |
| | Muniot |

# TRACK YOUR RESEARCH

Tracking your research results—both successful and unsuccessful—is important. If you record each research step, you will be able to analyze results and prepare further research plans. You can develop more advanced research skills and avoid duplicating your research effort.

## CENSUS RESEARCH KIT

Be prepared for census research at the library. Gather the following supplies and keep them in a dedicated tote bag, backpack, or briefcase:

- Family data (family group sheets; genealogy database on laptop or handheld computer).

- Summary of prior research (successful and unsuccessful).

- Photocopies of census index pages relevant to your research.

- Magnifying glass.

- Colored paper or film (to place on reader when handwriting is difficult to read). Do not use dark construction paper.

- Extraction forms.

- Self-stick removable notes (to place on copied census page and jot down ideas for follow-up research).

- Large rubber bands and paper clips.

- Coins for photocopy machines.

- Black pen (to record citation on photocopy).

- Red pen (to mark location of family on copied census page).

- Your copy of *Your Guide to the Federal Census*, containing census year maps, questions asked in each census year, Soundex code chart and rules, abbreviations, summary of population and non-population schedules, and other tips and information.

**Research Tip**

**The fact that you did *not* find something is just as important as a positive result.** When recording census research results, include
- date and place of research, including the Internet
- full citation to index or census researched, leading to positive or negative results
- spelling variants checked, leading to negative results

When you examine the image of the census, whether on microfilm, CD-ROM, or on the Internet, print a hard copy if possible. Immediately record the citation in your notes. You can later handwrite the citation on the face of the photocopy or print and affix a label to it.

File the copy according to your particular filing system. Some researchers file documents by number; some, by name of ancestor; others, by place. Refer to *Organizing Your Family History Search* by Sharon DeBartolo Carmack (Cincinnati: Betterway Books, 1999) for tips on organizing all of your genealogical research.

## Extraction Forms

Photocopying the census page (and the page before and after) showing your selected individual is ideal in census research. You retain the context of the neighborhood and maintain a record of the original handwritten census record for future reference.

When you cannot photocopy or print a census record, an alternative is to extract the information onto forms that duplicate the census questions. In fact, you may want to extract data even if you make a copy. This forces you to methodically review every item and can generate ideas for future research.

**You can download census extraction forms for free at**

- Ancestry.com
  www.ancestry.com/save/charts/census.htm
- Family Tree Magazine
  www.familytreemagazine.com/forms/download.html
- FamilySearch
  www.familysearch.org
- Genealogy.com
  www.genealogy.com/00000061.html

**Money Saver**

## Software for Organizing and Analyzing

Your computer is a tool for organizing census research. Spreadsheets, databases, and word processing programs can generate reports to help you organize census data. Some specialized software packages also make the task easier:

*Clooz*
    Ancestor Detective
    P.O. Box 6386
    Plymouth, MI 48170-8486
    www.clooz.com
        Clooz is an "electronic filing cabinet" for genealogical records, including census forms for the United States, Canada, Ireland, and the United Kingdom.
*Design Software*
    220 Stella
    Burleson, TX 76028-1642
    www.dhc.net/~design
    Information and ordering: (800) 303-1331
        The Genealogy Charts & Forms and the Family Census Research programs have templates for all census years and more than 210 ways to print the data.
*Census Tools*
    729 Graves Ave.
    El Cajon, CA 92021
    www.censustools.com

**Notes**

**CENSUS TRIVIA**

At least two hundred women were enumerators for the 1880 census and also found jobs tabulating statistics at the Census Bureau.

Census Tools is a collection of thirty-two free electronic census spreadsheets, created with Microsoft Excel, for the United States, Canada, England, Ireland, and Scotland. The U.S. collection is for all federal census records, as well as state censuses of Iowa, Kansas, Massachusetts, New York, and Wisconsin. A Census Tracker supplements the individual spreadsheets, allowing all census data for an individual to be summarized in one form.

**Case Study**

## Analyze Your Research
## Case Study: Census Summary and Analysis Chart

*Data contributed by Ann Lisa Pearson, Littleton, Colorado*

Collecting and analyzing information from every possible census year helps build a complete family profile and can sometimes provide clues or information not found in other records.

The Jesse Pearson family was located in the 1840 Meriweather County, Georgia, census when Jesse and his wife, Sarah Elizabeth, were twenty-two years old. Using census records from 1840 through 1900, you can follow their migration from Georgia through three counties in Alabama. Their family grew from two children in 1840 to a total of thirteen children by 1900.

Figure 8-1 illustrates how to compare census data and create a summary of the family. The birthplaces of the children helped estimate when the family moved from Georgia to Alabama. Only one census revealed that Elizabeth's full name was Sarah Elizabeth.

The Jesse and Sarah Elizabeth Pearson family is unusual for several reasons:

1. Jesse and his wife, Sarah Elizabeth, were found in the records of every available census for their adult lives. This is sometimes difficult to accomplish.

2. Jesse's and Sarah Elizabeth's ages are consistently correct. It is more common to find among censuses two to ten years' discrepancy in ages of individuals, especially women.

3. Jesse's and Sarah Elizabeth's places of birth are correctly reported as Georgia in every census. It is more common to find among censuses discrepancies in place of birth.

4. In the censuses, the spelling of Pearson is always the same—even with a name that can easily be misspelled.

Combining the census data, the complete family structure is as follows:

Husband: Jesse C. Pearson, born 1818, Georgia
Wife: Sarah Elizabeth [Hay] Pearson, born 1817, Georgia
Children:

| | | |
|---|---|---|
| William A. Pearson | b. about 1838 | Georgia |
| Sarah Ann Pearson | b. about 1840 | Georgia |
| John Pearson | b. about 1841 | Georgia |
| Samantha Pearson | b. about 1844 | Georgia |

| | | | | | | |
|---|---|---|---|---|---|---|
| **JESSE AND SARAH ELIZABETH PEARSON**<br>**CENSUS STUDY 1840 THROUGH 1900** | | | | | | |
| **Year** | **Place** | **Surname** | **Name** | **Sex** | **Age** | **Birthplace** |
| 1900 | Jefferson County, Alabama | Pearson | Jessee[1] | M | 82 | Georgia |
| | | | Elizabeth[2] | F | 82 | Georgia |
| 1880 | Shelby County, Alabama | Pearson | J.C.[1] | M | 62 | Georgia |
| | | | Elizabeth[2] | F | 62 | Georgia |
| | | | Francis V.[3] | F | 18 | Alabama |
| 1870 | Shelby County, Alabama | Pearson | J.C.[1] | M | 52 | Georgia |
| | | | Elizabeth[2] | F | 52 | Georgia |
| | | | M.K.[4] | F | 21 | Alabama |
| | | | Levi J.[5] | M | 19 | Alabama |
| | | | N.E.[6] | F | 14 | Alabama |
| | | | L.L.[7] | F | 16 | Alabama |
| | | | F.A.[3] | F | 9 | Alabama |
| 1860 | Shelby County, Alabama | Pearson | J.C.[1] | M | 42 | Georgia |
| | | | Elizabeth[2] | F | 42 | Georgia |
| | | | John[8] | M | 18 | Georgia |
| | | | Samantha[9] | F | 16 | Georgia |
| | | | Wenlock[10] | M | 14 | Alabama |
| | | | Howell[11] | M | 12 | Alabama |
| | William A. and his wife, Elizabeth resided with William's parents and siblings. | | Catharine[4] | F | 11 | Alabama |
| | | | Levi[5] | M | 9 | Alabama |
| | | | Nancy | F | 7 | Alabama |
| | | | Luisa[7] | F | 6 | Alabama |
| | | | Martha[6] | F | 4 | Alabama |
| | | | Lida | F | 2 | Alabama |
| | | | William A.[12] | M | 22 | Georgia |
| | | | Elizabeth | F | 20 | Alabama |
| 1850 | Tallapoosa County, Alabama | Pearson | Jesse C.[1] | M | 32 | Georgia |
| | | | Sarah E.[2] | F | 32 | Georgia |
| | The only census year that reveals Sarah Elizabeth's full name. | | William A.[12] | M | 12 | Georgia |
| | | | Sarah Ann | F | 11 | Georgia |
| | | | John[8] | M | 8 | Georgia |
| | A clue to the date of migration from Georgia to Alabama, i.e., about 1845. | | Samantha[9] | F | 6 | Georgia |
| | | | Wenlock[10] | M | 5 | Alabama |
| | | | Howell[11] | M | 4 | Alabama |
| | | | Katharine[4] | F | 2 | Alabama |
| 1840 | Meriweather County, Georgia | Pearson | Jesse[1] | M | 20–30 | N/A |
| | | | | F | 20–30 | N/A |
| | | | | M | Under 5 | N/A |
| | | | | F | Under 5 | N/A |

**Figure 8-1**
Jesse Pearson census summary and analysis chart. Superscript numerals identify family members in more than one census.

| | | |
|---|---|---|
| Wenlock Pearson | b. about 1845 | Alabama |
| Howell Pearson | b. about 1847 | Alabama |
| M. Katherine/<br>Catherine Pearson | b. about 1848 | Alabama |
| Levi J. Pearson | b. about 1851 | Alabama |
| Nancy Pearson | b. about 1853 | Alabama |

| | | |
|---|---|---|
| Luisa L. Pearson | b. about 1854 | Alabama |
| Martha E. Pearson | b. about 1857 | Alabama |
| Lida Pearson | b. about 1858 | Alabama |
| Francis V./A. Pearson | b. about 1861 | Alabama |

The 1900 census reported that Sarah Elizabeth Pearson was the mother of thirteen children, nine of whom were living in 1900. This confirms that all of the Pearson children were located in census record research.

Organizing and displaying family data in different formats helps you see patterns in names, ages, or places of birth. If a piece of data looks out of place, such as a parent and a child born about the same year, you know you have a problem to resolve.

Genealogical research involves constant evaluation and reevaluation of data. As you continue your research into other types of records, you will corroborate some facts, question others, and gradually develop a well-documented family history with census research as an integral part of the process. Stay organized throughout the process to make your job easier and more enjoyable.

## CITE CENSUS RECORDS

Your census research may be wasted unless you fully cite your sources throughout the research process. If you do not record exactly what index you checked and where you did or did not find your family, you may end up repeating the research.

More important, when you publish the results, proper citation will help you meet the standards of the genealogical field and allow others to locate the same census records you found.

*Evidence! Citation & Analysis for the Family Historian* by Elizabeth Shown Mills (Baltimore: Genealogical Publishing Co., 1997) outlines citation policy and styles for all types of records. Here is some advice from Mills regarding census records:

- **Abbreviations:** Do not abbreviate elements in the first citation to a record. Such abbreviations may not be recognized by beginning researchers. You may, however, abbreviate in subsequent citations to the same record.
- **Page numbers:** Some censuses have more than one page number—a stamped number and a handwritten number. If both are present, record both and identify which is which.
- **Line numbers:** Early census records do not have a dwelling or family number. In those cases, cite the line number.
- **Dwelling and family numbers:** When dwelling and family numbers are shown in the census record, cite both. The line number is not needed when citing dwelling and family numbers.
- **House number and street address:** It is not necessary to cite the house number and street address since the other identifiers can help anyone locate the source. However, this data should not be ignored when documenting your family. It can be important in proving relationships or identities of persons, and it can be useful in other genealogical research.

**Citing Sources**

The term "micropublication" can be modified to "microfilm publication" or "microfiche publication." The important element is to stay consistent in your citations.

- **1850 and 1860 population schedules:** Indicate whether the census schedule is for free or slave inhabitants.

  Hendrick Longstreet household, 1850 U.S. census, Monmouth County, New Jersey, free schedule, Raritan Township, page 213 (stamped), dwelling 400, family 417; National Archives micropublication M432, roll 456.

  Hendrick Longstreet household, 1850 U.S. census, Monmouth County, New Jersey, slave schedule, Raritan Township, page 45 (handwritten), lines 26–28; National Archives micropublication M432, roll 466.

- **Non-population schedules:** When citing a non-population schedule (agriculture; defective, dependent, delinquent [DDD]; industry and manufacturing; mortality; social statistics; veterans), include the type of schedule.

  1870 U.S. census, Cass County, Nebraska, agriculture schedule, page 7 (recto and verso), line 28; National Archives micropublication T1128, roll 1.

- **NARA and the Family History Library (FHL):** When citing census microfilm used through the Family History Library, remember that this film is a publication of the National Archives. Therefore, it should be cited as such, using NARA's publication number and roll number. If you wish, for your own file reference, you may also include the FHL film numbers; however, library cataloging numbers for published material are not conventionally part of formal citations.

  Phitts Garrold household, 1870 U.S. census, population schedule, Butler County, Missouri, Epps Township, page 33, dwelling 15, family 13; National Archives micropublication M593, roll 763, viewed at Family History Library.

- **Internet:** Federal census images viewed on the Internet are typically digitized copies of NARA-published microfilm. Cite the NARA film publication and roll numbers as well as the publisher of the digitized edition you used.

  Theodore Roosevelt household, 1900 U.S. census, population schedule, Nassau County, New York, Oyster Bay Township, E.D. 723, sheet 16A, dwelling 290, family 301; National Archives micropublication T623, roll 1079; digitally enhanced copies viewed at <www.genealogy.com> and <www.ancestry.com>.

- **Local or state copy:** When using a local or state copy of the federal census, do not cite the NARA microfilm numbers; local and state copies are not identical to the ones produced and held by NARA. A local or state copy should be cited as a manuscript or microfilm of the repository that holds that document.

  Charles C. Sammonds household, 1860 U.S. census, Pike County, Alabama, population schedule, Pea River post office, page 324, dwelling 1034, family

**Internet Source**

**NARA CATALOGS ONLINE**

To obtain the publication and roll numbers of NARA census microfilm, refer to the NARA Microfilm Catalog, available online at <www.nara.gov/publications/microfilm/census/census.html>. The catalogs can also be purchased online or by calling (800) 234-8861.

1046; county-level copy, probate judge's office, Pike County Courthouse, Troy, Alabama.

- **Soundex card:** A Soundex card needs to be cited as the source if the full census page is illegible or missing.

  1900 U.S. census, Texas, Individual Soundex card, R500, Mrs. Ryan; National Archives micropublication T1073, roll 220.

NARA micropublication numbers:

1790   M637
1800   M32
1810   M252
1820   M33
1830   M19
1840   M704
1850   M432
1860   M653
1870   M593
1880   T9
1890   M407 (population) and M123 (veterans)
1900   T623
1910   T624
1920   T625
1930   T626

## READY TO BEGIN

You are now ready to search census records. You've done your homework: gathering known facts about your family and acquiring maps to guide your research. You know what indexes are available. You have prepared a list of spelling variants for the surname and given names with corresponding Soundex codes.

You have decided on a system to organize your research results, including forms to track your research progress. And most important, you understand the need to cite your sources.

**Reminder**

**You are not in a race. Take your time and be deliberate.** If you run into problems, slow down and relax. Devote time to reading the census records page by page and line by line. Enjoy the research task, and do not jump to inaccurate conclusions. Your challenge is to make certain you are climbing the correct family tree, fully documenting your sources and conclusions along the way. Your reward is the satisfaction of solving a puzzle and learning more about your history.

# NINE

# Research Strategies

Census research is fun! It is challenging, but it is exceptionally rewarding when you locate your family and uncover new information. You are not a full-fledged genealogist until you suddenly shout out loud "I found him!" in a public library or archives. The general public might think you are weird, but fellow genealogists will share your joy and rush over to see your discovery.

## BEGINNING THE RESEARCH

Where do you begin? If you were born on or before 1 April 1930, begin with yourself because you appear in the 1930 census. If you were born after 1 April 1930, begin with your parents or grandparents—whichever relatives were alive in early 1930.

**The policy for all census research is to begin with the most current census record available for your research subject.** For example, if the person you are studying died in 1902, begin with the 1900 census. It is tempting to look for the person listed as a child first, but researching backward in time, one census at a time, is more logical and successful than leapfrogging. This also allows you to trace the movement of the family by checking each child's birthplace.

**Research Tip**

Exceptions to this policy occur, of course, when you must skip a census year because of difficulties in locating the family in census records. But the overall strategy should always be to work backward into time—essentially from the known to the unknown, as in all genealogical research.

## INDEX STRATEGIES

Census research is a continuous process. Every time you discover new data on your family or extend it another generation, your immediate follow-up response should be to search additional census records.

**Figure 9-1**
"Of Ward No. 1 Charleston," 1840 U.S. census, Charleston District, South Carolina, stamped page 17; National Archives micropublication M704, roll 509.

**Notes**

---

**CENSUS TRIVIA**

Some Confederate veterans were mistakenly listed in the 1890 Union Veterans Schedule. When the enumerators discovered their error, they often drew a line through the name, but most of these are still legible. See page 100 for an example.

Begin your census research by using indexes correlated to the time and place of the targeted individual or family. But recognize indexes for what they are—tools to shorten research time.

You might assume that if a person or family is not in the index that person or family is not in the census. This absence may simply mean that the handwriting was misinterpreted by the indexer or the surname was misspelled by the enumerator. The index that you are using may be a head-of-household index rather than an every-name index. A person may have been residing in an entirely different state than where you had thought and appears in a different index.

Your assumption may be correct: Your person may not appear in the census. No census has ever been 100 percent complete or accurate. Some people refused to participate, some were not home when the enumerator visited, and some may have been missed for a variety of other reasons. It is estimated that in most federal censuses, about 15 percent of the population was not counted—10 percent urban and 5 percent rural.

## HELP WITH HANDWRITING

Accurate indexing depends on good handwriting, but handwriting in census records ranges from illegible scratches to elaborate calligraphy—such as in the above example by Morris Goldsmith, census taker for 1840 in Charleston, South Carolina. Ink is smeared or faded in some census records, and some microfilm was poorly made or has been scratched. **To overcome some of these difficulties**

**Tip**

- Place pastel green, yellow, blue, or pink paper on the microfilm reader surface where the image is projected. This helps reduce the glare. Colored transparent film, such as that used for report covers, can also be used and is available at most office supply stores.
- Enlarge the image.
- Make negative and positive photocopies. Comparing these two types of copies may reveal a pen stroke visible on only one copy.
- Study other handwriting for the same neighborhood and compare it to the word or name that is causing difficulty. If necessary, create an alphabet

of the enumerator's handwriting by tracing each letter separately. Upper-case letters that are commonly misread for one another are

| | |
|---|---|
| *A* and *H* | *H* and *K* |
| *B*, *P*, and *R* | *K* and *R* |
| *C*, *G*, *O*, and *Q* | *L* and *S* |
| *E* and *G* | *M* and *W* |
| *F* and *T* | *T* and *Y* |
| *G*, *J*, and *Y* | *U*, *V*, and *W* |
| *H* and *N* | *X* and *H* |
| *I* and *J* | *Z* and *Q* |

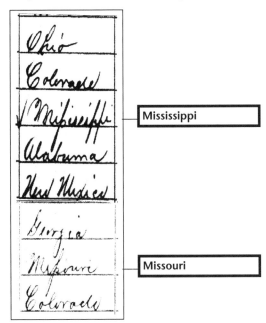

**Figure 9-2**

A common occurrence in census records is the use of the "leading *s*" in words with double *s*. The first *s* is written like a backward *f* and is often misinterpreted as an *f* or *p*. For example, the name Jesse might be misread by an inexperienced researcher as "Jefse" or "Jeffe." The example in figure 9-2 illustrates *Missouri* and *Mississippi* with the leading *s*.

- Focus only on the word you are trying to decipher. Place a piece of paper on each side of the word to cover the surrounding words.
- Stand up and read the word. Sometimes the increased distance and different angle make the word clearer.
- Walk away from the word for a while. A fresh mind can sometimes see things differently.
- Read the census on a different microfilm reader whose focus and light may be better.
- Read the census in another medium or on a different copy. The quality may be enhanced in CD-ROM format or on the Internet. The image on the same microfilm in another library may be clearer if the film has been used less often or has not suffered as much damage from old microfilm readers.

**Notes**

**CENSUS TRIVIA**

In 1800, enumerators were paid one dollar for every fifty persons counted in sparsely populated areas, one dollar for every one hundred persons recorded in rural areas, and one dollar for every three hundred persons recorded as residents in a town or city with a population of more than three thousand.

- Consult books that discuss early handwriting styles. Alphabets by time period and ethnicity are published in these books and can be compared with your example. See the bibliography on page 263.
- Ask the person at the neighboring reader to take a look. This may tap a more experienced eye or, at the very least, a fresh look at the word or phrase giving you problems. Most genealogical researchers are delighted to share with others what they know.

## SPELLING TEST

**Reminder**

The most common reason an individual cannot be located in an index is because the name was spelled differently than you had expected. **Be creative and persistent when using census indexes,** taking into account all possible spelling errors that could have been made by the enumerator or the transcriber. The fictional presidential examples on page 171, adapted with permission from Pat Hatcher, CG, FASG, illustrate how an enumerator can jumble names.

## RESEARCH STRATEGIES IN ACTION
### Not Found in 1870 Printed Index
### Reading the Census Line By Line

**Brick Wall Buster**

**Case Study: Surname Fitzgerald Recorded as Garrold**
*Contributed by Duane H. Duff Jr., Denver, Colorado*
Several attempts to locate Moses Christopher Fitzgerald in the 1870 Butler County, Missouri, census were unsuccessful. He was not in the printed indexes, nor was he located by scanning the Butler County census pages for the surname Fitzgerald. It was not until the census was *slowly* read line by line that Moses Fitzgerald was found—under the name "Garrold, Phitts." The names and ages of the children helped confirm that Phitts Garrold was Moses Fitzgerald. And, of course, he was in the index all the time, but under the surname Garrold. (See Figure 9-3 on page 172.)

### Not Found in 1920 Soundex Reading
### the Census Line By Line

**Case Study: Surname Ebetino Recorded as Betneio**
*Contributed by Sharon DeBartolo Carmack, CG, Simla, Colorado*
Immigrant surnames were often corrupted in census records when the enumerator spelled the surname phonetically. Italian immigrant Salvatore Ebetino is an excellent example of how important it is to read the census line by line when the family is not found through usual research methods.

Salvatore Ebetino, Soundex code E-135, was not found in the 1920 New York Soundex. Since it was known that he resided in Rye, Westchester County, the New York census was read line by line. The family was found—with the surname Betneio.

Not surprisingly, Salvatore Ebetino was also hidden in the 1910 census and could only be found by reading each page in Rye, Westchester County, New

| POTENTIAL ERRORS IN PRESIDENTIAL CENSUS ENUMERATIONS | | |
| --- | --- | --- |
| **Name of President** | **Fictional Census Enumerator's Rendering** | **Type of Variation** |
| George Washington | G⁽ᵉᵒ⁾ Washington | Superscript abbreviation for given name. May be ignored or missed by indexers. |
| John Adams | Jno Adams | Given name abbreviation. "Jno" might be misinterpreted by indexers as Joseph or Jonathan rather than John. |
| Thomas Jefferson | Tommy Jefferson | Nickname. |
| James Madison | Jens Madsen | Ethnic (Danish) variations of given name and surname. |
| James Monroe | J. Munro | Initial for given name. Ethnic (Scottish) variation of surname. |
| John Quincy Adams | Kwinzy Adams | Phonetic spelling of middle name. First name ignored. |
| Andrew Jackson | Drew Jackson | Nickname based on second syllable of given name. |
| Martin Van Buren | Mart V. Buren | Abbreviated given name. First half of surname is middle initial. Second half of surname is surname. |
| William H. Harrison | H. W. Harrison | Reversed initials for given and middle names. |
| James K. Polk | Jamie Polk | Nickname. |
| Zachary Taylor | Jack Tailor | Given name is an abbreviated soundalike. Variant spelling of surname. |
| Franklin Pierce | Frank Pearce | Variant spelling of surname. |
| James C. Buchanan | JayCee Buckanon | Given name and middle name initials combined into a phonetic spelling for given name. Variant spelling of surname. |
| Abraham Lincoln | Abe Lincin | Nickname. Phonetic spelling of surname. |
| Ulysses S. Grant | Euliss Grant | Phonetic spelling of given name. |
| Rutherford B. Hayes | Ford Hays | Nickname based on third syllable of given name. Vowel dropped in surname. |
| James A. Garfield | Jim Garfeld | Nickname. Vowel dropped in surname. |
| Grover Cleveland | Cleveland Grover | Reversal of given name and surname. |
| William McKinley | Bill Mac Inley | Nickname. Second part of surname recorded as surname, with first part of surname used as middle name. |
| Theodore Roosevelt | T. Rose Velt | Second part of surname recorded as surname, with first part of surname used as middle name. |
| William H. Taft | Billie Taft | Nickname. |
| Woodrow Wilson | W. Willson | Double consonant in surname resulting in spelling variant. |
| Warren G. Harding | G. Harding | Middle initial only used for given name. |

| Calvin Coolidge | Vinnie Coolidge | Nickname based on second syllable of given name. |
|---|---|---|
| Herbert Hoover | Huber Hoover | Nickname. |
| Franklin Delano Roosevelt | D. F. Roosevelt | Initials used for first and middle names and reversed. |
| Harry S. Truman | Hank Trumen | Nickname. Change of vowel in surname. |
| Dwight David Eisenhower | David Isenhaur | Middle name used for given name. Phonetic spelling of surname. |
| John Fitzgerald Kennedy | Jack Canady | Nickname. Phonetic spelling of surname. |
| Lyndon Baines Johnson | Len Johnston | Phonetic nickname of given name. Additional consonant in surname resulting in spelling variant. |
| Richard Milhous Nixon | Dick Nickson | Nickname. Substitute of *ck* for *x* in surname. |
| Jimmy Carter | James Carter | Known by nickname, but reports proper given name in census record. |
| George Herbert Walker Bush | George Washington Bush | Incorrect middle name added by enumerator. |
| Bill Clinton | William Clinton | Known by nickname, but reports proper given name. |
| George W. Bush | George Busch | Variant spelling of surname. |

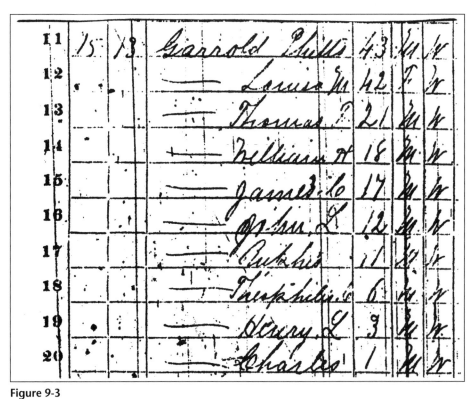

**Figure 9-3**
"Phitts Garrold" household, 1870 U.S. census, population schedule, Butler County, Missouri, Epps Township, page 33, dwelling 15, family 13; National Archives micropublication M-593, roll 763.

York. This time the enumerator had recorded his name as Salvatori Abitai.

Census research should not be rushed. More impatient researchers would have given up trying to find Moses Fitzgerald and Salvatore Ebetino. Only by repeated examination of the censuses and reading each page line by line were the problems resolved. The errors had been made by enumerators who had written down what they thought they had heard—a common occurrence regardless of the year or state.

## Find "Missing Family" on Missing Page
### Case Study: Jacob Hachenberg, 1830 Dauphin County, Pennsylvania
*Contributed by Birdie Monk Holsclaw, FUGA, Longmont, Colorado*

A routine search for Jacob Hachenberg in the 1830 Dauphin County, Pennsylvania, census was unsuccessful. The census records for the entire county were read page by page, carefully considering spelling variants and nicknames or initials. Since Jacob Hachenberg was not found, it was assumed he had been missed by the census marshal or had been living in someone else's household.

Supplemental research in land and tax records verified that Jacob Hachenberg resided in the county at the time of the census. Rather than give up on locating him, it was decided to find his neighbors, which would at least prove where he should appear in the census.

Names of neighbors were collected from earlier census records, tax lists, and a warranty map. Using the neighbor list, the census was again read line by line; it was discovered that some of Jacob's neighbors were also missing from the census though present in the preceding and following census enumerations.

---

### OTHER MISSING CENSUS PAGES

**1820 Virginia:** Nine pages in the 1820 Virginia census were not microfilmed. Gerald M. Petty's article "Virginia 1820 Federal Census: Names Not on the Microfilm Copy" in *The Virginia Genealogist* 18 (April–June 1974): 136–139 lists the names on the missing pages. The counties and page numbers are

| | |
|---|---|
| Accomac | page 6 |
| Monongalia | page 51a |
| Prince Edward | page 163a |
| Pittsylvania | page 63 |
| Randolph | page 266a |
| Shenandoah | pages 149a and 150 |
| Southampton | pages 111a and 112 |

**1850 Saint Clair County, Alabama:** Page 290 (stamped 144) of the 1850 Saint Clair County, Alabama, census was missed during microfilming. A transcription of the page appears in the *National Genealogical Society Quarterly* 77 (March 1989): 66–67 in the article "Missing Households: Saint Clair County, Alabama, 1850" by Dorothy Chambers Watts and Harry A. Nelms.

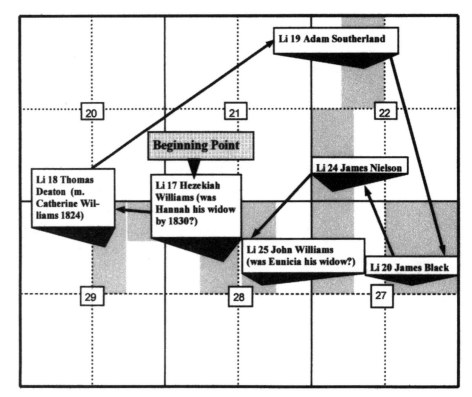

**Figure 9-4**
Map of Sections 20–22, 27–29 of Township 16 Range 5 West

Rather than assume that an entire neighborhood had been missed by the enumerator, the researcher considered the possibility of a census page having been lost. The handwritten and stamped page numbers were reviewed, revealing that handwritten page 128 (stamped page 81) of Londonderry Township was missing from the microfilm.

A letter of inquiry was sent to the National Archives, asking them to examine the original census. The staff found that page 128 did exist and confirmed that it had been missed in the microfilming. The National Archives form "Order for Reproduction Services" was submitted, and a 4″ × 5″ (10cm × 13cm) black-and-white negative and an 8″ × 10″ (20cm × 25cm) black-and-white photographic print of page 128 were made.

The missing page included not only Jacob Hachenberg but also twenty-five other households that do not appear on any indexes to this 1830 census or on the microfilm copy of the census.

## Plot the Census Taker's Route
### Case Study: 1830 Jefferson County, Alabama
*Contributed by Mary McCampbell Bell, CLS, CGL, Arlington, Virginia*
Census takers did not have to follow any particular route when they canvassed a district. In rural areas, the census taker usually rode horseback from neighbor to neighbor and cut across fields or roads to get to each household by the shortest route.

It is commonly assumed that names that follow one another on a census page represent neighbors. This is not necessarily true. Yes, the people lived in the same county or district, but they may not have been close neighbors. The path of the census taker may have made a loop that ended at the point he began, thereby making people in his last entry neighbors of those in the first entry.

Descriptions of land from early land patents were plotted onto a map of sections 20–22 and 27–29 of Township 16 Range 5 West (see Figure 9-4) in Jefferson County, Alabama. By comparing the entries on the 1830 census with the plotted landowners, it was possible to trace the path of the census taker.

1830 U.S. census, Jefferson County, Alabama, page 181, lines 17–25; National Archives micropublication M19, roll 1

| Line Number | Head of household |
|---|---|
| 17 | Hannah Williams |
| 18 | Thomas Deaton |
| 19 | Adam Southerland |
| 20 | James Black |
| 21 | Richard Adams |
| 22 | Allen Rogers |
| 23 | Benjamin Miller |
| 24 | James Nelson |
| 25 | Eunicia Williams |
| 26 | Richard Smith |

There were no land patents available for the heads of the families listed on lines 21 through 23 and line 26 (Adams, Rogers, Miller, and Smith). They may have been renters or may have purchased their land later.

After plotting the census taker's path, you can see that the Williams families on lines 17 and 25 are neighbors, with their land adjoining. This exercise does not prove a relationship between Hannah Williams and Eunicia Williams, but it shows a possibility that they may be the widows of two Williams men, Hezekiah and John, who patented land in Jefferson County in the 1820s.

## Track the Census Enumerator in the City
### Case Study: Molly Brown's Residence, 1900 Denver, Colorado
*Contributed by Janice S. Prater, Denver, Colorado*

In April 1894, the Unsinkable Molly Brown of *Titanic* fame, and her husband, James Joseph Brown, purchased a four-year-old three-story home at 1340 Pennsylvania Street, Denver, Colorado. (See <www.mollybrown.org> for the history of the Molly Brown House and for photographs of the Brown family.)

The 1900 census enumerator recorded the household at 1340 Pennsylvania Street:

Brown, James J., Head, W/M, Nov 1854, 45, married 14 yrs., Pennsylvania, Ireland, Ireland, mine owner.

Brown, Margaret, Wife, W/F, July 1868, 31, married 14 yrs., 2/2, Missouri, Ireland, Ireland.

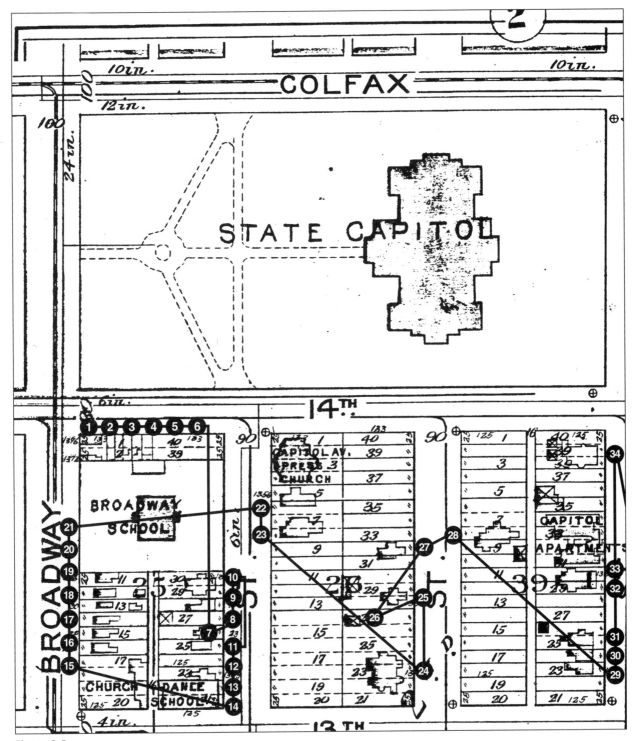

**Figure 9-5**
1900 Census Enumerator Route, E.D. 82, Denver, Colorado. Baist's Real Estate Atlas of Surveys of Denver, 1905. Map courtesy of Denver Public Library Western History/Genealogy Department.

> Brown, Lawrence P., Son, W/M, Aug 1887, 12 yrs., Missouri, Pennsylvania, Missouri.
> Brown, Helen, Daughter, W/F, July 1889, 10 yrs., Missouri, Pennsylvania, Missouri.

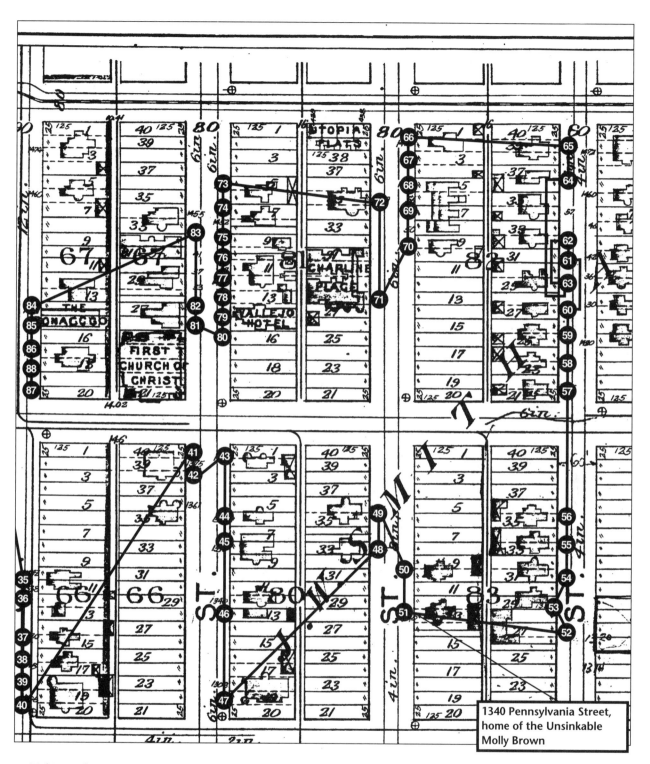

1340 Pennsylvania Street, home of the Unsinkable Molly Brown

Tobin, Johanna, M-in-Law, W/F, March 1825, 75, Ireland, Ireland, Ireland.

Bondestel, Mary, Ward, W/F, April 1884, 16, California, Germany, France.

Becker, Frank A., Nephew, W/M, Jan 1882, 18, Missouri, New York, Missouri.

Mulligan, Mary C., Housekeeper, W/F, Oct 1863, 36, Kansas, Ireland, Ireland.

Reynolds, Harry, Servant, W/M, Feb 1875, 25, Massachusetts, New Hampshire, Canada.

James J. Brown household, 1900 U.S. census, Arapahoe County, Colorado, population schedule, Denver, Precinct 5, Ward 10, E.D. 82, sheet 3A, dwelling 51, family 56; National Archives micropublication T623, roll 119.

Using Molly Brown's census entry as the focal point, the path of the enumerator was tracked on a real estate map (see Figure 9-5). This exercise added insight into the makeup and history of the neighborhood:

- There were eighty-eight dwellings in precinct 5, ward 10, Denver enumeration district 82, spanning twelve pages.
- The enumerator, Florence Wilbur, began her route with her own residence—dwelling number 1 on the map. Florence was a twenty-seven-year-old single kindergarten teacher who resided with her widowed mother and fifteen-year-old brother. Miss Wilbur probably taught at Broadway School since her home was next door.
- The government allowed one month for the 1900 census to be taken; Florence completed her task in two weeks.
- The Brown household (dwelling number 51 on the map) was enumerated on 4 June 1900. According to Kristen Iversen's *Molly Brown: Unraveling the Myth* (Boulder, Colo.: Johnson Books, 1999), pp. 121–122, Molly and J.J. Brown were in Ireland in June 1900, and their children were attending school in Paris. Molly's mother, or perhaps one of the servants, most likely provided the information to enumerator Florence Wilbur.
- In 1900, only four houses were in the 1300 block of Pennsylvania Street; two on the east side and two on the west. A stone stable was located behind Molly Brown's house.
- Joshua and Victoria Monti (dwelling 50) lived next door to Molly Brown and were immigrants from Switzerland and France.
- Mrs. Sayer, who lived across the street (dwelling 49), was born in Missouri, and her parents were born in Ireland—just like Molly Brown. Iversen (page 123) declares that the two families are related and cites the 1900 census as the source. The 1900 census does not report relationships between neighbors; therefore, one should be careful in jumping to such a conclusion. Iversen may be correct, but proof of such a relationship needs to be established through other documents.
- John and Mary Milheim, the remaining neighbors on Pennsylvania Street (dwelling 48), were born in Switzerland. Therefore the four families living in the 1300 block of Pennsylvania Street were Irish, Swiss, and French.
- The only children living in the 1300 block of Pennsylvania Street were Molly Brown's ten-year-old daughter and twelve-year-old son, plus the sixteen-year-old ward residing in the Brown home.
- Broadway School was five blocks west of Molly Brown's residence, but the Brown children did not attend the neighborhood school. According to Iversen (page 119), both children attended Sacred Heart College, a

**Research Tip**

**TAX RECORDS**

Supplement your census research with research of tax records. Annual real estate, personal property, and poll tax records can fill the gap between each census. Tax records can help you prove relationships, distinguish persons with the same name, and establish migration patterns.

Catholic school in Denver, and boarding schools in France. Helen also attended the prestigious Wolcott School for Girls in Denver.

- The five households (dwellings 52–56) that shared the back alley of Molly Brown's house were those of a jeweler born in Louisiana, a music company manager born in New York, a lawyer born in Maine, a landowner born in Vermont, and a stockyard manager born in Missouri. Only one child under age twelve lived in these five residences.
- The First Church of Christ Scientist was within walking distance (about 1½ blocks) of the Brown residence, although this was not their church. The Browns were Irish Catholics.
- The Smith family resided in dwelling 71—a family-owned hotel that is not named in the census record. The census named eighteen employees/servants and seventeen boarders. The name of the hotel, Charline Place, was determined by matching the dwelling's address on the map with the census enumeration and confirming with the 1900 Denver city directory. The Smith family included a seventeen-year-old daughter named Charline. Was the hotel named after her?

Many of these observations could not have been made without combining information from the census record with the graphic images of the map. You can re-create your ancestor's neighborhood in a similar fashion and gain new insight into his community and lifestyle. Sanborn Fire Insurance Maps are an excellent resource for more than twelve thousand U.S. cities from 1867 to 1970. See <http://sanborn.umi.com/>.

## Use Immigration Data to Locate Passenger List
### Case Study: 1879 Immigration of Theresa Huck,
### Cincinnati, Hamilton County, Ohio
*Contributed by Julie Miller, Broomfield, Colorado*
The 1900, 1910, and 1920 censuses asked foreigners to give their year of immigration. Usually the year is consistent among the censuses, but sometimes the date varies slightly. In the case of Theresa Huck, born in 1834 in Germany, the year of immigration was always reported as 1879:

1920: Theresa Huck, grandmother in the household of George C. Coors, 1920 U.S. census, Hamilton County, Ohio, population schedule, Cincinnati, E.D. 400, sheet 1, dwelling 10, family 10, line 45; National Archives micropublication T625, roll 1394. *Year of immigration: 1879.*

1910: Theresa Huck, mother in household of Elizabeth Hagmeier, 1910 U.S. census, Hamilton County, Ohio, population schedule, Cincinnati, E.D. 268, sheet 13B, dwelling 126, family 183, line 61; National Archives micropublication T624, roll 1194. *Year of immigration: 1879.*

1900: Theresa Huck, mother in the household of Elizabeth Hagmeier, 1900 U.S. census, Hamilton County, Ohio, population schedule, Cincinnati, E.D. 268, sheet 3, dwelling 47, family 68, line 75; National Archives micropublication T623, roll 1179. *Year of immigration: 1879.*

Using the 1879 immigration date, Theresa Huck's passenger arrival information was found in P. William Filby's, *Germans to America: Lists of Passengers Arriving at U.S. Ports*, Volume 34 (Wilmington, Del.: Scholarly Resources, Inc., 1996), 398. Follow-up research with the passenger list:

> Therese Huck entry, *SS City of New York* Passenger Manifest, 29 Nov. 1879, page 5, line 244; in *Passenger Lists of Vessels Arriving at New York, NY 1820–1897*; records of the U.S. Customs Service, Record Group 36, National Archives micropublication M237, roll 421.
>
>> Therese Huck, age 45, female, widow, no occupation
>> Elisa, female, age 17, spinster
>> Franz, male, age 15, laborer
>> Marie, female, age 11, child
>> Joseph, male, age 10, child
>> Catharina, female, age 7, child
>> All Germany to United States

The passenger list gave a nonspecific place of birth: Germany. The 1880 and 1920 censuses, however, reported Baden, a region in Germany, which is another clue in continuing research into this German family.

## Use Immigration Data to Locate Naturalization Record
### Case Study: 1900 Naturalization of Walter H. Gresham, Cleveland, Cuyahoga County, Ohio
*Contributed by Lou-Jean Rehn, Denver, Colorado*

The 1900 through 1930 censuses reported the immigrants' arrival year and their citizenship status, e.g., "Al" for alien, "Pa" for first papers (Declaration of Intention) filed, and "Na" for naturalized. The year of naturalization is reported in the 1920 census—the only year that this information is provided.

The citizenship data from the census records provided important clues to locate naturalization documents for Walter H. Gresham. According to the 1900, 1910, and 1920 censuses, Walter H. Gresham, born in 1871 in England, immigrated in 1888 when he was about seventeen years old. The naturalization data, however, conflicted—the 1920 census reported the year of naturalization as 1892, but in 1900 he was reported an alien:

> 1920: Walter Gresham household, 1920 U.S. census, Summit County, Ohio, population schedule, Akron City, E.D. 167, sheet 2A, dwelling 24, family 28; National Archives micropublication T625, roll 1439. *Year of immigration: 1888. Citizenship: naturalized 1892.*
>
> 1910: Walter Gresham household, 1910 U.S. census, Summit County, Ohio, population schedule, Akron City, E.D. 148, sheets 4–5, dwelling 81, family 93; National Archives micropublication T624, roll 1233. *Year of immigration: 1888. Citizenship: naturalized.*
>
> 1900: Walter Gresham household, 1900 U.S. census, Cuyahoga County, Ohio, population schedule, Cleveland City, E.D. 161, sheet 17, line 4 (dwell-

ing and family numbers illegible); National Archives micropublication T623, roll 1258. *Year of immigration: 1888. Citizenship: alien.*

## Steps to Locate Naturalization Record

With the conflicting naturalization data in the census records, it appeared that Walter became a citizen in 1892 or between 1900 and 1910. The first step to locate Walter's naturalization records was to examine the Family History Library catalog. Two indexes that covered the appropriate time periods for Cuyahoga County, Ohio, were searched for the surname Gresham:

> Naturalization Index 1859–1901, Cuyahoga County, Ohio, Probate Court; original records at Cuyahoga County Archives, Cleveland, Ohio. Family History Library film number 1,818,696:
>> No Walter Gresham

> Naturalization Index 1818–1931, Cuyahoga County, Ohio, Court of Common Pleas; original records at Cuyahoga County Archives, Cleveland, Ohio. Family History Library film number 1,819,030:
>> Walter H. Gresham, 33 Edwards, Cleveland, Ohio. Petition No. 17233, Common Pleas, Cuyahoga Co., Ohio; born 6 November 1871 in Great Britain; arrived 7 May 1887; naturalized 27 October 1900.

The 1892 naturalization date reported in the 1920 census was incorrect. Walter's alien status in the 1900 census was correct because the census was taken in June and he became naturalized in October. It is interesting to note that Walter consistently reported 1888 as his date of arrival into the United States; however, the naturalization index card and the petition for naturalization (also on microfilm at the Family History Library) gave a date of 7 May 1887. Incorrect dates such as this are common in census records since the information may have been gathered from someone other than the named individual.

## Siblings

When researching the naturalization indexes, all persons with the surname Gresham were noted—an excellent procedure in all genealogical research. As a result, four siblings who were thought to have been residing in England were unexpectedly discovered. The family story had been that Walter traveled to the United States alone and left behind his six brothers and two sisters, except for one brother who migrated to Canada.

The naturalization and census records established a profile of a family that immigrated separately, between 1886 and 1909, but with the same destination: Cleveland, Ohio. City directories and marriage, newspaper, and birth records helped prove relationships among these men:

| Name | Date of Birth | Date of Arrival |
|---|---|---|
| Charles D. Gresham | April 1860 | 27 July 1886 |
| 1900 and 1910 census reported 1886 arrival | | |
| Not found in 1920 Ohio census | | |

Harry E. Gresham       11 December 1865     17 November 1886
1900 census reported 1884 arrival
1910 census reported 1890 arrival
1920 census reported 1900 arrival

Walter H. Gresham       6 November 187     17 May 1887
1900, 1910, and 1920 censuses reported 1888 arrival

Samuel E. Gresham       5 September 1869     9 September 1890
1900 census reported 1891 arrival
1910 census reported 1890 arrival
Not found in 1920 Ohio census

Harold E. Gresham       10 August 1874     11 February 1892
1900 census reported 1888 arrival
Not found in 1910 and 1920 Ohio censuses

Will Gresham
Walter's brother Will Gresham was residing with Walter in 1910, an immigration date of 1909 was reported. Follow-up research in the Ellis Island passenger records <www.ellisislandrecords.org> indicated that Willy Steele Gresham, age forty-five years, arrived 29 December 1909 from Sheffield, England, on the ship *Furnessia*. He had departed from Glasgow, Scotland.

The census and naturalization records were genealogically rich for this family. Besides the immigrant data, the 1900 and 1920 censuses for Walter H. Gresham had another bonus. In 1900 his widowed mother-in-law was reported as residing with his family. In 1920 she was again reported as living with them and as a widow, but she had a new surname. This indicates a marriage between 1900 and 1920, the death of one of her spouses prior to 1900, and the death of the other spouse between 1900 and 1920.

Also note that two naturalization indexes covering the same time period were examined. Do not stop after just one index when searching naturalization, census, or other types of genealogical sources.

## Compare and Analyze Pre-1850 Census Statistics
### Case Study: William Lowe, 1810 Through 1830 Censuses, Warren County, Kentucky
*Contributed by J. Mark Lowe, CG, Springfield, Tennessee*
Organizing pre-1850 census statistics in a comparative format will help you see discrepancies and irregularities. By aligning individuals in age ranges, you can narrow estimated birth dates and correlate them with other available data.

William Lowe and his family lived in Warren County, Kentucky. The following census data was reported (data regarding slaves has been omitted for this example):

William Lowe household, 1810 U.S. census, Warren County, Kentucky, page 259, line 22; National Archives micropublication M252, roll 8.
1 0 0 1 0-3 0 0 1 0

William Lowe household, 1820 U.S. census, Warren County, Kentucky, page 53, line 14; National Archives micropublication M33, roll 28.
3 1 0 0 1 0-2 1 2 1 1

William Lowe household, 1830 U.S. census, Warren County, Kentucky, page 111, line 3; National Archives micropublication M19, roll 42.
1 1 0 3 1 0 0 0 0 0 0 0 0 0-0 1 2 0 0 0 1 0 0 0 0 0 0

The comparison form was completed by transcribing the census data into the appropriate census year column from top to bottom. The census research began with 1830 and moved backward in time, but the comparisons are made going forward in time.

Male information is recorded on the upper portion of the comparison form; female information, on the lower portion. There should be a box for each item. The notes column may be used to identify family members or to include data from later census records.

The appearance or disappearance of individuals in a census year provides a beginning date to look for changes (*e.g.*, death, marriage, migration). The questions "What happened?" or "Where did they go?" should be answered if possible. The disappearance of the three girls (Elizabeth, Edy, and Sally) from the 1820 census to the 1830 census corresponds with their individual marriages between 1820 and 1830. It also appears that William Lowe, the head of the household, died between 1830 and 1840. The older female appearing in the 1830 census may have joined the family because of the death of a spouse or other family member.

Although no estate settlement is known to survive for William Lowe, an equity (chancery) court case reported his estate. Eleven children were mentioned by name. The eldest son, Isaac Walker Lowe, served as administrator of the estate and removed to Illinois before this court case was filed. (*Prior P. Lowe, et al. vs Isaac W. Lowe, Admr., et al.*, Warren County, Kentucky, Equity Court Case 1177, Folklife and Manuscript Collection, Western Kentucky University, Bowling Green, Kentucky.)

Upon review of the census comparison, three sons may have been born between 1810 and 1820, but only two were identified through the equity court record and other known records. Because the census records indicate a third son living in 1830, additional court records were reviewed. A debt case against $W^m$ G. Lowe was dismissed in the research earlier as being against sibling William J. Lowe. Upon reexamination of the case, Williamson G. Lowe, born about 1814, was the other son of William Lowe. This young man died on a river raft trip to New Orleans in 1834, shortly after his father. Because this son had purchased a new suit of clothing on credit, his estate was sued for the debt. Williamson G. Lowe died without issue (children), and the debt was paid out of his father's estate before distribution to the other heirs. (*Potter, Smith & Co.*

## 1800-1840 Census Comparison Form

| Birthyear to -> from | 18 00 | 18 10 | 18 20 | 18 30 | 18 40 | Notes / Names<br>© 2001 by J. Mark Lowe cg, 505 Josephine St., Springfield, TN 37172  All Rights Reserved |
|---|---|---|---|---|---|---|
| 1840 | | | | | | |
| 1835 | | | | | | |
| 1830 | | | | | | |
| 1825 | | | | 1 | | John H (b. 1828) |
| 1820 | | | | 1 | | Hobson (b. 1824) |
| 1815 | | | 3 | 0 | | William J (b. 1816) |
| 1810 | | | | 3 | | Prior (b. 1810)      **UNIDENTIFIED INDIVIDUAL** |
| 1804 | | | 1 | | | |
| 1802 | | 1 | 0* | 1 | | Isaac Walker (b. 1806) |
| 1800 | | | 0* | | | |
| 1794 | | 0 | | | | |
| 1790 | | | | 0 | | |
| 1784 | | 0 | | | | |
| 1780 | | | 1 | 0 | | William (b. 1780) |
| 1774 | | | | | | **probably died between 1830 and 1840** |
| 1770 | | 1 | | 0 | | |
| 1765 | | | | | | |
| 1760 | | | | 0 | | |
| 1755 | | | | | | |
| 1750 | | 0 | 0 | 0 | | |
| 1740 | | | | 0 | | |
| 1730 | | | | 0 | | |
| bef 1730 | | | | 0 | | |

\* An individual age 16-18 would be reported twice in this census year. Use top box for them.

| | 18 00 | 18 10 | 18 20 | 18 30 | 18 40 | |
|---|---|---|---|---|---|---|
| 1840 | | | | | | |
| 1835 | | | | | | |
| 1830 | | | | | | |
| 1825 | | | | 0 | | |
| 1820 | | | | 1 | | Martha (b. 1822) |
| 1815 | | | | 2 | | Julia (b. 1819) |
| 1810 | | | 2 | 0 | | Nancy P. (b 1806) |
| 1804 | | | 1 | | | Edy (b. 1804) |
| 1802 | | 3 | | 0 | | Elizabeth (b. 1803) **married between 1820 and 1830** |
| 1800 | | | 2 | | | Sally (b. 1801) |
| 1794 | | 0 | | | | |
| 1790 | | | | 0 | | |
| 1784 | | 0 | | | | |
| 1780 | | | 1 | 1 | | Nancy (b. 1780) |
| 1774 | | 1 | | | | |
| 1770 | | | | 0 | | |
| 1765 | | | | | | |
| 1760 | | | | 0 | | |
| 1755 | | | | | | |
| 1750 | | | | 0 | | |
| 1740 | | 0 | 1 | 0 | | **older unidentified female (mother, aunt, in-law?)** |
| 1730 | | | | 0 | | |
| bef 1730 | | | | 0 | | |

**Figure 9-6**

*vs. Estate of Wm. G. Lowe*, Equity Court Case [loose papers], Folklife and Manuscripts Collection, Western Kentucky University, Bowling Green, Kentucky.)

## Correlate Census and Mortality Schedule
### Case Study: Eliza Terry, 1850 Cecil County, Maryland
*Contributed by Elissa Scalise Powell, CGRS, Wexford, Pennsylvania*

Eliza Terry, wife of William P. Keetley Sr., was born in October 1849 in Maryland. She died in April 1903 at age fifty-three years and was interred at the Union Methodist Episcopal Churchyard in Fremont, Chester County, Pennsylvania.

The research goal was to determine the names of Eliza's parents. The 1900 and 1880 Chester County, Pennsylvania, censuses reported Eliza's birthplace as Maryland. The 1900 census reported that her father was born in Maryland and her mother, in Pennsylvania; however, the 1880 census gave a birthplace of Maryland for both parents.

Eliza Terry and William Keetley married after 1870; therefore they each should have been residing with their respective parents in 1870. At the time of this research, there was no statewide census index to 1870 Maryland, but there was for 1860, so it was checked for Terry surnames.

By studying all the families with the surname Terry in the 1860 Maryland census, the following family offered the closest profile, although Eliza was reported as twelve years old rather than ten and the mother was reported as having been born in Ireland. But upon closer examination, it was noted that the wife of Thomas Terry was reported as thirty years old and his oldest son, George, was reported as twenty years old. This suggested that Margaret was a second wife and not the mother of the older children and perhaps not the mother of Eliza, even though Margaret would have been eighteen years old when Eliza was born.

> Thos. Terry household, 1860 U.S. census, Cecil County, Maryland, population schedule, Fifth District, pages 239 and 240, dwelling 1691, family 1711; National Archives micropublication M653, roll 472.
>
> Thos. Terry, 50, M, farmer, $3600, $700, Maryland
> Margaret, 30, F, Ireland
> George, 20, M, Maryland
> Eliss M., 15, M, Maryland, school
> Amanda, 14, F, Maryland, school
> Eliza, 12, F, Maryland, school
> Ellen, 7, F, Maryland, school
> Samuel, 6, M, Maryland, school
> Margaret, 4, F, Maryland
> Homard, 2, M, Maryland

This family looked promising for two reasons: They had a daughter named Eliza who was within two years of a "correct" age, and they had a son named Homard. Eliza's son and grandson each had this unusual name, so this suggested that the research was on the right track. Continuing backward in time, the 1850 Cecil County, Maryland, census showed

> Thomas Terry household, 1850 U.S. census, Cecil County, Maryland, population schedule, 2nd Subdivision, 5th Election District, page 124, dwelling 591, family 597; National Archives micropublication M432, roll 290.
>
> Thomas Terry, 38, M, farmer, $470, Maryland
> George W. Terry, 10, M, Maryland
> Mary L. Terry, 8, F, Maryland
> Ellis M. Terry, 5, M, Maryland
> Amanda Terry, 3, F, Maryland
> Eliza Terry, $^{10}/_{12}$, F, Maryland
> Ann Fletcher, 26, F, England

The 1850 census gave a more accurate age for Eliza, so the 1860 census data demonstrate how ages in census records are often estimates rather than exact. Note the absence of the mother. Since Eliza was a ten-month-old baby at the time, the first assumption is that the mother died during or shortly after childbirth. The 1850 mortality schedule proved this hypothesis:

> 1850 Maryland Mortality Schedule, page 177, line 24; Family History Library film number 1,429,789.
>
> Eliza Terry, age 38, F, Married, born Pennsylvania, died in October of Confinement lasting 6 months.

Eliza Terry was apparently named for her deceased mother, who died from complications of giving birth ("confinement" refers to her pregnancy). Eliza's mother was reported as having been born in Pennsylvania, which matches the information in the 1900 census.

While one mystery was solved, another developed. Eliza, the mother, died in October 1849. On the next line in the mortality schedule is a three-month-old child named Slayton, with what appears to be ditto marks for the surname, indicating Terry. If so, the three-month-old child, who died in December 1849, may have been a twin of Eliza. Since Eliza was named after her mother, could it be that Slayton is a family surname? Perhaps the maiden name of the mother? This is a mystery that needs to be solved through further research.

## Correlate Census and DDD Prisoner Schedule
### Case Study: Robert Goodlett, 1880 Greenville County, South Carolina
*Contributed by Penelope J. Cansler, Greenville, South Carolina*
Robert Goodlett, fifty years old per the 1880 Greenville County, South Carolina, census, was reported as being "In U.S. penitentiary" at the time of the census. A wife is not listed, although his five children, ages three to thirteen, are named:

> Robert Goodlett household, 1880 U.S. census, Greenville County, South Carolina, population schedule, Highland Township, E.D. 92, page 33, lines 28–33; National Archives micropublication T9, roll 1231.

Robert Goodlett, B, M, 50, in U.S. penitentiary, SC, SC, SC, cannot read/
write

Mary Goodlett, B, F, 13, daughter, laborer, SC, SC, SC

Richard Goodlett, B, M, 11, son, SC, SC, SC

Lucy Goodlett, B, F, 7, daughter, SC, SC, SC

Benjamin Goodlett, B, M, 6, son, SC, SC, SC

Robert Goodlett, B, M, 3, son, SC, SC, SC

The immediate questions are, Why was Robert Goodlett in prison? and Were
his children living alone? How long was he to be in prison? Was the thirteen-
year-old caring for this family, or was there a relative nearby? Where was the
mother of the children? Was she deceased or merely absent?

Armed with the information that Robert Goodlett was in the penitentiary in
the summer of 1880, the "Inhabitants in Prison" DDD schedule number 6 was
searched (see chapter four for information about these schedules). Using the
enumeration district and page number from the population schedule, Robert
Goodlett was located in the prisoner schedule:

> 1880 U.S. census; Greenville County, South Carolina, Supplemental Sched-
> ule No. 6 for the Defective, Dependent, and Delinquent Classes, Inhabitants
> in Prison; Highland Township; E.D. 92. South Carolina State Archives mi-
> crofilm CN632, roll AD280; viewed at South Carolina Room, Greenville
> County Public Library, Greenville, South Carolina.

*Inhabitants in Prison*

| | |
|---|---|
| Column 1 | Number of page from Schedule 1: Page 33 |
| Column 2 | Line number from Schedule 1: Line 28 |
| Column 3 | Name: Robt Goodlett |
| Column 4 | Residence when at home, city or town: Greenville |
| Column 6 | Place of imprisonment, state penitentiary or prison, county penitentiary or jail, workhouse, house of correction, city prison, stationhouse, lockup or calaboose: Albany, NY, U.S. |
| Column 16 | Date of incarceration: 8 [?] Sept 1879 |
| Column 17 | Alledged offense: Illicit Distilling |
| Column 20 | Number of years in penitentiary: 1 and $\frac{3}{12}$ |

The prisoner schedule reported that Robert Goodlett had been in prison since
September 1879 and would not be released for another six months. "Illicit
distilling" was a federal offense, which explains why Robert was not in a local
jail.

It first appeared from the census that the five children had been living alone.
But closer examination taught an important lesson. Paying attention to the
dwelling and family numbers, it was discovered that the Robert Goodlett family
was *not* living alone. Three families were sharing the same dwelling:

*Dwelling 282, Family 288 (Lines 21–23)*

| | |
|---|---|
| Linda Henson | B, F, 52, keeping house, SC, SC, SC, cannot read/write |
| Mack Henson | B, M, 13, son, laborer, SC, SC, SC |
| Jesse Henson | B, M, 12, son, laborer, SC, SC, SC |

*Dwelling 282, Family 289 (Lines 24–27)*

| | |
|---|---|
| Coaela Jones | B, F, 30, boarder, laborer, SC, SC, SC, cannot read/write |
| Ella Jones | B, F, 11, daughter, SC, SC, SC |
| Harriett | B, F, 3, daughter, SC, SC, SC |
| Minnie | B, F, 1, daughter, SC, SC, SC |

*Dwelling 282, Family 290 (Lines 28–33)*

| | |
|---|---|
| Robert Goodlett | B, M, 50, in penitentiary, SC, SC, SC, cannot read/write |
| Mary Goodlett | B, F, 13, daughter, laborer, SC, SC, SC |
| Richard Goodlett | B, M, 11, son, SC, SC, SC |
| Lucy Goodlett | B, F, 7, daughter, SC, SC, SC |
| Benjamin Goodlett | B, M, 6, son, SC, SC, SC |
| Robert Goodlett | B, M, 3, son, SC, SC, SC |

The profile of these families residing in the same dwelling presents new questions:

- Are there any family relationships between the Henson, Jones, and Goodlett families? Families residing in the same house or dwelling were not necessarily related, but often they were. The place of birth of individuals and/or their parents can gives clues, but in this case everyone was born in South Carolina, so there is no marker to suggest relationships.
- Could the thirty-year-old female (Coaela Jones) have been the daughter of Robert Goodlett? Coaela was twenty years younger than Robert, so it is possible. That would mean that he had an eleven-year-old granddaughter and an eleven-year-old son.
- Was fifty-two-year-old Linda Henson a sister of Robert Goodlett or unrelated?

The only male adult listed for this dwelling of thirteen persons is the absent fifty-year-old Robert Goodlett. With Robert away in the federal penitentiary, the only adults were the fifty-two- and thirty-year-old females, who were caring for ten children. This profile certainly presents an image of hardship.

Robert Goodlett was also enumerated in the 1880 New York population schedule as a prisoner in the Albany County Penitentiary. He was therefore counted twice (once in South Carolina and once in New York) with additional information about his imprisonment reported in the South Carolina DDD schedule. The Albany Penitentiary was not included in the New York DDD schedule.

It helps to place events into historical and geographical context when researching a family. In this case, Highland Township, South Carolina, is in the upper part of Greenville County—in the mountains. It is part of a section called the Dark Corner, home of feuds and stills. Even as late as World War I, local residents sometimes shot at visiting military recruiters.

Follow-up research could include investigation of previous census records to perhaps link relationships between the Henson, Jones, and Goodlett families. Local court records and newspaper reports might give details of Robert's arrest and conviction.

## Correlate Polygamy Court Record With Census
### Case Study: Hector S. Wisner

Hector S. Wisner was convicted of bigamy in the district court of the first judicial district of the territory of Utah on 17 September 1879 and sentenced to two years in the Utah Penitentiary. The records of his criminal case are in National Archives Record Group 21, Records of District Courts of the United States, District of Utah, territorial files 1870–1896, box 51, entry 1, case number 2540; National Archives and Records Administration, Rocky Mountain Region, Denver, Colorado.

The grand jury found that Hector S. Wisner had married Minnie E. Babcock on 31 August 1871 in New York and had married again on 14 February 1877 in Sevier County, Utah. They charged that "while he was so married to said Minnie E. Babcock and while his said wife Minnie E. Babcock was living and remained his wife, feloniously and unlawfully did marry and took for wife one Ede Tutton."

The 1880 census confirmed Hector's prison sentence, but it also reported that he was a doctor. His second wife and two-year-old son were living with her parents; however, the first wife was not located.

> Hector S. Wisner entry, 1880 U.S. census, Salt Lake County, Utah, population schedule, Sugar House Precinct, U.S. Utah Penitentiary, E.D. 54, page 224D, dwelling 80, family 80; National Archives micropublication T9, roll 1337.
>
> Hector S. Wisner, W/M/S, doctor, NY, NY, Massachusetts

> George Tutton household, 1880 U.S. census, Sevier County, Utah, population schedule, Richfield City and Precinct, E.D. 69, page 479B, dwelling 124, family 132; National Archives micropublication T9, roll 1338.
>
> Tutton, George, W/M/57, married, musician and bristlemaker, Isle of Guernsey, England, England, England
>
> Tutton, N. Margaret, W/F/56, wife, married, NY, NY, NY
>
> Wisner, Eda A.E., W/F/23, daughter, married, Ohio, Guernsey, NY
>
> Wisner, Jos. I., W/M/2, grandson, Utah, NY, Ohio

Note that Hector was reported as single, whereas Eda was shown as married.

**Figure 9-7**
*Bringing Your Family History to Life Through Social History* by Katherine Scott Sturdevant (Cincinnati: Betterway Books, 2000).

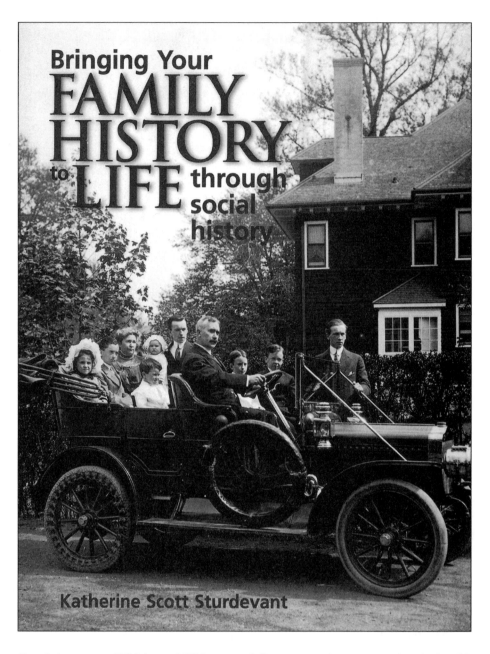

One is incorrect. Which one? This type of discrepancy is common, but it should never be ignored.

If the census enumeration for Eda had been the first record encountered in the research, the clue for further research would have been the fact that she was married but her husband was not named.

This case study demonstrates how the census is a mainstream record type that can confirm data from other records yet still provide new information.

## Identify Family in Photograph Using Census Research
### Case Study: William H. McKiernan, Brooklyn, New York
*Adapted with permission from Katherine Scott Sturdevant, M.A., Colorado Springs, Colorado*

Katherine Scott Sturdevant dated and identified the cover photograph on *Bringing Your Family History to Life Through Social History* by using Brooklyn city directories, the 1900 census, and reference books on automobiles. A case study appears on page 89 of Sturdevant's book and has been adapted for presentation in this discussion of census research.

The only identifying information for the photograph was "William H. McKiernan, Brooklyn." Before searching for the family in a city directory or in census records, it was necessary to date the photo. By researching automobiles of the early twentieth century, historian Rick Sturdevant hypothesized that the car was a 1909 Studebaker A Suburban. The curved fenders and placement of the brake or shift handles were key in narrowing the time period and model.

The Irish family of William H. McKiernan (note spelling variation from photograph) was located in the 1900 and 1910 censuses of Brooklyn. By correlating the persons in the photograph with the sex and age of each family member in the censuses, it appears the correct family has been identified.

By comparing the photograph with the family members listed in the 1910 census—the closest to the date of the photograph—we can identify each person. The forty-two-year-old father is sitting in the driver's seat and his wife, Agnes, is standing near the rear of the car holding her one-year-old daughter, Agnes. The four oldest sons (ages eighteen, sixteen, twelve, and ten) are grouped around the car, and eight-year-old James and four-year-old John are sitting in the rear seat. Gertrude, six years old, is wearing the big bonnet.

| 1900 Census: 61 Clifton Place | 1910 Census: 1835 Caton Avenue |
|---|---|
| Wm. H. McKiernan household, 1900 U.S. census, Kings County, New York, population schedule, Brooklyn, Ward 7, E.D. 81, sheet 2B, dwelling 10, family 42; National Archives micropublication T623, roll 1046. | Wm. H. McKiernan household, 1910 U.S. census, Kings County, New York, population schedule, Brooklyn, E.D. 928, sheet 2, dwelling 29, family 29; National Archives micropublication T624, roll 982. |
| Wm. H. McKiernan, husband, Dec 1868, 31, married 10 yrs., NY, Ireland, Ireland, news paster | William H. McKiernan, husband, 42, married 20 yrs., NY, Ireland, Ireland, real estate speculator |
| Agnes McKiernan, wife, Apr 1868, 32, married 10 yrs., 6 children/5 living, NY, Ireland, Ireland | Agnes M. McKiernan, wife, 42, married 20 yrs., 10 children/8 living, NY, Ireland, Ireland |
| Mary McKiernan, daughter, May 1890, 10 yrs. | William A. McKiernan, son, 18 yrs. |
| William McKiernan, son, June 1891, 8 yrs. | Thomas J. McKiernan, son, 16 yrs. |
| Thomas McKiernan, son, July 1893, 6 yrs. | Raymond L. McKiernan, son, 12 yrs. |
| Raymond McKiernan, son, August 1897, 2 yrs. | *Charles McKiernan, son 10 yrs. |
| *James McKiernan, son, September 1899, 8 months | *James D. McKiernan, son, 8 yrs. |
| | Gertrude McKiernan, daughter, 6 yrs. |
| | John McKiernan, son, 4 yrs. |
| | Agnes McKiernan, daughter, 1 yr. |

*This shows a contradiction in the age of James McKiernan, reported in 1900 as eight months old and in 1910 as eight years old. James *should* have been ten years old in 1910 rather than eight. There are two possible explanations, the most likely being that the names of the eight- and ten-year-old sons are reversed in the 1910 census. This is a common error in census enumerations. Another scenario could be that James is the middle name of ten-year-old Charles. Additional research in censuses and other record types could resolve this conflict.

Agnes McKiernan was the mother of ten children, although only eight were still living at the time of the 1910 census. All eight are in the photograph. One child died prior to 1900, as noted in Agnes's census report that she had had six children, five of whom were living in 1900. Their oldest daughter, Mary, died between 1900 and 1910, since she is the only child missing when comparing the two census schedules.

According to the 1910 census, the McKiernan family owned their home at 1835 Caton Avenue. Perhaps that is the house in the background of the photograph. If the home is still standing, a personal visit to the neighborhood would verify this. If not, neighborhood photos or Sanborn Fire Insurance Maps would help reveal more information about the family and the photo.

## Research an Enumerator
### Case Study: G.W. Hackenberger, Assistant Marshal, 1870 Lancaster County, Pennsylvania

*Contributed by Birdie Monk Holsclaw, FUGA, Longmont, Colorado*

George W. Hackenberger was the assistant census marshal in Lancaster County, Pennsylvania. His 1870 enumeration appears on National Archives micropublication M593, roll 1354 (Conoy Township, stamped pages 209–221) and roll 1359 (West Donegal Township, stamped pages 421–435).

To determine what employment or personnel records the federal government may have, *Preliminary Inventory of the Records of the Bureau of the Census, Inventory 161* (Washington, D.C.: National Archives and Records Service, 1964) was examined. This inventory, arranged by census year, lists the following items related to enumerators in 1870:

Entry 40    Record of Pay Certificates. 1870, 1 vol., 3 in.
Pay accounts of marshals, deputies, and assistants, apparently prepared in order to determine the amounts due them for taking the ninth census. Each entry gives the name of the marshal or assistant and the number of his subdivision; the number of inhabitants, farms, dwellings, and business establishments enumerated by him; the number of miles he traveled in making the enumeration; his rate of compensation; and the total amount due him. Arranged alphabetically by state, thereunder by marshal's district, and thereunder by name of marshal or assistant.

Entry 41    Record of Final Payments. 1871–72, 1 vol., 2 in.
A record book showing the final payments made to marshals and assistants for their services in taking the ninth census. The record shows the number of the subdivision for which each marshal or assistant was responsible, the name of the marshal or assistant, his post office, the amount of compensation due him, the date when the Census Office received the voucher, the date of payment, and in some cases, remarks concerning the payment. The entries are arranged alphabetically by state, thereunder by marshal's district, and thereunder

Entry 42      alphabetically by name of marshal or assistant.

Entry 42      Descriptions of Enumeration Subdivisions. 1870, 1 vol., 3 in. The description for each subdivision gives its number; the name of the county or parish in which it was situated; the civil divisions composing it; an industrial description of the subdivision, such as "commercial" or "agricultural"; the number of square miles in the subdivision; and the name and address of the marshal, deputy, or assistant marshal. The descriptions are arranged alphabetically by state and thereunder by marshal's district.

A letter to the National Archives and Records Administration cited the entry numbers and requested photocopies of the pages pertaining to George W. Hackenberger. The National Archives sent the "Order for Reproduction Services" form to be completed and returned with the appropriate fee. Four pages of pay records that included the following details about George's employment as an assistant marshal were received:

Area: 28 square miles

Schedule 1 (population; $0.02 per name): 3,120 names; 622 dwellings

Schedule 2 (mortality; $0.02 per name): 48 names

Schedule 3 (agriculture; $0.10 per farm): 239 farms

Schedule 4 (industry; $0.15 per establishment): 39 establishments

Schedule 5 (social statistics; 2 percent of Schedule 1): [blank]

Payment: George was paid $183.46, which is worth about $2,400 in today's dollars.

## SUMMARY OF CENSUS RESEARCH STRATEGIES

**Tip**

- Begin with the most current census year available relevant to your subject and work backward in time.
- Locate all direct *and* collateral ancestors in every possible census record.
- Use maps throughout your census research, paying attention to boundary changes.
- Consult all available indexes, but do not rely solely upon them.
- Pay attention to neighbors—they may have been related or later married into the family.
- Compare census research results to find inaccurate or conflicting data.
- Use population and non-population schedules concurrently.
- Correlate results with other types of records to reach sound genealogical conclusions.
- Cite your sources.
- Slow down.
- Enjoy your successes.

# TEN

# Research Special Populations

**Important**

B lacks, Indians, Catholic sisters and brothers, and military personnel are more difficult to locate in census records than other individuals. The policies of how these special populations were to be counted or recorded varied by census year; therefore, it is important to understand census procedures specific to each of these groups.

## AMERICAN INDIANS (NATIVE AMERICANS)

**Prior to 1870 the enumerators were instructed to include only Indians who were taxed, meaning those who did *not* live on reservations.** This includes the few who may have severed their tribal affiliations or mingled with the white population—marrying into white families or residing in huts or tepees on the outskirts of towns or settlements.

The Indians who lived on government reservations were considered "Indians not taxed" and consequently not counted in the censuses. Thousands of Indians roamed the frontier and were not named in census records. Indians residing in Indian Territory (Oklahoma) in 1860 may be included in the 1860 Arkansas census titled Persons on Indian Lands West of Arkansas, although the census primarily counted whites living on Indian lands.

Some Indians were included in the early census reports, but it is difficult to accurately identify them until the 1870 census, when Indian was finally added as a race category. Prior to 1870, the choices were white, black, or mulatto, although enumerators sometimes added "I" or "In" for Indians. It is likely that some Indians were included in one of the three defined race categories.

Indians are sometimes referred to in general terms within the reports of the enumerators. For example, William F. Wheeler, assistant census marshal, 1870 Big Horn County, Montana Territory, pg. 16, named fourteen white male employees of the Crow Agency and then added the following note concerning the Crow and Sioux Indians:

In my trip down the Missouri River in April last and at Ft. Buford, I saw several men who had spent the winter among the Crow Indians, hunting buffalo for robes and they informed me that there were no white men except occasional hunters who lived with the Indians and a few near the Crow Agency anywhere on the Yellow Stone or it's [sic] tributaries. It was supposed there were quite a large number of white men—about 400—in the southern part of the county, who started to explore the Big Horn and other streams for gold, from Cheyenne on the U.P.R.R. [Union Pacific Railroad] in May or June last; and it was feared they had been destroyed by Sioux Indians. Except with the Crows, it is not safe for white men anywhere in the county. All with whom I conversed agree in representing the Valley of the Yellow Stone and it's [sic] tributaries as the most fertile imaginable. The grass grows to the height of four and six feet and like all the grass in Montana, cures in the stalk before frost comes and retains its nutriment all winter so that all game and domestic cattle [can feed] in the winter as well as in the summer. Coal abounds the whole length of the Yellow Stone.

## Indians in 1880

National Archives micropublication M1791 (five rolls), *Schedules of a Special Census of Indians* is a special 1880 enumeration of all Indians not taxed. This census is an enumeration of Indians living near military reservations in Washington Territory (Yakima Agency; Tulalip Agency; Fort Simcoe; Fort Madison; Swinomosh, Muckleshoot, and Lummi Reservations), Dakota Territory (Standing Rock Agency), and California (Round Valley Agency).

Information in the *Special Census of Indians* includes
- name of tribe, reservation, agency, and post office
- number living in household and description of the dwelling
- Indian name
- translation of Indian name
- relationship of each person to head of family
- marital and tribal status
- personal description
- occupation
- health
- education
- personal property
- landownership
- sources of subsistence

Other Indians might appear in the regular population schedules in the localities where they resided, although their race may not always have been recorded as Indian. A federal census was not taken in 1880 Indian Territory (now Oklahoma).

## Indians in 1900 and 1910

The most complete and valuable census records pertaining to American Indians are the 1900 and 1910 censuses because they included "special inquiries relating to Indians." Indians answered the same questions as the general population, plus

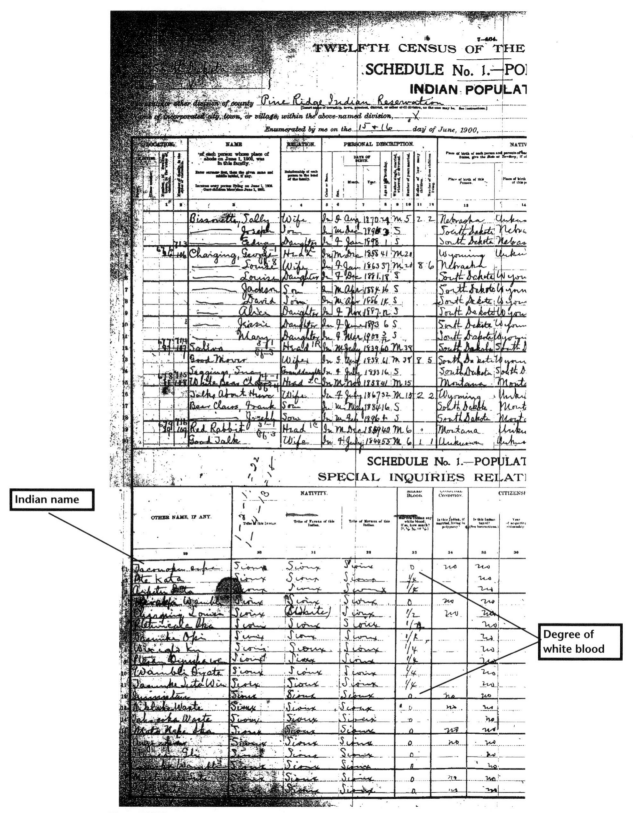

**Figure 10-1**
1900 U.S. census, Pine Ridge Indian Reservation, [county not stated], South Dakota Indian population schedule, supervisor's district [S.D.] 1, enumeration district [E.D.] 46, sheet 73A (stamped); National Archives micropublication T623, roll 1556.

8008 (68)

IE UNITED STATES.

POPULATION.

LATION.

73 - A

| Supervisor's District No. | 1 | Sheet No. |
| Enumeration District No. | 46ᵉ | 10-7 |

Name of Institution, ............ X

Ward of city, ......... X

W. B. Dew ......., Enumerator.

| NATIVITY. | | CITIZENSHIP. | OCCUPATION, TRADE, OR PROFESSION | EDUCATION. | OWNERSHIP OF HOME. | |
|---|---|---|---|---|---|---|
| Place of birth of Father of this person. | Place of birth of Mother of this person. | Year of immigration to the United States. / Number of years in the United States. / Naturalization. | OCCUPATION of each person TEN YEARS of age and over. (See instructions below.) | Months not employed. / Attended school (in months). / Can read. / Can write. / Can speak English. | Owned or rented. / Owned free or mortgaged. / Farm or home. | |
| 14 | 15 | 16 17 18 | 19 | 20 21 22 23 24 | 25 26 27 | |
| known | Unknown | | Ration Indian | yes yes yes | | |
| ebraska | Nebraska | | Old Age - R | | | |
| raska | Nebraska | | Under Age - R | | | |
| known | Unknown | | Ration Indian | no no no | O F H | 4 |
| | | | Ration Indian | no no no | | 5 |
| young | Nebraska | | Ration Indian | 1 yes yes yes | | 6 |
| young | Nebraska | | Ration Indian | 6 yes yes yes | | 7 |
| young | Nebraska | | Ration Indian | 6 yes yes yes | | 8 |
| young | Nebraska | | Ration Indian | 10 yes yes yes | | 9 |
| young | Nebraska | | Old Age - R | 3 | | 10 |
| young | Nebraska | | Under Age - R | | | 11 |
| h Dakota | South Dakota | | Ration Indian | no no no | O F H | 12 |
| young | Wyoming | | Ration Indian | no no no | | 13 |
| th Dakota | South Dakota | | Ration Indian | 10 yes yes yes | | 14 |
| ontana | Montana | | Ration Indian | no no no | O F H | 15 |
| nknown | Unknown | | Ration Indian | no no no | | 16 |
| ontana | Wyoming | | Ration Indian | 10 yes yes yes | | 17 |
| ntana | Wyoming | | Under Age - R | | | 18 |
| nknown | Unknown | | Ration Indian | no no no | O F H | 19 |
| known | Unknown | | Ration Indian | no no no | | 20 |

"Ration Indian" means the person was wholly dependent on the government for support.

LATION—Continued.

ATING TO INDIANS.

| IZENSHIP | | DWELLINGS | INSTRUCTIONS FOR FILLING THIS SCHEDULE. |
|---|---|---|---|
| Year of acquiring citizenship. / War citizenship acquired by allotment. | | Is the Indian living in a fixed or in a movable dwelling? | |
| 36 | 37 | 38 | |

This modified form of Schedule No. 1 is to be used in making the enumeration of Indians, both those on reservations and those living in family groups outside of reservations.

Detached Indians living either in white or negro families outside of reservations should be enumerated on the general population schedule (Form 7-224) as members of the families in which they are found; but detached whites or negroes living in Indian families should be enumerated on this schedule as members of the Indian families in which they are found. In other words, every family composed mainly of Indians should be reported *entirely* on this schedule, and every family composed mainly of persons not Indian should be reported *entirely* on the general population schedule.

This schedule contains on each side twenty horizontal lines, each running twice across the page, and it is consequently possible to enumerate on it only forty persons (twenty persons on the A side and twenty persons on the B side). Each Indian should be carried through from the beginning to the end of the line on which he is entered, as line 1, line 2, etc., and each inquiry from column 1 to column 38 which applies to the individual case should be answered.

COLUMNS 1 TO 28.—These columns are identical with those on the general population schedule. Fill each column, so far as the inquiry applies, in accordance with the instructions for filling the corresponding columns in the general population schedule, but note the following additional instructions in relation to filling columns 1, 2, and 19:

COLUMNS 1 AND 2.—If you are canvassing a given territory with both the general population schedule (Form 7-224) and this schedule for Indian population, make two independent series of numbers for these columns, one series in each kind of schedule, so that the last numbers on the two schedules when added together will correctly give the whole number of dwellings and of families visited and enumerated in your entire district.

COLUMN 19.—If the Indian has no occupation and is wholly dependent on the Government for support, write "Ration Indian." If he is partly self-supporting and partly dependent upon the Government, write the occupation and then the letter "R" (for ration). If the Indian is under ten years of age and receives rations, write "Under age—R."

INSTRUCTIONS CONTINUED ON "B" SIDE OF SHEET.

Dwellings column (handwritten): Fixed, Fixed, Fixed, Fixed, Fixed, Fixed, Fixed, Fixed, Fixed, Fixed, Fixed, Fixed, Fixed, Fixed, Fixed, Fixed, Fixed, Fixed, Fixed, Fixed

- Indian name, if the person had one.
- Tribe of the Indian.
- Tribe of the father of the Indian.
- Tribe of the mother of the Indian.
- Degree of white blood. (In 1910 this was revised to report degree of Indian, white, or Negro blood.)
- If married, whether living in polygamy. (In 1910 an additional question of number of times married was added as was, if living in polygamy, whether the wives were sisters.)
- Graduate of what educational institution (1910 question).
- Whether Indian was "taxed." An Indian was considered taxed if he was detached from the tribe and living among white people as an individual or if living with the tribe but having received an allotment of land and thereby having acquired citizenship. An Indian was considered not taxed if he was living on a reservation without an allotment, or roaming over unsettled territory.
- Whether living in a fixed or moveable dwelling.

The Indian schedules are interspersed with the general population census, although sometimes they appear at the end of an enumeration district or county or at the end of the state. The NARA *1900 Federal Population Census Catalog* lists the following specific locations of Indian schedules in micropublication T623. The 1910 catalog does not identify the location of the Indian schedules.

| | |
|---|---|
| Arizona (roll 48) | Colorado River, Navajo, Fort Apache, Hualpai, and Supai Indian Reservations |
| Idaho (roll 234) | Nez Perce Reservation |
| Minnesota (roll 798) | White Earth Indian Reservation |
| Montana (roll 910) | Fort Belknap, Fort Keogh, and Tongue River Indian Reservations |
| North Dakota (roll 1234) | Standing Rock Indian Reservation |
| Oklahoma (roll 1344) | Oklahoma Territory Indian Reservation |
| Oregon (roll 1353) | Indian population schedules |
| Rhode Island (roll 1513) | Indian population schedules |
| South Carolina (roll 1545) | Indian population schedules |
| South Dakota (roll 1556) | Pine Ridge and Rosebud Indian Reservations; Indian population schedules |
| Washington (roll 1754) | Indian population schedules |

## Five Civilized Nations
### Cherokee, Chickasaw, Choctaw, Creek, and Seminole
The 1900 Indian population of the Five Civilized Nations is recorded in a separate National Archives publication (T623, rolls 1843–1854) and Soundex (T1082, rolls 1–42).

## Indians in 1920

Indians are reported in the 1920 regular population schedule. To locate reservations (not individuals), use the 1920 Soundex for institutions, found on the last roll for each state. Individuals are named in the population Soundex. *No* special Indian schedule was created in 1920.

## Indians in 1930

The Census Bureau instructed enumerators to report the degree of Indian blood of American Indians and the names of their tribes. Since there was not a place on the form for this information, they were instructed to use the columns intended for the birthplaces of the father and mother.

A person of mixed white and Indian blood was to be reported as an Indian except when the percentage of Indian blood was very small or when she was regarded as white in the community.

As stated earlier, someone who was part Indian and part Negro was to be reported as Negro unless the Indian blood predominated and the person was generally accepted as an Indian in the community.

## Indian Census Rolls for 1885 Through 1940

Beginning in 1884, Congress required Indian agencies to take an annual census of Indian reservations. These tribal censuses are unrelated to the decennial census schedules and are stored in National Archives RG 74, Bureau of Indian Affairs, micropublication M595 (692 rolls). The data normally includes

- Indian and/or English name
- age or date of birth
- sex
- relationship to head of household

Beginning in 1930, additional data was included:
- degree of Indian blood
- marital status

The tribal census collection is not complete. It neither includes every reservation nor every year. Several tribes were exempt, including the Five Civilized Tribes. New York did not participate in these annual census returns because it had state reservations rather than federal. The only Indians named in these records are those who maintained a formal affiliation with a tribe under federal supervision.

To use these censuses, you must know the tribe and agency because the rolls are arranged alphabetically by the name of the Indian agency and the name of the tribe and then numerically by year. **A list of 205 tribes and their affiliations is included in NARA's** *American Indians: A Select Catalog of National Archives Microfilm Publications.*

The Family History Library holds many of these records. For more information, see chapter eleven, "Records of the Native Americans" in *Guide to Genealogical Research in the National Archives of the United States*, third edition,

**Notes**

**CENSUS TRIVIA**

The 1790 population was estimated to be about 64 percent white, 16 percent Indian, 11 percent black, and 4 percent Polynesian. Of the whites, nearly half were of English heritage.

**Sources**

2001; and Chapter 14, "Tracking Native American Family History" by Curt B. Witcher and George J. Nixon in *The Source: A Guidebook of American Genealogy*, Revised Edition, 1997.

## Find Indians in Census Indexes

Census entries for Indians often do not include surnames—not because the enumerator failed to record them, but because Indians usually did not have surnames. Each tribal nation had its own ideas about names and naming procedures, and many Indians did not keep the same name over a lifetime. Only with strong European influence did they begin to use "English" names which may or may not have been translations of their tribal names.

**Research Tip**

**This is why some indexes include the surname Indian, even when two names were reported on the census.** For example, the 1870 Wisconsin index (Bountiful, Utah: Heritage Quest, 2000) lists on page 27, Waupaca County, six heads of household with the surname Indian. Use the chart below to compare these index entries with the census page; you can see that each head of household had one name and the indexer used Indian for the surname. This is not true for all Indian census entries, but it is an important point to remember when studying indexes.

In 1880, the Soundex cards that did not have a surname, i.e., "Not Reported," were grouped together and filed after the last card having a Soundex code beginning with Z. In the case of California (T737, roll 34), the majority

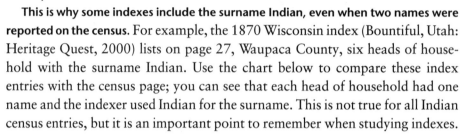

| 1870 WISCONSIN INDEX | | | 1870 WAUPACA COUNTY, WISCONSIN CENSUS PAGE 27 | | |
|---|---|---|---|---|---|
| INDIAN | | | 6/6 | Chapuadock | 60/M/I |
| Chapuadock | Waupaca County | 27 | | ——— Squaw | 60/F/I |
| John | Waupaca County | 27 | | ——— Keekipa | 20/F/I |
| Oncoat | Waupaca County | 27 | | ——— Mitchone | 18/F/I |
| Sougnaw | Waupaca County | 27 | | ——— Chame | 14/M/I |
| Tekon | Waupaca County | 27 | | ——— Joseph | 10/M/I |
| Waupaca | Waupaca County | 27 | | ——— John | 2/M/I |
| | | | 7/7 | Sougnaw | 26/M/I |
| | | | | ——— Squaw | 26/F/I |
| | | | | ——— Susana | 6/F/I |
| | | | 8/8 | Tekon | 40/M/I |
| | | | | ——— Susana | 38/F/I |
| | | | | ——— John | 16/M/I |
| | | | | ——— Joshua | 14/M/I |
| | | | | ——— Milo | 14/M/I |
| | | | | ——— Waupatosh | 8/M/I |
| | | | | ——— James | 4/M/I |
| | | | | ——— Frank | 4/M/I |
| | | | | ——— Bill | 2/M/I |
| | | | 9/9 | John | 28/M/I |
| | | | | ——— Wichcom | 30/F/I |
| | | | 10/10 | Oncoat | 50/M/I |
| | | | | ——— Waupaca | 80/F/I |

Note: The index identifies Waupaca as head of her household, but she was not. Oncoat, thirty years her junior, was the actual head of household according to the original ennumeration.

of the "Not Reported" cards were for Indians. They were filed alphabetically by first names such as

(N.R.) Baby
(N.R.) Boy
(N.R.) Child
(N.R.) Girl
(N.R.) Infant
(N.R.) Male

Some Soundex cards in this same collection have the surname Indians and are arranged alphabetically by given name:

Indians
    (N.R.) Abby
    (N.R.) Abe
    (N.R.) Ableta
    (N.R.) Adam
    (N.R.) Addie
    (N.R.) Adolphus
    (N.R.) Agners

The lesson with this wide range of methods of indexing Indians: If you know the geographical area where your Indian family resided, read the census schedules slowly and page by page. If you use indexes or the Soundex, search for the surname Indian, search for given names listed as surnames, and search for no surnames, which are filed at the beginning of the alphabet.

## Example of Indian Enumeration: Unnamed Tribe in California

The unnamed Indian tribe in 1880 Plumas County, California (Plumas Township, E.D. 81, pages 23 and 24 [handwritten]; National Archives micropublication T9, roll 70), is a good example of how difficult it is to locate Indians in the census. The tribe of eighty-seven persons lists the twenty-four adult males between the ages eighteen and seventy first, followed by sixty-three women and their minor children. Some of the men have full names such as Jim Chandler or Aleck Dixon, but others are simply named Bill, Jake, Mike, Joe, etc.

The females are usually identified only by first names such as Mary. The children are *not* named; they are identified only as, for example, Mary's son or Mary's daughter and by race, age, and sex. It is therefore difficult to determine at the beginning of the enumeration which female is married to which male.

The enumerator also added the following comments in the occupation column:

> Near the list of twenty-four adult males: "Indian bucks occupied in hunting, fishing, and working occasionally on the ranches."

> Near the list of women on page 23: "Indian Squaws and their children."

> Near the list of women on page 24: "Indian Squaws and their families."

# SLAVES, BLACKS, AND COLORED PERSONS

There are many misconceptions and incorrect assumptions about slaves, blacks, and colored persons in census records:

- Slaves were not always black or mulatto; some were Indian, Chinese, and other races.
- Free blacks or people of color sometimes had Indian or black slaves.
- Some Indians owned African slaves.
- A colored person is not necessarily a person of African descent. For example, the *New York Herald*, 25 January 1861, reported the following birthplaces of colored persons in the 1860 New York City census:

| | |
|---|---|
| Africa | Haiti |
| at sea | Ireland |
| Austria | Madagascar |
| Barbados | Mexico |
| Bermuda | New Brunswick |
| Brazil | Nova Scotia |
| Canada | Port-au-Prince, Haiti |
| Cuba | Portugal |
| Denmark | St. Domingo (Haiti) |
| East Indies | Scotland |
| England | South America |
| France | Spain |
| Germany | West Indies |

## Slaves and Blacks Before 1870

Prior to the Civil War and abolition of slavery, black persons were recorded as

1. free (free blacks, free colored, or other free persons), or
2. slave

## Free Blacks

A free black was an individual whose ancestors had never been slaves, such as descendants of indentured servants; one born to a free parent(s); one who had been manumitted; one who had bought his own freedom; or one who was a successful runaway. According to David T. Thackery, author of "Tracking African American Family History" in *The Source: A Guidebook of American Genealogy,* revised edition, at least one out of ten African Americans was already free when the Civil War began.

Free blacks who were heads of household were individually identified in census records from 1790 through 1840. Those who were not heads of household were counted in the category of "other free persons" in 1790 through 1810 and "free colored" in 1820 through 1840.

In 1850 and 1860, the names of all free household members were listed—including free blacks, who were identified as either black or mulatto.

Free blacks struggled economically, as evidenced in the description of a large free black community in the 1860 Prince Edward County, Virginia, census

## BLACK RESEARCH AIDS

Burroughs, Tony. *Black Roots: A Beginner's Guide to Tracing the African American Family Tree*. New York: Fireside Book/Simon & Schuster, 2001.

Carmack, Sharon DeBartolo. *A Genealogist's Guide to Discovering Your Immigrant & Ethnic Ancestors*. Cincinnati: Betterway Books, 2000.

National Archives Trust Fund Board. *Black Studies: A Select Catalog of National Archives Microfilm Publications*. Washington: NATFB, 1996.

Newman, Debra. *List of Free Black Heads of Families in the First Census of the United States, 1790*. Washington, D.C.: National Archives and Records Service, 1973.

Streets, David H. *Slave Genealogy: A Research Guide With Case Studies*. Bowie, Md.: Heritage Books, 1986.

Witcher, Curt Bryan. *African American Genealogy: A Bibliography and Guide to Sources*. Fort Wayne, Ind.: Round Tower Books, 2000.

Woodtor, Dee Parmer. *Finding a Place Called Home: A Guide to African-American Genealogy and Historical Identity*. Rev. ed. New York: Random House, 1999.

population schedule, Farmville, page 963; National Archives micropublication M653, roll 1371:

> The real estate consists of 350 acres of land subdivided amongst them. The personal property of most of the negroes is so small as not to require statement of amount. This settlement of Free Negroes is quite an interesting one, as an experiment made under most favorable circumstances by their owners and it would appear to demonstrate that the "free negroe" [*sic*] is only minimally in a free white community and that under the most favorable circumstances there will be degeneracy and degradation. The old negroes informed me that the number liberated in 1811 was upwards of 100 with about an equal division of the sexes. The number now, all told on Israel Hill and in Farmville and elsewhere does not exceed 150. T.B. McRoberts, Assistant Marshal (1860).

According to Herbert Clarence Bradshaw's *History of Prince Edward County, Virginia* (Richmond: Dietz Press, 1955), 278–279, Richard Randolph of Bizarre (Cumberland County) freed his slaves by his will, which was probated in 1797. The freed Negroes were given land known as Israel Hill in Prince Edward County. The 1860 census entry quoted above describes this group of free blacks. Bradshaw further explains that free Negroes were required to register at the county clerk's office every three years, and they had to have a certificate of registration to obtain employment. Prince Edward County records document the members of this community.

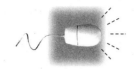

**Internet Source**

**AFRICAN-AMERICAN CENSUS SCHEDULES ONLINE**

AfriGeneas at <www.afrigeneas.com/aacensus/> posts transcriptions and indexes to African Americans in census records. Remember to follow up the transcription with a photocopy of the original census page—the transcriber may have misread the handwriting, and the neighbors shown on the page may have been relatives of your target individual.

You can also download and print blank 1860 slave and mortality schedules from this Web site.

## Slaves

Slaves were reported statistically with their slave owners from 1790 through 1840 and in the slave schedules in 1850 and 1860 (see chapter four for examples and further discussion). Slaves were enumerated as follows:

### 1790 through 1810

- Total number of slaves—no division by sex or age—per slave owner was reported.

### 1820

- Males and females were reported separately and by age:
    under 14
    of 14 and under 26
    of 26 and under 45
    of 45 and upwards

### 1830 and 1840

- Males and females were reported separately and by age:
    under 10
    of 10 and under 24
    of 24 and under 36
    of 36 and under 55
    of 55 and under 100
    of 100 and upwards
- In 1840, the total number of deaf and dumb slaves and free blacks was reported in three age ranges: under 14, of 14 and under 25, and of 25 and upwards.

### 1850 and 1860 slave schedules

- See Figure 3-9 in chapter three for an example of an 1850 slave schedule. Each slave was reported separately under the name of the slave owner. A line on the census form was dedicated to each slave, but the slaves were not named. The slaves were usually listed in chronological order, not necessarily by family grouping. Information for each slave included
- age
- sex
- color
- whether slave was a fugitive
- whether slave was deaf, dumb, insane, or idiotic
- total number of slaves manumitted (granted freedom)
- number of slave houses owned

If a slave died between 1 June 1849 and 31 May 1850 or between 1 June 1859 and 31 May 1860, he may have been reported by name in the respective mortality schedule (see chapter four).

## Blacks After 1870

**The first post–Civil War census, taken in 1870, is important in black research because for the first time former slaves were identified by full name.** Be aware, however, that the race was not always reported consistently or correctly in census records. White persons have been recorded as black and vice versa. Indians and people of other races were sometimes classified as black. To confuse matters even more, the term *mulatto* had many meanings according to instructions to the enumerators:

| | |
|---|---|
| 1880 | Quadroons, octoroons, and all persons having any perceptible trace of African blood were to be reported as mulatto. |
| 1890 | Black persons were to be reported as black, mulatto (one-half Negro blood), quadroon (one-quarter Negro blood), or octoroon (one-eighth Negro blood). |
| 1900 | A Negro or anyone of Negro descent was to be reported as black. |
| 1910 and 1920 | A person of mixed blood, with any trace of Negro, was to be reported as mulatto. |
| 1930 | Any mixture of white and nonwhite was to be reported according to the nonwhite parent. A person of mixed white and Negro blood was considered Negro, no matter how small the percentage of Negro blood. Mixtures of colored races were to be reported according to the race of the father, except Negro-Indians. A person who was part Indian and part Negro was also to be listed as Negro unless the Indian blood predominated and the person was generally accepted as an Indian in the community. |

## CATHOLIC SISTERS (NUNS) AND BROTHERS (MONKS)

Researching sisters (nuns) and brothers (monks) of the Catholic church can be difficult because they often discontinue use of their birth name and assume a new spiritual name. Sisters and brothers are sometimes indexed (in both print and Soundex) with a surname of Sister or Brother.

The 1920 Illinois Soundex cards coded S-236 (for the "surname" of Sister) were filed at the end of the code without alphabetizing the given names, as the first twelve S-236 cards show:

| | | |
|---|---|---|
| (Sister) M. Bernarda | Cook County | Angel Guardian Orphanage |
| (Sister) M. Teresilla | Cook County | Angel Guardian Orphanage |
| (Sister) Emerentia | Kankakee County | Emergency Hospital Assist |
| (Sister) M. Chilipine | Will County | Teacher—School |
| St. Theresa (Sister) | Kankakee County | Emergency Hospital Assist |
| (Sister) Nicola Mary | Cook County | Not reported |

| REPORTED RACE IN CENSUS SCHEDULES | | | | | | | | | |
|---|---|---|---|---|---|---|---|---|---|
| 1790–1810 | white | other free | slaves | | | | | | |
| 1820 | white | slaves | free colored | all other except Indians not taxed | | | | | |
| 1830 and 1840 | white | slaves | free colored | | | | | | |
| 1850 and 1860 | free white | free black or free mulatto | slaves (indicate if black or mulatto) | | | | | | |
| 1870 and 1880 | white | black | mulatto | Indian | Chinese | | | | |
| 1890 | white | black | mulatto, quadroon, octoroon | Indian | Chinese | Japanese | | | |
| 1900 | white | black | | Indian | Chinese | Japanese | | | |
| 1910 | white | black | mulatto | Indian | Chinese | Japanese | other | | |
| 1920 | white | black | mulatto | Indian | Chinese | Japanese | other | Filipino | Hindu | Korean |
| 1930 | white | Negro | mulatto | Indian | Chinese | Japanese | other (write race in full) | Filipino | Hindu | Korean |

| (Sister) Theckla | Cook County | St. Francis Hospital |
| (Sister) Anne | Cook County | Convent and parochial residence |
| (Sister) Natalie | Cook County | Convent and parochial residence |
| (Sister) Lullus | Cook County | Convent and parochial residence |
| (Sister) M. Pulcharia | Cook County | Angel Guardian Orphanage |
| (Sister) Sebastiana | St. Clair County | St. Teresa Academy |

When a nun did report a surname in the census records, the Soundex card may not be where you would expect, i.e., alphabetically under Sister or a given name such as Mary or Anne. In this example, the Soundex cards for sisters with the surname Driscoll and other surnames with the Soundex code D-624 are filed at the beginning of the code:

1920 Soundex Code D-624, New York
National Archives Micropublication M1578, Roll 214
Driscoll, (N.R.) [This is a husband with wife and two children.]

Dorscoll (N.R.) Cholida (Sister)
Driscoll (N.R.) Euphrasa (Sister)
Driscoll (N.R.) (Sister) Veronica
Dorschel (N.R.) M. Rosalie (Nun)
Dorschlag, Abraham

The Soundex cards following Abraham Dorschlag are alphabetical by given name, as expected and as they should be.

Brothers (monks) are indexed in the same style as sisters (nuns); however, priests retain their surnames and are found as other individuals are.

## MILITARY AND NAVAL POPULATION

Genealogical records are full of exceptions and variables that prevent clear-cut rules or absolute statements about location and content. This is especially true for research of military persons in census records. For example, in 1880 the enumerators were instructed to report all soldiers of the U.S. Army, civilian employees, and other residents at posts or on military reservations in the district in which they normally reside. In other words, these people were supposed to have been reported in the census with their families, but you may not find them with their family on a military base—or in both places.

The published instructions for enumerations after 1880 do not state how military persons were to be reported. Generally speaking, they were counted with others at the military base or ship, but sometimes they were also reported at their home residence.

## VETERAN STATUS REPORTED IN THE CENSUS

Only the 1840, 1890, 1910, and 1930 censuses made distinct inquiries of veterans:

1840    The names and ages of Revolutionary or military pensioners or their widows were reported in the 1840 census. The names were recorded on the back of the original census page. (It is easy to ignore or miss this back page when viewing microfilm because it is often blank.) The results were published in *A Census of Pensioners for Revolutionary or Military Services, as Returned Under the Act for Taking the Sixth Census in 1840* (1841; reprint, Baltimore: Genealogical Publishing Co., 1954). This report is also reproduced in National Archives Microfilm Publication T498, 1790 census, roll 3, and in an Internet version at <www.usgennet.org/usa/topic/colonial/census/index.html>. Do not assume that the published index is 100 percent correct. For example, the pensioner in figure 3-6 (page 40) is not in the index.

1890    The 1890 population schedule asked whether a person was a Union or Confederate soldier, sailor, or marine during the Civil War or the widow of such a person. Most of these schedules were destroyed in

**Notes**

**CENSUS TRIVIA**

The 1840 census gives full names and exact ages of Revolutionary War pensioners, which included both veterans and veterans' widows.

**Research Tip**

**SERVING IN THE CIVIL WAR UNDER ASSUMED NAME**

Persons who enlisted and served in the Civil War under assumed names and afterward reassumed their legal names are listed in the 1890 Veterans Schedule under their real names followed by their aliases.

the 1921 fire (see chapter three).

The 1890 Special Union Veterans and Widows supplemental schedules gave the veteran's rank, company, regiment or vessel, dates of enlistment and discharge, length of service, post office address, and nature of any disability. Schedules survive for Washington, DC; about half of Kentucky; and all states alphabetically beginning with Louisiana. (See chapter four, page 100 for an example.)

1910    The 1910 census enumerators were instructed to ask all males over fifty years old who were born in the United States and all foreign-born males who immigrated to the United States before 1865 if they were survivors of the Union Army ("UA"), Union Navy ("UN"), Confederate Army ("CA"), or Confederate Navy ("CN").

1930    The 1930 census asked if a person was a veteran of the U.S. military or naval force and excluded persons who served only during peacetime. Persons who had served in a war or expedition were asked which one:

Civil War (Civ): 1863–1865
Spanish-American War (Sp): 1898
Philippine Insurrection (Phil): 1899–1902
Boxer Rebellion (Box): 1900
Mexican Expedition (Mex): 1916
World War (WW): 1917–1918

## ACTIVE-DUTY MILITARY AND NAVAL
### 1900 Census First to Count U.S. Population Abroad

The 1900 census was the first in which American citizens abroad, including armed forces personnel and civilian government employees, were counted. This population group is indexed in a separate Soundex titled "Military and Naval," National Archives micropublication T1081, rolls 1–32, with accompanying full census schedules in micropublication T623, rolls 1838–1842.

NARA catalog descriptions of the contents of the 1900 census rolls indicate that some military or naval enumerations are mixed with the state records:

Maine: Roll 603 includes Fort McClary and the Portsmouth Navy Yard and Marine Barracks.

North Dakota: Roll 1234 includes military and naval population schedules.

Oklahoma: Roll 1344 includes military and naval population schedules.

The 1900 military and naval population schedules are similar in content to the regular population schedules, but with additional data:

- Identifying information such as name of miliary station or naval vessel and name of company or troop, regiment, and branch of service.
- Rank, grade, or class of each individual.
- Residence in the United States, i.e., city, state, and street address including number.

**Notes**

**CENSUS TRIVIA**

The first time an area outside the continental states and territories (Alaska and Hawaii) was included in the federal census was 1900. This was also the first census to count American citizens abroad, including armed forces personnel and civilian government employees.

## Case Study: Sailor Counted Twice in 1900

The 1900 Military and Naval Soundex (National Archives micropublication T1081, roll 7) for Soundex Code D-100 had two entries for Benjamin Duff:

**Case Study**

Duff, Benjamin
born Aug 1878
21 yrs. old
born New York
Port of Gibraltar
U.S.S. *Buffalo*
Vol. 7, E.D. 9, sheet 2, line 34

Duff, Benjamin
born Aug 1878
22 yrs. old
born New York
Port of China
U.S.S. *Monocacy*
Vol. 7, E.D. 52, sheet 1, line 157

The two entries appear to be for the same person since both give an August 1878 birth date and a New York birthplace. (See page 218 in chapter eleven for a discussion on duplicate census entries.)

Follow-up research of the full census schedules confirmed that both entries were for the same person as both enumerations gave his home residence as Seventy-third Street, Brooklyn, New York. He was counted twice because he was on different ships in different ports when each crew was enumerated. Benjamin Duff was in the port of Gibraltar on 2 June 1900 and in the port of Tonghua, China, on 13 October 1900. This also explains why Benjamin was reported as twenty-one years old in one entry and twenty-two in the other—he had a birthday between those enumerations.

To determine if Benjamin Duff was also enumerated with his family at Seventy-third Street in Brooklyn, New York, the enumeration district or the names of his parents (head of household) would be needed. With either of those pieces of information, the census schedule or the Soundex could be researched.

Since Benjamin was born in August 1878, he would have been about one year old at the time of the 1880 census. By using the FamilySearch 1880 census index, the family was easily located in Brooklyn, New York, records. Benjamin Duff was the son of James and Ellen Duff and had three older brothers and two older sisters.

The 1900 Soundex listed James and Ellen Duff, thereby providing the identifiers to locate the full census schedule. Benjamin's parents are listed in the census in Brooklyn, Kings County, New York, enumeration district 553, sheet 13B. James and Ellen had resided on Seventy-third Street—the same address Benjamin reported in the military and naval census schedule. He was *not* named with his parents and siblings.

## 1910 Military and Naval

One roll of microfilm—roll number 1784, the last roll of the series—contains census schedules for military and naval personnel in the Philippines, in hospitals, aboard ships, and at stations. There is no separate Soundex or Miracode for these census reports.

## 1920 Overseas Military and Naval Forces

The military and naval population has a separate Soundex—M1600, rolls 1–18. The full schedules, T625, are in four volumes:

Volume 1: U.S. Military Forces, American Red Cross in Europe, Philippine Islands, European Forces in Germany, and Philippine Islands
Volume 2: U.S. Naval Forces
Volume 3: U.S. Naval Forces
Volume 4: U.S. Consular Service

There are also separate Soundexes for the Canal Zone (3 rolls), Puerto Rico (165 rolls), Guam (1 roll), American Samoa (2 rolls), and the Virgin Islands (3 rolls). The Canal Zone/Panama includes civilians in the Canal Zone in addition to the military and naval forces. The Virgin Islands Soundex includes St. Croix, St. John, St. Thomas, and the U.S.S. *Vixen*.

**Case Study**

## Case Study: Band Leader Enumerated in Germany and Minnesota in 1920

The 1920 overseas and military census of European forces in Germany listed the family of Wheeler W. Sidwell in Coblenz, Germany, Eighth Infantry Headquarters. Wheeler Sidwell was a thirty-five-year-old band leader, and residing with him were his wife, Edna, and their twelve- and thirteen-year-old daughters. His home residence was reported as 2509 Minnesota Avenue, Duluth, Minnesota.

Wheeler W. Sidwell and his wife and children were located in the 1920 Duluth, St. Louis County, Minnesota, census with his father-in-law, Arthur L. Nutting, at the same address—2509 Minnesota Avenue. No occupation was given for Wheeler, nor were any clues or indications that Wheeler was in Germany with his wife and children.

This example confirms the need for careful and thorough genealogical research. It would be easy to miss the military enumeration without oral history or clues from other records that suggested military service. Records speak to us, but not always in complete sentences.

## 1930 Population Schedule

There are two separate rolls of microfilm for the Consular Service—rolls 2630 and 2638. There is no Soundex for these records. Since very few 1930 census records have been indexed (see chapter seven), it is necessary to study enumeration district descriptions to locate military and naval bases within the general population schedules.

The census is a record that you will use throughout your research on these special populations. For further instructions and resources on researching Indians, blacks, Catholic sisters and brothers, and military and naval personnel, see the bibliography on page 263. Nonfederal census records can also help in this type of research. See chapter twelve for details.

# ELEVEN

# Census Anomalies

W *ebster's Tenth New Collegiate Dictionary* defines *anomaly* as a "deviation from the common rule; irregularity"; or "something different, abnormal, peculiar, or not easily classified." Ask an experienced genealogist if she has ever found anything odd or unusual in the census, and invariably the answer will be an enthusiastic yes.

Census research can be like a treasure hunt without a map. Census anomalies are hidden clues and gems just waiting for discovery. The treasures can be extra data or comments added by a conscientious enumerator. An enumerator's failure to follow instructions can end up helping your research rather than hindering it. This chapter highlights just a few anomalies—your research will uncover more.

## EXACT PLACE OF BIRTH

Beginning in 1850, census enumerators were instructed to record the state or country of birth of each individual. Occasionally, the enumerator went beyond the government's instructions and recorded a more precise birthplace. If you have any hint of a relative residing in the areas in the following chart, be sure to examine the census. It may contain the clue you need to extend your family tree. See the chart on page 212.

## ENUMERATOR COMMENTS

Sometimes a census enumerator added comments about specific individuals within his district or general comments about his experience. These comments may not add genealogical data to your family tree, but they place census taking into historical context and give us a glimpse into the attitudes and experiences of the time period.

| CENSUS SCHEDULES SHOWING EXACT BIRTHPLACE | | | |
|---|---|---|---|
| **State** | **Year** | **County** | **Town, District, Township** |
| Connecticut | 1850 | Windham | Brooklyn, Canterbury, Killingly, Plainfield, Sterling, Thompson |
| Georgia | 1850 | Baker | Eleventh District only |
| | 1850 | Jefferson | District 48 |
| | 1850 | Muscogee | All but Columbus |
| | 1850 | Tattnall | Entire county (intrastate only) |
| | 1850 | Telfair | Entire county (intrastate only) |
| Illinois | 1850 | Edgar | District 19; Grandview and Embarrass precincts |
| Indiana | 1860 | Allen | Wayne Township |
| | 1860 | Cass | Clinton, Deer Creek, Jackson, Miami, and Washington Townships, and part of Eil Township |
| Kentucky | 1850 | Caldwell | District 1, pages 279–340 (mostly intrastate) |
| | 1850 | Green | District 1 |
| | 1860 | Breathitt | Entire county (mostly intrastate, with some Virginia data cited) |
| | 1860 | Clay | Entire county |
| Maryland | 1850 | Frederick | Fifth & tenth election districts and Emmitsburg (intermittent data; mostly intrastate) |
| | 1850 | St. Mary's | All five election districts (intrastate data only) |
| Massachusetts | 1850 | Plymouth | Rochester and Wareham (lists Mass. cities and some out-of-state towns) |
| Missouri | 1860 | St. Louis | Ward 2 |
| New Jersey | 1860 | Bergen | Harrington and New Barbadoes Townships |
| New York | 1850 | Cortland | Part of Cortlandville |
| | 1860 | Allegany | Genessee (first eight pages include town and county names for all states and foreign countries) |
| | 1880 | Albany | Albany, Sixteenth Ward |
| North Carolina | 1850 | Caswell | Entire county (intrastate data only) |
| | 1850 | Catawba | Entire county |
| | 1850 | Guilford | Entire county |
| | 1850 | Orange | Part of First District |
| | 1850 | Warren | Part of Sandy Creek District |
| | 1850 | Wayne | South side of Neuse River |
| | 1860 | Cherokee | Entire county |
| Ohio | 1860 | Cuyahoga | Bedford, Brecksville, Parma, and Royalton Townships |
| Pennsylvania | 1850 | Fayette | Jefferson, Luzerne, Redstone, and Washington Townships; Bridgeport and Brownsville boroughs |
| | 1850 | Mercer | East and West Lackawannock, Findley, Hickory, Shenango, and Springfield Townships; also Sharon borough |
| | 1850 | Perry | Jackson, Madison, and Toboyne Townships; borough of New Germantown |
| South Carolina | 1850 | Charleston | St. John Berkley Parish |
| | 1850 | Fairfield | Entire county |
| | 1850 | Lexington | First page only |
| | 1850 | Marion | Entire county (intrastate data only) |
| | 1850 | York | Entire county |
| | 1860 | Pickens | Fifth Regiment |
| | 1860 | York | Entire county; intermittently |

| Texas | 1850 | Anderson | Entire county (intrastate data only) |
|---|---|---|---|
| | 1850 | Houston | Entire county (intrastate data only) |
| | 1850 | Van Zandt | Entire county (lists cities/towns/counties in other states and countries also) |
| Virginia | 1850 | Charlotte | Entire county |
| | 1850 | Powhatan | Entire county |
| | 1850 | Prince Edward | Entire county |
| | 1850 | Russell | Entire county |
| | 1860 | Calhoun | Entire county |
| | 1860 | Charlotte | Entire county |
| | 1860 | Culpeper | Northern and southern subdivisions (intrastate data only) |
| | 1860 | James City | Williamsburg |

Adapted and updated with permission from Alycon Trubey Pierce, CG, based on her articles "In Praise of Errors Made by Census Enumerators," *NGSQ* 81 (March 1993): 51–55, and "Update: More Praise for Census 'Errors,'" *NGSQ* 82 (September 1994): 216–220.

## Posting Census Book in Private Home

*Contributed by Patricia Law Hatcher, CG, FASG, Dallas, Texas*
From 1790 through 1820, the government required that the census be posted in a public place for local residents to examine for errors or exclusions (see chapter five). The "public place" was most often a tavern or store, but in this case, the census marshal declared his home the most public place.

1810 U.S. census, Oxford County, Maine, page 22; National Archives micro-publication M252, roll 12.

> I do hereby certify that Timothy Howe has posted up in my House (it being one of the most public places in the Eastern part of Oxford County) a Book purporting to be a true coppy [*sic*] of the schedule of the whol [*sic*] number of persons within the district aloted [*sic*] to Timothy Howe by the Marshall of the District of Main, [*sic*] signed with his name & their [*sic*] suffers it to remain. Livermore Nov 27th 1810 Barzillai White

## Unable to Personally Visit Family

1830 U.S. census, Wayne County, Michigan, page 31; National Archives micro-publication M19, roll 69.

> I Nathaniel Champ do solemnly affirm that the number of persons set forth in the return made by me, [illegible] to the provisions of the Act entitled, An Act to provide for taking the fifth Census of Enumeration of the Inhabitants of the United States, have been ascertained by an actual inquiry at Every dwelling house or a personal inquiry of the head of every family [illegible] conformity with the provisions of Said Act; And that I have, in every respect, fulfilled the duty required of me by Said Act to the best of my ability, and that the return aforesaid is correct and true according to the best of my knowledge and belief, Excepting the family of David Clark, who resides on an Iseland [*sic*] at the mouth of the Detroit River. On being informed there was no opportunity or chance of conveyance on the Iseland

[*sic*] to his house, I took the account of his family from his next neighbour [*sic*], who said he knew the family well, and could give them in as correct as I could get them from him or the family. Their number consists of five whites. See page 27, 7th line from top. Detroit. November 27th 1830. N. Champ.

### Apology for Inability to Report German Nativity

1870 U.S. census, Saratoga County, New York, Quaker Springs; National Archives micropublication M593, roll 1088. Letter from N.T. Howland at end of roll:

Quaker Springs, Aug. 25th, 1870

Dear Sir,

I send today my first set of returns. There are a few Germans on the list who have recently arrived in the Country and I could not ascertain from what part of Germany they came as they spoke English very imperfectly. So I was forced to enter them as natives of Germany without [ink smear]ing the state. In all other respects I believe my returns are correct. Hoping they will prove satisfactory. I remain yours respectfully, N.T. Howland, Sub. 314.

### Apology for Wet Census Pages

*Contributed by Marcia Yannizze Melnyk, Rowley, Massachusetts*
1880 U.S. census, Sumner County, Mississippi, population schedule, Fifth Supervisor's District, E.D. 180, blank page following page 17 (handwritten). The page after the blank page has handwritten number 21 crossed out and replaced with 18. Ancestry.com did not digitize this page. When trying to view this page, you will receive the message "Page cannot be displayed."

Pages 18th, 19th & 20th of this Schedule got wet by my horse falling with me in the creek and could not write upon said pages while wet and I continued the enumeration on page 21st. Robt. C. McDaniel, Enumerator

### Plea for Military Pension

*Contributed by Birdie Monk Holsclaw, FUGA, Longmont, Colorado*
Abier Fellows household, 1830 U.S. census, St. Joseph County, Michigan, Brady Township, page 180, line 4, National Archives micropublication M19, roll 69.

This man is sixty-five of age has nineteen Living Children two of which is under his care was a soldier in the Revolution is a man of Sober Habits of unusual enterprise and great strength of mind has never Received any thing from our government for his cares and Youthful Strugle [*sic*] for Independence. Is it to late to hope?!

### Gruesome Deaths

*Contributed by Roger D. Joslyn, CG, FASG, New Windsor, New York*
1870 U.S. census, Madison County, New York, mortality schedule, Nelson,

page 63. New York State Library microfilm (no film or roll number); viewed at New York Genealogical and Biographical Society Library, New York, New York.

> I find this a very healthy town. Face of the country very hilly. Not one death in a hundred Inhabitants (14 deaths to 1733). In case No. 2 William Taylor was killed by a lathe bolt. It caught the Buzz saw flew back struck him in the bowels, lived 10 hours. Case 318 [Joseph Button] was injured by being crushed by a canal boat, 15 years ago. Took nearly one ounce of Opium per day. Left it off and died in a short time in great agony.

## 1860 Occupation of "Wife"

*Contributed by Dawne Slater-Putt, CG, M.L.S., Wake Forest, North Carolina*
1860 U.S. census, Henry County, Illinois, population schedule, National Archives micropublication M653, roll 182.

Relationships to head of household were not reported until 1880; however, Ben Graham, enumerator of the 1860 Henry County, Illinois, census, listed "wife" in the occupation column for all wives in the county. For example, a head of household may have been reported with an occupation of farmer, and his wife was reported with the occupation of wife. Other relationships such as son or daughter were not reported.

## Twenty Children, Over Four Hundred Descendants

*Contributed by Dawne Slater-Putt, CG, M.L.S., Wake Forest, North Carolina*
John Summers household, 1820 U.S. census, Delaware County, Indiana, page 33, line 26; National Archives micropublication M33, roll 14.

> This man is 114 years old never lost sight or hearing has upward of four hundred descendants and has had two wives by each had ten children.

## Large Five-Year-Old Child

*Contributed by Gordon L. Remington, FASG, Salt Lake City, Utah*
1820 U.S. census, Delaware County, New York, Town of Tompkins, stamped page 90; National Archives micropublication M33, roll 54.
(See Figure 3-4, chapter three.)

> This boy was but 5 years old on the 26th day of last June and weighs more than one hundred pounds. I measured his height which was four feet & seven inches. He is a well made and healthy child. When but three years old he was able to carry one side of a two bushel basket filled with corn, potatoes or any kind of produce. He is about the size of Most boys of fourteen years of age. His parents are of the ordinary size.

## Small Fourteen-Year-Old Child

*Contributed by Dawne Slater-Putt, CG, M.L.S., Wake Forest, North Carolina*
Daniel Nestle household, 1860 U.S. census, Allen County, Indiana, Wayne Township, page 785; National Archives micropublication M653, roll 243.

Charles Nestle, age 14: Tom Thumb of Ft. Wayne. Weighs 23 pounds, 29 inches high and speaks German, French, and English; born in Ft. Wayne, Indiana.

### Recent Arrivals Looking for Work
*Contributed by James Jeffrey, Denver, Colorado*
1880 U.S. census, Arapahoe County, Colorado, population schedule, Denver, E.D. 5, page 47 (handwritten), page 120C (stamped); National Archives micropublication T9, roll 88.

The occupation column for about one-half of the census page is blank except for the enumerator's explanation, "Recent arrivals at Precinct. All looking for work." The twenty-one adult males were not born abroad, but in various states. This unusual census information would help prove the migration dates of these individuals or families. It appears they were all residing in a hotel or boarding house, although a facility name is not reported.

### Detailed and Humorous Occupation Descriptions
*Contributed by Marcia Yannizze Melnyk, Rowley, Massachusetts*
1870 U.S. census, Ellsworth County, Kansas, population schedule, Ellsworth, page 30 (stamped); National Archives micropublication M593, roll 434.

| Name | Age/Sex/Race | Occupation |
| --- | --- | --- |
| Carrie Wilburne | 28/F/B | Keeping house & washes |
| Phebe Taylor | 22/F/B | Cook & keeping house |
| Benj. L. Conley | 25/M/B | Farmer (hauling coal at mines) |
| Solomon Brown | 22/M/M | Laborer (without employment) |
| George Dobbs | 23/M/B | works about a Store |
| Joseph Anderson | 50/M/W | Keeps sleeping rooms |
| Thomas Anderson | 26/M/W | Keeping Restaurant on Train |
| John Metzler | 36/M/W | (Saddler) works on his farm |
| Libby Thompson | 18/F/W | "Diddles" |
| Harriet Parmenter | 23/F/W | Does Horizontal work |
| Ettie Baldwin | 23/F/W | "Squirms" in the dark |
| Lizzie Harris | 24/F/W | "Ogles" fools |

Did you guess that the last four females were prostitutes?

### "Sins With Marlin"
*Contributed by Julie Miller, Broomfield, Colorado*
William Marlin household, 1870 U.S. census, Webster County, Missouri, population schedule, Washington Township, page 29 (handwritten), page 362 (stamped), dwelling 209, family 211; National Archives micropublication M593, roll 826.

*The household of William Marlin:*
Marlin, William    44/M/W/Farmer/$2000/$500/Farmer/Tennessee

| Marlin, Isabelle | 41/F/W/Keeping House/Tennessee |
| Marlin, Mary A. | 18/F/W/At Home/Missouri |
| Marlin, James | 13/M/W/Works on Farm/Missouri |
| Pack, Elizabeth | 23/F/W/Sins with Marlin/Missouri |

## Prostitutes on the Frontier

*Contributed by Diane E. Greene, AG, Boulder City, Nevada*

The 1870 Virginia City, Storey County, Nevada census, pages 389–447, names 122 prostitutes born in Alabama, California, Maine, Maryland, Massachusetts, Missouri, New Hampshire, New York, Ohio, Virginia, Canada, China, France, Germany, Ireland, Italy, Mexico, Nova Scotia, and Santiago. Most of them are labeled "prostitute," although a few are called "harlot" or "hurdy-gurdy dancer." One is called a "prostitute of the worst order."

## Indians on the Frontier

*Contributed by Barbara L. Brown, Overland Park, Kansas*

The 1870 Wabaunsee County, Kansas, census (page 278B, Wabaunsee Township) names Indians with occupations of scalper, thief, beast of burden, and "murders white women in summer time; at government expense in winter."

## Reasons for Incarceration: Massachusetts

*Contributed by Marcia Yannizze Melnyk, Rowley, Massachusetts*

1860 U.S. census, Essex County, Massachusetts, population schedule, Ipswich town, pages 210–213 (handwritten), dwelling 1721 (House of Correction) and dwelling 1722 (Insane Asylum); National Archives micropublication M653, roll 499.

The prison (House of Correction) and insane asylum in Ipswich, Massachusetts were enumerated on the same day with information on one following the other on the census schedule. In fact, John C. Cross, dwelling 1719, was the superintendent for both institutions. The census taker listed eighty-nine prisoners (including eleven females) with their date of incarceration and reason for imprisonment. The crimes included polygamy, assault, disturbing the peace, nuisance, larceny, adultery (including one female offender), drunkenness, vagabond, perjury, common drunkard, burglary, and nightwalker (a black woman).

Immediately following this listing are twenty-three males and twelve females who were in the insane asylum. The enumerator again listed the year of incarceration and the cause of insanity. These included religious excess, self-pollution, intemperance, fall from horse, wound, jealousy, weight, and disappointment.

## Reasons for Incarceration: Iowa

*Contributed by Marsha Hoffman Rising, CG, CGL, FASG, Springfield, Missouri*

The Iowa State Penitentiary in Fort Madison, Lee County, Iowa (pages 605–609) lists 139 prisoners chronologically by date of sentencing. Column 14 (Deaf and Dumb) was used by the enumerator to report the reason for incarceration.

The earliest conviction was in 1854 and for rape. All the prisoners were males, age seventeen to sixty. Crimes included horse stealing, counterfeiting, forgery, rape, mayhem, robbing mail, arson, and murder.

### North Dakota Artist

*Contributed by Dawne Slater-Putt, CG, M.L.S., Wake Forest, North Carolina*
This drawing appears in the right-hand corner of a blank page (sheet 6B) of the 1910 Pierce County, North Dakota, census, E.D. 142, Village of Barton. The enumerator was Ole J. Ried.

**Figure 11-1**
Is this a self-portrait of the enumerator or a drawing of a local resident?

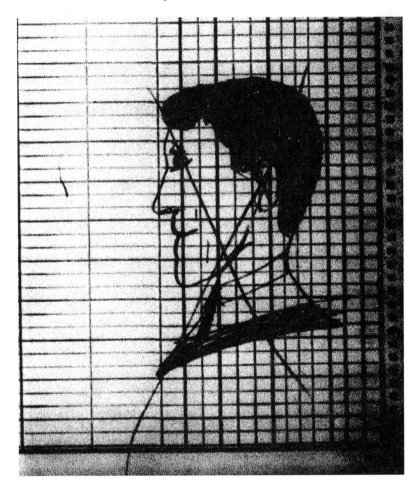

## DUPLICATE ENTRIES

Census taking is not a perfect process, especially when the information must be gathered over an extended period of time. Although enumerators were instructed to be certain to report data as of the official census date (see page 26, chapter two), it is clear from census examples that those instructions were not always followed.

Discovering your person in the census more than once is a research bonus. Sometimes the entries vary in content, and by combining the answers you may gather new clues or information.

**The following case studies of double entries vary by type:**

- One individual appearing in the census three times in the same census year and city. Are these entries for the same person?
- A family reported at exactly the same address but enumerated on two different dates by two different enumerators.
- Same family enumerated twice in the same township; however, in the first record the first and middle names of the husband and wife are reversed, making it more difficult to realize the entries are for the same family.
- A female is named with her siblings in her parents' home, but she was also enumerated with her husband.
- The same family was enumerated in two different states. They left Tennessee after being counted, migrated to Illinois, and were counted again.
- An entire neighborhood was duplicated several months later.

## Case Study: Same City, Different Addresses and Dates

*Contributed by James Jeffrey, Denver, Colorado*

Three individuals named Albert May were enumerated in the 1920 Denver, Colorado, census. Are the three census entries for one person who moved around? Or are two of the three for the same person? Or perhaps were there really three different persons named Albert May in Denver in 1920?

The three entries, abstracted in the chart on page 220, appear to represent the same person: Each time Albert was reported to be forty-two years old with a California birthplace. But other conflicting information puts his identity in question.

Denver city directories for 1919 through 1921 were consulted to help separate the identities reported in these three census entries:

> *Ballenger & Richards Denver Directory*, 1919 (Denver: Gazetteer Publishing and Printing Co., 1919), 1429.
>> May Albert janitor Colfax Hotel 325 W Colfax av
>> May Albert L porter Brown Palace Hotel rms 1659 Broadway

> *Ballenger & Richards Denver Directory*, 1920 (Denver: Gazetteer Publishing and Printing Co., 1920), 1553.
>> **May Albert watchman American Wholesale Drug Co 427 W Colfax av**
>> [Matches census entry number 1]
>>
>> May Albert E mach SMCo rms 1419 Larimer

> *Ballenger & Richards Denver Directory*, 1921 (Denver: Gazetteer Publishing and Printing Co., 1921), 1458.
>> **May Albert watchman Scholtz r 427 W Colfax**
>> [Matches census entry number 1]

The question of whether the three census entries represent one, two, or three different persons remains unsolved. The city directories suggest that there may have been two men named Albert May, but the census and directories are not proof. Only with more in-depth research will this puzzle be unraveled.

| | Entry Number 1 | Entry Number 2 | Entry Number 3 |
|---|---|---|---|
| **DUPLICATE CENSUS ENTRIES FOR ALBERT MAY** | | | |
| **1920 DENVER, COLORADO** | | | |
| Date | 16 Jan 1920 | 3 Feb 1920 | 9 Feb 1920 |
| Enumerator | Margaret Duff | Douglas Washburn | Orlando Keing |
| Address | 427 W. Colfax | 2161 Larimer | 1519 Champa St. |
| Name | Albert May | Albert May | Albert May |
| Relationship to Head | Head; living alone, renting | Lodger (Unnamed hotel with thirty-seven persons) | Lodger (Unnamed hotel with 216 persons) |
| Age | 42 | 42 | 42 |
| Marital Status | Married | Single | Single |
| Place of Birth | California | California | California |
| Father's Place of Birth | Iowa | California | Illinois |
| Mother's Place of Birth | Louisiana | Wisconsin | Illinois |
| Occupation | Watchman at a Wholesale House | R.R. Fireman | Watchman at a Furniture Store |

**Entry Number 1:** Albert May, 1920 U.S. census, Denver County, Colorado, population schedule, Denver, E.D. 154, sheet 14A, dwelling 192, family 476; National Archives micropublication T625, roll 160.
**Entry Number 2:** Unnamed Hotel, 1920 U.S. census, Denver County, Colorado, population schedule, Denver, E.D. 171, sheet 10A, dwelling 35, family 36 (Albert May, lodger); National Archives micropublication T625, roll 161.
**Entry Number 3:** Unnamed Hotel, 1920 U.S. census, Denver County, Colorado, population schedule, Denver, E.D. 152, sheet 21A, dwelling 60, family 332 (Albert May, lodger); National Archives micropublication T625, roll 160.

The census sometimes presents new questions rather than solving old ones. Distinguishing the identities of persons with the same name is a common problem and requires careful analysis of every potentially relevant record.

### Case Study: Same Address, Different Dates
*Contributed by Sherril Erfurth, Evergreen, Colorado*
The George Shaw family was counted twice in the 1920 census in Georgetown Township, Vermilion County, Illinois. In this case, the street address is the same in both entries, but in the second enumeration, the Shaw residence was the only household on Kelly Avenue counted. Several residences on Kelly Avenue were included in the first enumeration, done 5 January 1920. This may be a case of one enumerator having crossed over into the territory assigned to another. If you find a situation similar to this, track on a city map the route of each enumerator and determine why the family was counted twice.

These duplicate enumerations are genealogically useful because of the differ-

| | Entry Number 1 | Entry Number 2 |
|---|---|---|
| **DUPLICATE CENSUS ENTRIES FOR THE GEORGE SHAW HOUSEHOLD**<br>**1920 VERMILION COUNTY, ILLINOIS**<br>(Note: Facts that were reported differently in the two enumerations are underlined.) | | |
| Date(s) | 5 January 1920 | 22 and 26 January 1920 |
| Enumerator | Walter Doublesky | Louis A. Turner |
| Address | [no number; between 1508 and 1511] E. Kelly Ave. | [no number] Kelly Ave. |
| Shaw, George | Head, owns home/ mortgaged, male, <u>63</u> years, married, <u>immigrated 1882</u>, naturalized. Born England; parents born England. Janitor for schoolhouse. | Head, owns home/ mortgaged, male, <u>64</u> years, married, <u>immigrated 1881</u>, <u>naturalized 1883</u>. Born England; parents born England. Janitor for schoolhouse. |
| Shaw, Elizabeth | Wife, female, 58 years, married, <u>immigrated 1883</u>, naturalized. Born England; parents born England. No occupation. | Wife, female, 58 years, married, <u>immigrated 1882, naturalized 1883</u>. Born England; parents born England. No occupation. |
| Shaw, John | Son, male, 20 years, single. Born Illinois; parents born England. Coal miner. | Son, male, 20 years, single. Born Illinois; parents born England. Coal miner. |
| Shaw, Chester | Son, male, <u>23</u> years, widowed. Born Illinois; parents born England. <u>Driver at coal mine</u>. | Son, male, <u>22</u> years, widowed. Born Illinois; parents born England. <u>Coal miner</u>. |
| Shaw, Chester | <u>Son</u>, male, 2⁹⁄₁₂, single. Born Illinois; parents born Illinois. | <u>Grandson</u>, male, 2⁹⁄₁₂, single. Born Illinois; parents born Illinois. |
| Shaw, <u>Hellen</u> [entry number 1]<br>Shaw, <u>Ellen</u> [entry number 2] | Dother [sic], female, 14 years, single. Born Illinois; parents born England. | Daughter, female, 14 years, single. Born Illinois; parents born England. |
| Shaw, <u>Hellen</u> [entry number 1]<br>Shaw, <u>Ellen</u> [entry number 2] | Granddaughter, female, <u>10</u> years, single. Born Illinois; parents born Illinois. | Granddaughter, female, <u>11</u> years, single. Born Illinois; parents born Illinois. |

**Entry Number 1:** George Shaw household, 1920 U.S. census, Vermilion County, Illinois, population schedule, Westville Village, Georgetown Township, E.D. 180, sheet 4A, dwelling 43, family 43; National Archives micropublication T625, roll 412.
**Entry Number 2:** George Shaw household, 1920 U.S. census, Vermilion County, Illinois, population schedule, Belgium Village, Georgetown Township, E.D. 150, sheet 16A, dwelling 324, family 336; National Archives micropublication T625, roll 411.

| DUPLICATE CENSUS ENTRIES FOR THE WILLIAM HENRY BARNES HOUSEHOLD—1880 FLOYD COUNTY, GEORGIA | | |
|---|---|---|
| | **Entry Number 1** | **Entry Number 2** |
| Date | 19 June 1880 | 21 June 1880 |
| Enumerator | James A. Clement | James A. Clement |
| Name and Race/Sex/Age | Barnes, Henry W. W/M/30<br>Barnes, Evaline W/F/27<br>Barnes, Andrew W/M/9<br>Barnes, Fred W/M/7<br>Barnes, James W/M/5<br>Barnes, Hattie W/F/3 | Barnes, William H. W/M/33<br>Barnes, Lucretia E. W/F/33<br>Barnes, Andrew W/M/8<br>Barnes, Frederick W/M/6<br>Barnes, James L. W/M/4<br>Barnes, Hattie M. W/F/2 |
| **Entry Number 1:** Henry W. Barnes household, 1880 U.S. census, Floyd County, Georgia, population schedule, Etowah District (1048), E.D. 72, page 52 (handwritten), page 348C (stamped), dwelling 474, family 474; National Archives micropublication T9, roll 146.<br>**Entry Number 2:** William H. Barnes household, 1880 U.S. census, Floyd County, Georgia, population schedule, Etowah District (1048), E.D. 72, page 55 (handwritten), page 349B (stamped), dwelling 508, family 508; National Archives micropublication T9, roll 146. | | |

ences between them. The chart above details the two enumerations and their differences. Of prime importance is the year of naturalization (1883) reported only in the second enumeration. This information is helpful in a search for passenger arrival and naturalization records.

## Duplicate Census Entries

### Case Study: Same Family; Adults' First and Middle Names Reversed

*Contributed by Judith Wade Anderson, Tahlequah, Oklahoma*

The William Henry Barnes family of Floyd County, Georgia, was listed twice in 1880 in the Etowah District by the same enumerator—two days apart. Because the first and middle names of the husband and wife are reversed, this example demonstrates how eagle-eyed you need to be when reading the census. Without watching for the first and middle names in the census using both to search an index, you might miss the double listing. Note too that ages for all the family members are different after two days.

## Duplicate Census Entries

### Case Study: Same Person in Two Different Households

*Contributed by Mary Ann Abbe, Athens, Georgia*

Mary E.A. Horton married Benjamin B. Speed on 5 September 1850, when she was fifteen years old. When the census was taken in November, Mary's parents included her in the list of their children—as they should have since the official date of the census was 1 June 1850. (The government allowed five months for this census to be taken; however, the enumerator in Sumter County, Alabama, collected data in November.) Mary wed in September, and she was also enumerated in her marital home with her husband. This resulted in Mary's being counted twice—as a daughter with her parents and as a wife with her husband:

| DUPLICATE CENSUS ENTRIES FOR MARY HORTON SPEED—1850 SUMTER COUNTY, ALABAMA | | |
|---|---|---|
| | **Entry Number 1** | **Entry Number 2** |
| Date | 15 November 1850 | 27 November 1850 |
| Enumerator | Danl. L. Ayers | Danl. L. Ayers |
| Name, Age, (Occupation), (Value of Real Estate), Birthplace | Stephen Horton, 40, farmer, $1500, Georgia<br>Elizabeth Horton, 37, Georgia<br>Sarah A. Horton, 18, Alabama<br>Mary E.A. Horton, 15, Alabama<br>Frances S.A. Horton, 14, Alabama<br>John W.W. Horton, 7, Alabama<br>Margaret A. Horton, 6, Alabama | Benjamin B. Speed, 24, manager, South Carolina<br>Mary A.E. Speed, 16, Alabama<br>(Note: The enumerator reversed Mary's middle initials. Her name is Mary E.A. (Horton) Speed. |
| **Entry Number 1:** Stephen Horton household, 1850 U.S. census, Sumter County, Alabama, population schedule, Belmont, page 303, dwelling 711, family 725; National Archives micropublication M432, roll 15.<br>**Entry Number 2:** Benjamin B. Speed household, 1850 U.S. census, Sumter County, Alabama, population schedule, Black Bluff, page 309, dwelling 803, family 818; National Archives micropublication M432, roll 15. | | |

Ironically, the same thing happened with Mary's sister Sarah A. Horton. Sarah Ann married John T. Caldwell on 16 March 1850. John and Sarah Caldwell are family number 728 in Belmont, three households from Sarah's parents. In Sarah's case, the parents should *not* have reported their daughter Sarah with their household, because she married prior to the June 1 census date.

## Duplicate Census Entries
### Case Study: Same Family in Two Different States
*Contributed by Stanley C. and Patricia D. Smith, Garden City, Kansas*
The family of Allen J. Bridges was enumerated in 1830 in Smith County, Tennessee, and again in Greene County, Illinois. Data in the two census entries is as follows:

One more male was counted in Illinois than was in Tennessee. The age of the head of household (sixty and under seventy is the same in both enumerations, as is the number of females. It is unknown if the additional male counted in the Illinois census was due to an error in recording the family data. Another plausible explanation for the count difference is that a married son who was enumerated in the next household in Illinois was also included with his parents in Illinois. Other scenarios for the extra male include that a person was living temporarily with the family, for any of a number of reasons.

To better understand how this duplication occurred, it helped to study the census procedures and analyze the census data. The 1830 census enumeration officially began 1 June 1830, but the census takers were allowed twelve months to collect the data. Both reports were signed in November 1830: The Smith County, Tennessee, report is dated November 1830 (without a day); and the Greene County, Illinois, report is dated 27 November 1830.

Allen Bridges was enumerated about midway through the Smith County, Tennessee, census—entry number 1,443 out of 2,466 households. With about

| DUPLICATE CENSUS ENTRIES FOR ALLEN J. BRIDGES AND FAMILY—1830 TENNESSEE AND ILLINOIS | | |
|---|---|---|
| | Entry Number 1<br>Smith County, Tennessee | Entry Number 2<br>Greene County, Illinois |
| Males 5 years and Under 10 years | 1 | 0 |
| Males 10 years and Under 15 years | 1 | 2 |
| Males 15 years and Under 20 years | 2 | 2 |
| Males 20 years and Under 30 years | 2 | 3 |
| Males 60 years and Under 70 years | 1 | 1 |
| Females 5 years and under 10 years | 1 | 1 |
| Females 30 years and under 40 years | 1 | 0 |
| Females 40 years and Under 50 years | 0 | 1 |
| Totals | 7 males; 2 females | 8 males; 2 females |

**Entry Number 1:** Allen Bridges household, 1830 U.S. census, Smith County, Tennessee, page 85, line 15; National Archives micropublication M19, roll 181.
**Entry Number 2:** Allen Bridges household, 1830 U.S. census, Greene County, Illinois, page 50, line 20; National Archives micropublication M19, roll 24.

41 percent of the county remaining to be counted, the Bridges family was probably visited in late summer or early fall.

On the other hand, in Greene County, Illinois, the Allen Bridges family and Flemmon Bridges, Allen's son, were the last two households to be counted. The approximate date of migration for the Bridges family, based on the two census reports, is likely to be between June and November 1830.

The strongest proof that Allen J. Bridges in Tennessee and Illinois are the same person comes from the Widow's Revolutionary Pension Application #W8159. Allen J. Bridges declared in Greene County, Illinois, open court on 4 March 1834 that he had resided in these locations following the Revolution:

> Wilkes County, Georgia
> Oglethorpe County, Georgia
> Jackson County, Georgia
> Tennessee
> Greene County, Illinois

## Duplicate Census Entries
### Case Study: Neighborhood Double-Counted
*Contributed by Julie Miller, Broomfield, Colorado*
Many residents of Geauga County, Ohio, appear to have been counted twice in 1870. This was discovered when all Geauga County entries for the surname Potter were abstracted. Duplicate entries for Potter families, shown in the chart on page 225, were found on pages 66 and 103, 109 and 119, 126 and 147, and 174 and 185. Neighbors were also listed twice, although the sequences were not identical.

| DUPLICATE CENSUS ENTRIES FOR POTTER FAMILIES—1870 GEAUGA COUNTY, OHIO | |
| --- | --- |
| Page 66<br>Miles Potter, 31, m, w, Ohio, farmer<br>Annette S. Potter, 28, f, w, New York<br>Hiram Potter, 4, m, w, Ohio | Page 103<br>Milo Potter, 31, m, w, Ohio, farmer laborer<br>Annette Potter, 28, f, w, New York<br>Hiram Potter, 5, m, w, Ohio |
| Page 109<br>Elwood Potter, 24, m, w, Ohio, farm laborer | Page 119<br>Elwood Potter, 24, m, w, Ohio, farm laborer |
| Page 126<br>Abbie Potter, 21, f, w, Ohio, domestic<br>Rosa Potter, 2 months, f, w, Ohio | Page 147<br>Abby Potter, 21, f, w, Ohio, dom. servant<br>Rosa Potter, 2 months, f, w, Ohio |
| Page 174<br>Wm. Potter, 16, m, w, Ohio, farm laborer | Page 185<br>Willie Potter, 16, m, w, Ohio, farm laborer |
| 1870 U.S. census, Geauga County, Ohio, pages 66–185; National Archives micropublication M593, roll 1204. | |

Was this a simple mistake? Was it an official second enumeration? (See chapter five for discussion on second enumerations in 1870 for Indianapolis, New York City, and Philadelphia.)

The first enumeration was taken 24 June–23 July 1870). The community was counted again eight months later, 18–23 March 1871. Six enumerators participated: L.G. Griske (pages 66 and 174), P.M. Cowles (page 103), David Gates (pages 109 and 126), Walter Johnston (page 119), Harlow N. Spencer (page 147), and S.E. Bodman (page 185).

For more examples of duplicate entries, see the series of articles titled "Duplicate Census Enumeration: An Overview" in *The American Genealogist* 62 (April 1987): 97–105; (July 1987): 173–181; and (Oct 1987): 241–244.

## Other Census Anomalies
### Three Swedish Families Without Names
*Contributed by Karen E. Livsey, Falconer, New York*

Three Swedish families in Busti, Chautauqua County, New York, are listed in the 1870 census, but none of the eighteen persons are identified by name. The age, sex, occupation, and birthplace of each are given, but the name column is blank—except the first entry, which reads, "Swedes Can't talk."

Column 18 for reporting deaf and dumb persons is blank; therefore it is unlikely that these Swedish families could not talk. The Swedes probably could not speak English, and the enumerator probably gave up on trying to understand their names. It is unknown whether the enumerator guessed the ages and other information or someone within these households was able to communicate that information.

The twenty-five-, forty-, and fifty-year-old Swedish husbands all were farm hands with no real estate and with personal property of very low value. The entry directly preceding them is for a sixty-six-year-old farmer and his wife, a nineteen-year-old invalid son, and a seventeen-year-old daughter. Perhaps the Swedish families were farmhands for this farmer, but that is only speculation.

**Figure 11-2**
1870 U.S. census, Chautauqua County, New York, population schedule, Busti, page 35 (stamped), dwellings 406–408, families 354–356; National Archives micropublication M593, roll 912.

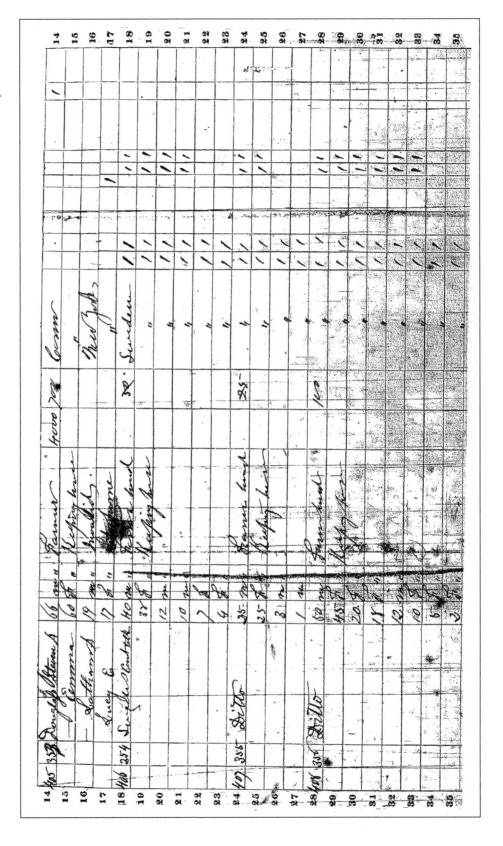

Data on this neighborhood in the 1880 census may help identify this family more clearly.

This example demonstrates how individuals or families can be in the census but not in any index. The value of reading census pages line by line is obvious.

## Court Case Against Enumerator

*Contributed by Janice S. Prater, Denver, Colorado*

Court papers concerning the indictment of Thomas Bailey for failure to make a proper return of the enumeration of the inhabitants of Baltimore, Maryland, in 1800 were microfilmed with the census manuscript (National Archives micropublication M32, roll 9). The documents (three pages) appear between the end of Baltimore and the beginning of Calvert County on the same roll of microfilm.

A court or file number does not appear on the documents. Only the heading "The United States of America District of Maryland vs. Thomas Bailey" identifies them.

The sixteen members of the grand jury are named, as well as the judge, attorney, and clerk. Some of these names are also in the census; some are not. The digitized census images at Ancestry.com do not include these pages—note that extra notes or documents in the microfilmed census records may not be included in digitized versions.

## Male Reported as Female

*Contributed by Elaine M. Turk, Macon, Georgia*

A common error in census recordings occurred when enumerators wrote down what they *heard*; this often resulted in badly misspelled surnames. In this case, an enumerator's misunderstanding of a ten-year-old boy's name caused him to report the boy as a girl.

In the 1920 Wilcox County, Georgia, census (Pope City District, E.D. 154, sheet 2, dwelling 173, family 176; National Archives micropublication T625, roll 229), Reuben Amory Futch, born in 1909, is named in his father's household as "Rubie Mae Futch, daughter, age 10."

## Born "on the Plains"

*Contributed by Kay Germain Ingalls, CGRS, Sunnyvale, California*

The government advised the enumerators in 1900 through 1930 to report "at sea" if a person was born at sea. Although the enumerators did not have similar instructions in earlier census years, Spencer Raymond, seventeen years old at the time of the 1870 Weber County, Utah, census (Plain City, page 10, stamped page 515, dwelling 71, family 71; National Archives micropublication M593, roll 1613), was recorded as born "on the plains or Nebraska." Spencer was born in about 1853, and Nebraska did not become a state until 1867—three years prior to the 1870 census. That may explain why the family reported "or Nebraska."

### 1880 Seminole Indian Village Includes Adopted Black Female

*Contributed by Alvie L. Davidson, CGRS, Lakeland, Florida*

A Seminole Indian village in Polk County, Florida (1880 U.S. census, Polk County, Florida, Catfish Lake Settlement, E.D. 129, page 66 [handwritten], page 34C [stamped]; National Archives micropublication T9, roll 131) was enumerated in March 1881.

A handwritten note at the bottom of the page explains why this small group of Indians was included in the census:

> This page contains the names of the Seminole Indians in Polk County, as enumerated by Clay McCanley, Special Agent of the office. General Walker decided that these Indians should be counted as part of the constitutional population of the State and this schedule is therefore inserted in district #129. This settlement being located in that district. C.W. Seaton, Chief Clerk.

The listing of a tribe of twenty-eight Indians in Catfish Lake Settlement begins with a ninety-year-old man and his sixty-five-year-old wife. All the names are written in the Seminole language. On line 26 is a forty-five-year-old black female who was "adopted into the tribe when a child—doesn't speak." She had a twenty-year-old daughter and twenty-three-year-old son residing with her. The race of the daughter is difficult to read—appears to be "I" for Indian and then overwritten with "B" for black. The son, however, is listed as "I½" meaning one-half Indian.

### Unorganized Census Pages

*Contributed by Susan Hertzke, Broomfield, Colorado*

When the census manuscripts were microfilmed years ago, they were not always in correct order, and some pages would be missed in microfilming. The case study "Find 'Missing Family' on Missing Page" on page 173 in chapter nine confirms that this happened.

The microfilm of the 1860 census of Douglas County, Oregon, (M653, roll 1055) is a good example showing that the original pages were not in the correct order when they were microfilmed. Note that the stamped numbers are in order, but the handwritten numbers are completely out of sequence:

| Handwritten Page Number | Stamped Page Number |
| --- | --- |
| 4 | 114 front |
| 3 | 114 back |
| 5 | 115 front |
| 6–12 | 115 back to 118 back |
| 1–2 | 119 front to 119 back |
| 51–56 | 120 front to 122 back |
| 49–50 | 123 front to 123 back |
| | *Family ends on handwritten page 49 |
| 39–46 | 124 front to 127 back |

**Notes**

**CENSUS TRIVIA**

The 1910 census was the first census for which enumerators took competitive examinations to qualify for the job. From 1880 to 1900, enumerators took noncompetitive tests, and prior to 1880, no tests were administered.

| | |
|---|---|
| 57–62 | 128 front to 130 back |
| 13–18 | 131 front to 133 back |
| 76 | 134 front |
| 75 | 134 back |
| 77–82 | 135 front to 137 back |
| 20 | 138 front |
| 19 | 138 back |
| 21–38 | 139 front to 147 back |
| 47–48 | 148 front to 148 back |
| | *Family begins on handwritten page 48 |
| 64 | 149 front |
| 63 | 149 back |
| 65–74 | 150 front to 154 back |

*A family begins on handwritten page 48 and is continued on page 49, but the disorganization of the original census pages splits this family data on the microfilm. A hurried genealogist might miss information in a case such as this if she does not pay attention to page numbers.

## Slaves Listed in Free Schedule in 1850 for Collin County, Texas

*Contributed by Beverly Rice, Coos Bay, Oregon*

The slaves were supposed to be reported on a separate slave schedule; however, the enumerator in 1850 for Collin County, Texas, included the data with each household. Unfortunately he did not include the names of the slaves.

## Incomplete, Confusing, and Peculiar Census Entries in 1810 for Columbus County, North Carolina

*Contributed by Helen F.M. Leary, CG, CGL, FASG, Raleigh, North Carolina*

In 1810 in Columbus County, North Carolina, the census taker clearly marched to his own drummer. With few exceptions he failed to provide the given names (supplying only an initial) of the heads of household, and he omitted all mention of the householder in the family statistics. Thus, one cannot tell whether the principal person in a family was male or female, and some households appear to have been composed entirely of a few children under ten.

Because no column headings are included in the microfilmed version, you cannot determine what the enumerator intended by his peculiar entries in the areas that were supposed to be used for manufacturing statistics (the number of looms, stills, grist mills, etc., and production statistics from each). What ought to be the number of looms in the house, for example, is followed not by a number like 100 or 200 (representing yardage produced) but by an inexplicably low number. Entries in this section are so unorganized, in fact, that one cannot tell what the figures represent.

Columns at the extreme right-hand side of the page appear to have been used to record livestock statistics (hogs, cattle, sheep, horses, etc.), although there is no notation to that effect. Judging by the handwriting, the enumerator was an educated man, so whatever he wrote he *meant*. One does wish, however, that he had told us what he was doing.

### 1820 Census Marshal Added Identifiers

*Contributed by Kay Germain Ingalls, CGRS, Sunnyvale, California*

William Handley, Assistant Marshal of the 1820 census in Monroe County, Virginia (National Archives micropublication M33, roll 133), added occupational, geographical, or relationship information for a few residents. This data was not required by law and can help distinguish the identities of persons with the same name. Little extras such as these examples are uncommon, but not rare:

> Pages 178 and 814 (handwritten), page 164 (stamped), line 20
> Campbell, John—milright [*sic*]

> Pages 180 and 816 (handwritten), page 165 (stamped), line 24
> Campbell, William—Indian Creek

> Pages 196 and 832 (handwritten), page 173 (stamped), line 2
> Harvey, John—Hands Creek

> Pages 198 and 834 (handwritten); page 174 (stamped), line 4
> Joens, John, B.S. [blacksmith?]

> Pages 204 and 840 (handwritten), page 177 (stamped), line 9
> Mann, James, D.L. [Doctor of Law]

> Pages 222 and 858 (handwritten), page 186 (stamped), lines 17 and 25
> Tracy, Jeremiah—Classical teacher
> Wiseman, Isaac—Son of Joseph

> Pages 224 and 860 (handwritten), page 187 (stamped), line 4
> Wickline, Jacob—Son of George

> Pages 232 and 868 (handwritten), page 191 (stamped), line 25
> Tracy, Jarimiah—Clasecle teecher [*sic*]
> [This is a duplication of page 222. Note the spelling difference of the given name and the misspelling of the occupation.]

## DISCOVERING MORE CENSUS ANOMALIES

The variety of census anomalies reflects the vastness of data that can be gleaned from census records. Many of your census discoveries will be routine, but occasionally you may uncover an anomaly that will enhance your family history. Although each census enumeration is a snapshot of your family at a particular time and place, it is also rich in content beyond mere names and dates.

Be persistent and use census records as a cornerstone of your research. You will not regret the time and energy you use to be successful.

# TWELVE

# Other Census Records

C olonial, state, and local censuses are not as well known as the federal enumerations, but they can be just as valuable in your research. The content varies from exceptionally limited data to more information than a federal schedule has. The availability ranges from several enumerations for some states to none for others.

Locating your family in these other census records may provide information or clues not found in the federal censuses. For example, the addition or presence of a child may narrow a birth date or place, or maybe prove a death. Many state and local census records report how long the individual or family resided locally, providing important migration or immigration information.

**Ann Lainhart's *State Census Records* (Baltimore: Genealogical Publishing Co., 1992) is the most comprehensive inventory of and guide to these records available.** Lainhart reports each state's collection of census records chronologically, including information on locations enumerated and availability of the records. Some entries include a full description of the contents or questions asked in a particular census.

The balance of this chapter merely touches on state and other census records and is intended to encourage your exploration and use of these resources. To learn more about their availability and content, use Lainhart's book and the tools described in chapter seven.

**For More Info**

## PRE-1790 CENSUSES
### 1699 Through 1732: Louisiana
*The Census Tables for the French Colony of Louisiana From 1699 Through 1732* (Baltimore: Genealogical Publishing Co., 1972) by Charles R. Maduell Jr. is a compilation of the twenty-eight earliest census records of Louisiana. In addition to census records, the publication includes the names of 1,704 mar-

---

**INTERNATIONAL CENSUSES**

Census taking is an international endeavor; therefore, you can research your immigrant ancestors in census records in their homelands. To determine what international census records exist, examine how-to guides for your country of interest and check the Family History Library catalog for those records available on microfilm.

Cyndi's List <www.cyndislist.com/census2.htm> is an excellent resource for finding references to foreign census records. This Web site has over one hundred worldwide census-related links to indexes and digitized images.

---

riageable girls, a list of persons requesting Negroes (1,726), landowners, and a list of persons massacred at Fort Rosalie in 1729.

## 1723: Mississippi
See Winston DeVille's article "Natchez 1723 Census" in the *National Genealogical Society Quarterly* 59 (1971): 94.

## 1762 and 1765: Detroit, Michigan
French and English censuses were taken for Detroit and have been published as
- Stuart, Donna Valley. "Detroit 1762 Census," *National Genealogical Society Quarterly* 68 (1980): 15.
- ———. "1765 Census of Detroit, Wayne County, Michigan," *Detroit Society for Genealogical Research Magazine* 43 (1979): 19.

## 1776: Maryland
The state census of Maryland in 1776 names the head of household with the remainder of the household listed statistically by sex and age. But some enumerators listed all members of the household and their ages, and occasionally they gave the names and ages of the blacks in each household. This census has been published twice:
- Brumbaugh, Gaius Marcus. *Maryland Records, Colonial, Revolutionary, County and Church From Original Sources*, 2 vols. (1915–28; reprint. Baltimore: Genealogical Publishing Co., 1967).
- Carothers, Bettie Stirling, compiler. *1776 Census of Maryland*. Rev. ed. (Westminster: Family Lines Publications, 1989).

## 1782: Delaware
The tax collectors took a census that listed the name of the head of household and grouped other members of the household by males over and under age eighteen and females over and under age eighteen. See Harold B. Hancock's *The Reconstructed Delaware State Census of 1782* (Wilmington, Del.: Delaware Genealogical Society, 1983).

## 1779 Through 1787: Illinois

See <www.iltrails.org/amercen.htm> for "List of Americans in Illinois, September 7, 1787; Total Men and Children 1779–1786" from Illinois Historical Collections. Footnotes at the end of the list give for some of the families additional information such as death dates, ancestry or relationships, and migration.

## 1790: New Mexico

The 1790 Spanish census of New Mexico gives the name; age; ethnic derivation; occupation; marital status; wife's name and age; and the number, age, and sex of children. Other relatives and servants within the household are also named. This is much more comprehensive than the 1790 U.S. census which, of course, did not include the area that became New Mexico.

# GOLD MINERS
## 1852: California

The 1852 Special Census of California is similar in format to the 1850 federal census, but instead of estimating the property value, the previous residence of each individual was recorded. The original and a microfilm copy of this census are housed at the California State Archives.

## 1862–63: Montana

A census of miners has been published as "List of Early Settlers: A List of All Persons (Except Indians) Who Were in What Is Now Montana During the Winter of 1862-63, Which Was the First Winter After the Gold Mines of This Region Had Become Noised Abroad," *Contributions to the Historical Society of Montana,* vol. 1. (Helena, Mont.: Rocky Mountain Publishing Co., 1876).

# MILITARY CENSUSES
## 1777: Rhode Island Military Census

Rhode Island took a military census of all males over age sixteen years who were both able and unable to bear arms. The census includes names of men who were already in the state militia or in Continental battalions, transient persons, Indians, Negroes, and Quakers. This list of about 8,500 Rhode Island men has been published as *The Rhode Island 1777 Military Census* (Baltimore: Genealogical Publishing Co., 1985).

## 1863: Georgia

The governor of Georgia ordered a military census of all males, including children. The census was to include the name and age (in years and months) of each male and indicate whether they owned a rifle, a shotgun, and/or a horse and tack. A transcription of Taylor County can be found at <www.rootsweb .com/~gataylor/cen1863.htm>.

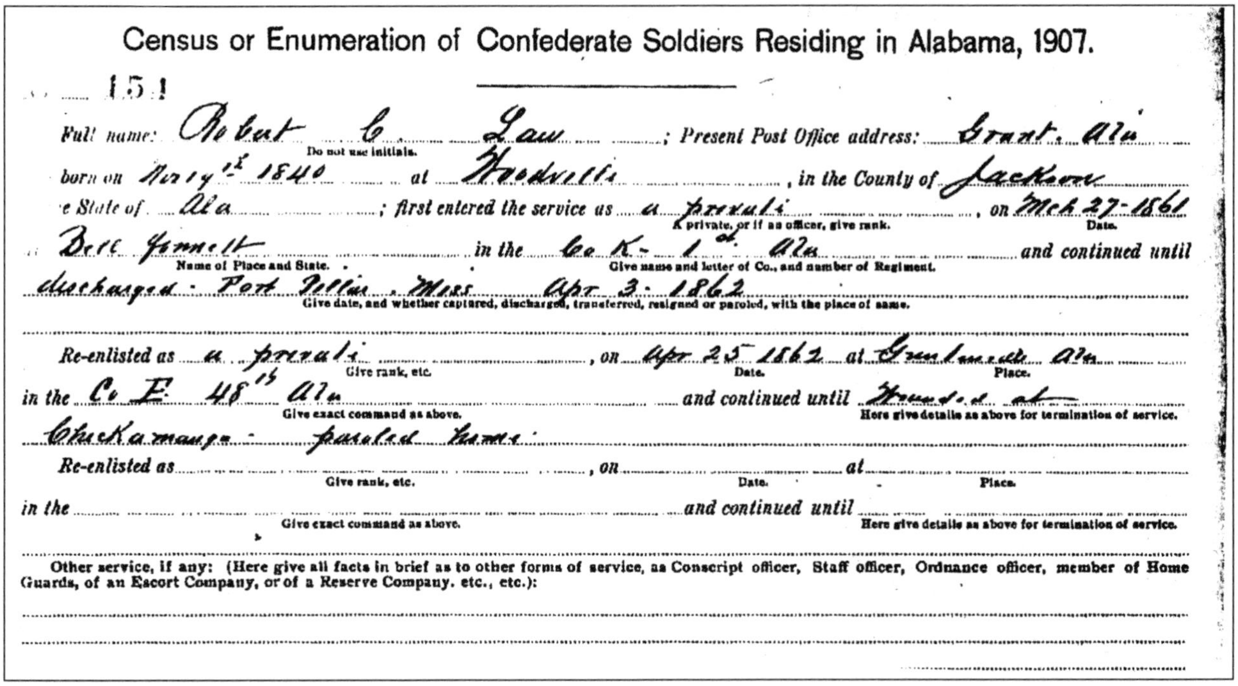

**Figure 12-1**
Robert C. Law, 1907 Census of Confederate Soldiers Residing in Alabama, Marshall County, Alabama, page number 51, entry number 153; Alabama Department of Archives and History, Montgomery, Alabama.

## 1907: Alabama Confederate Veterans

In 1907 the county tax assessors canvassed all persons in Alabama who were receiving a pension for Confederate service. Originals of this census are available at the Alabama Department of Archives and History, Montgomery, Alabama, and a microfilm copy is kept at the Family History Library. Information includes full name, post office address, exact date and place of birth, and Confederate military service.

## 1911: Arkansas Confederate Veterans

In 1911 each Arkansas county tax assessor was asked to collect information on Confederate veterans, including name, address, date and place of birth, date and place of enlistment, names and birthplaces of parents and grandparents, maiden name of wife, date and place of marriage, names of wife's parents, and a list of children. Records survive for forty-four of the seventy-five counties and are published in Bobbie Jones McLane and Capitola Glazner's *Arkansas 1911 Census of Confederate Veterans*, 3 vols. (1977–81). See <www.arkansasresearc h.com/Desmil.htm> for information on the index to the three volumes and on ordering.

## 1917: Connecticut State Military Preparedness Census

A census of all male inhabitants and all nurses over age sixteen was taken from 1917 through 1918. This census is available at the Family History Library, and the original manuscript is housed at the Connecticut State Library. The nurses (student nurses, practical nurses, and nurse's aides) completed nineteen questions that included birthplace and a relative's or friend's permanent address. The regular questionnaire for males asked for

- Present trade, occupation, or profession.
- Experience in other trades, occupations, or professions.
- Age, height, weight.
- Marital status.
- Number of dependents.
- Whether a citizen of the United States.
- If not a citizen, whether filed first papers.
- If not a citizen, nationality.
- Whether ever a military or naval serviceman for any other country. If so, where, for how long, and in what branch.
- Any serious physical disabilities.
- Whether able to do any of the following: ride a horse; handle a team; drive an automobile; ride a motorcycle; understand telegraphy; operate wireless; handle a boat, power, or sail. Any experience with a steam engine? Any experience with electrical machinery? Any experience in simple coastwise navigation? Any experience with high-speed marine gasoline engines? Able to swim well?

## 1921: Alabama Confederate Veterans

The census of Confederate pensioners in Alabama was taken by mail. Each pensioner was asked to complete the form and return it to the state. The original forms may be examined at the Alabama Department of Archives and History, Montgomery, Alabama.

## POST-1930 STATE CENSUS RECORDS

These state census records are open to the public since the federal privacy laws do not apply to state records.

## 1935 and 1945: Florida

The name, address and whether it was inside or outside city limits, age, sex, race, relationship, place of birth, degree of education, home ownership, and occupation were reported in the 1935 Florida state census. See <www.rootsweb .com/~flgilchr/1935gcc/CENSINDX.htm> for a sample transcription of the 1935 records for Gilchrist County. The originals are at the Florida State Archives and have not been indexed.

## 1935: Rhode Island

The Rhode Island State Archives has the original manuscript of the 1935 census that names all members of the household and lists sex, race, place of birth, date of birth, marital status, if they can read and write English, citizenship, if at school and name of school, grade in school, physical disabilities, and employment information.

### 1935 and 1945: South Dakota

Information collected on 3″×4″ (8cm×10cm) cards for each resident included name; age; sex; occupation; whether owned or rented home; place of birth; number of years resided in South Dakota and in the United States; whether naturalized; birthplaces of parents; education; military service (wars fought, state, company, regiment, and division); marital status; maiden name of wife; year married; church affiliation; ethnicity (color); whether can read and write; and if blind, deaf, idiotic, or insane. The index cards are at the South Dakota State Historical Society in Pierre, South Dakota.

## SCHOOL CENSUSES

School districts take school censuses to predict enrollment and plan expenditures for staff and textbooks. The content generally includes the name and age of each child and the names and address(es) of the parents. School census records are at county courthouses, state archives, or local libraries. Many have been microfilmed and are available at the Family History Library. The FHL catalog includes nearly one thousand school census titles. A few of these are

1854: Nacogdoches County, Texas
1880: Buffalo County, Nebraska
1890: Sabine County, Texas
1894–1900: Kittitas County, Washington
1898–1918: Anderson County, Kentucky
1900–1912: Galveston County, Texas
1912–1919: Muskogee County, Oklahoma
1913–1926: Adams County, Idaho
1912–1918: Ottawa County, Oklahoma
1927 and 1939: Amite County, Mississippi
1933–1946: Ellis County, Texas
1950–1984: Taylor County, Iowa

## THE CENSUS COUNTS—NO MATTER WHAT

A census record can be a decennial federal enumeration, a territorial or state collection of data, an early colonial list of residents, or a survey of local school-age children.

Regardless of the reason for the counting or who did the counting, the fact remains that the need for government to count the population has created for genealogists the largest and most valuable collection of records that spans over two hundred years and covers the entire United States, including territories.

The census counts—again and again. Use the census—again and again.

# National Archives and Its Regional Facilities

## www.nara.gov/nara/gotonara.html

### National Archives and Records Administration

700 Pennsylvania Ave. NW
Washington, DC 20408-0001
*Research Hours:*
Monday and Wednesday: 8:45 A.M.–5:00 P.M.
Tuesday, Thursday and Friday: 8:45 A.M.–9:00 P.M.
Saturday: 8:45 A.M.–4:45 P.M.

### Alaska

NARA's Pacific Alaska Region (Anchorage)
654 W.Third Ave.
Anchorage, AK 99501-2145    (907) 271-2443
E-mail: alaska.archives@nara.gov
*Research Hours:*
Monday through Friday: 8:00 A.M.–4:00 P.M.
Saturday: Call for schedule.

### California

NARA's Pacific Region (Laguna Niguel)
24000 Avila Rd., First Floor, East Entrance
Laguna Niguel, CA 92677-3497    (949) 360-2641
E-mail: laguna.archives@nara.gov
Research Hours:
Monday through Friday: 8:00 A.M.–4:30 P.M.
First and Third Saturdays: 8:00 A.M.–4:30 P.M.
Second and Fourth Tuesdays: 4:30 P.M.–8:30 P.M.
NARA's Pacific Region (San Francisco)
1000 Commodore Dr.
San Bruno, CA 94066-2350    (650) 876-9009
E-mail: sanbruno.archives@nara.gov
*Research Hours:*
Monday through Friday: 7:30 A.M.–4:00 P.M.
Wednesday: 4:00 P.M.–8:00 P.M.

### Colorado

NARA's Rocky Mountain Region
Building 46, Denver Federal Center
W. Sixth Ave. and Kipling St.
Denver, CO 80225-0307    (303) 236-0817

E-mail: denver.archives@nara.gov
*Research Hours:*
Monday, Wednesday, Friday: 7:30 A.M.–3:45 P.M.
Tuesday and Thursday: 7:30 A.M.–8:45 P.M.
First and Third Saturdays: 8:30 A.M.–4:45 P.M.

### Georgia
NARA's Southeast Region
   1557 St. Joseph Ave.
   East Point, GA 30344-2593   (404) 763-7474
   E-mail: atlanta.center@nara.gov
   *Research Hours:*
   Monday through Friday: 7:00 A.M.–4:00 P.M.
   Tuesday: 4:00 P.M.–8:00 P.M.

### Illinois
NARA's Great Lakes Region (Chicago)
   7358 S. Pulaski Rd.
   Chicago, IL 60629-5898   (773) 581-7816
   E-mail: chicago.archives@nara.gov
   *Research Hours:*
   Monday, Wednesday, Thursday, Friday: 8:00 A.M.–4:15 P.M.
   Tuesday: 8:00 A.M.–8:30 P.M.

### Massachusetts
NARA's Northeast Region (Boston)
   380 Trapelo Rd.
   Waltham, MA 02452-6399   (781) 647-8104
   E-mail: waltham.archives@nara.gov
   *Research Hours:*
   Monday, Tuesday, Friday: 8:00 A.M.–4:30 P.M.
   Wednesday and Thursday: 8:00 A.M.–9:00 P.M.
   First and Third Saturdays: 8:00 A.M.–4:30 P.M.
NARA's Northeast Region (Pittsfield)
   10 Conte Dr.
   Pittsfield, MA 01201-8230   (413) 445-6885
   E-mail: pittsfield.archives@nara.gov
   *Research Hours:*
   Monday, Tuesday, Thursday, Friday: 8:00 A.M.–4:00 P.M.
   Wednesday: 8:00 A.M.–9:00 P.M.

### Missouri
NARA's Central Plains Region (Kansas City)
   2312 E. Bannister Rd.
   Kansas City, MO 64131-3011   (816) 926-6272
   E-mail: kansascity.archives@nara.gov

*Research Hours:*
Monday, Thursday, Friday: 8:00 A.M.–4:00 P.M.
Tuesday & Wednesday: 7:30 A.M.–5:30 P.M.
Third Saturday (except December): 9:00 A.M.–4:00 P.M.

## New York

NARA's Northeast Region (New York City)
201 Varick St.
New York, NY 10014-4811    (212) 337-1300
E-mail: newyork.archives@nara.gov
*Research Hours:*
Monday, Wednesday, Thursday, Friday: 8:00 A.M.–4:30 P.M.
Tuesday: 8:00 A.M.–8:00 P.M.
Third Saturday: 8:30 A.M.–4:00 P.M.

## Pennsylvania

NARA's Mid-Atlantic Region (Center City Philadelphia)
900 Market St.
Philadelphia, PA 19107-4292    (215) 597-3000
E-mail: philadelphia.archives@nara.gov
*Research Hours:*
Monday through Friday: 8:00 A.M.–5:00 P.M.
Second and Fourth Saturdays: 8:00 A.M.–4:00 P.M.

## Texas

NARA's Southwest Region
501 W. Felix St., Building 1
Fort Worth, TX 76115-3405    (817) 334-5525
E-mail: ftworth.archives@nara.gov
*Research Hours:*
Monday, Wednesday, Thursday, Friday: 6:30 A.M.–4:00 P.M.
Tuesday: 6:30 A.M.–8:45 P.M.
First and Third Saturdays: 8:00 A.M.–4:00 P.M.

## Washington

NARA's Pacific Alaska Region (Seattle)
6125 Sand Point Way NE
Seattle, WA 98115-7999    (206) 526-6501
E-mail: seattle.archives@nara.gov
*Research Hours:*
Monday, Wednesday, Thursday, Friday: 7:45 A.M.–4:15 P.M.
Tuesday: 7:45 A.M.–8:00 P.M.
First Saturday: 9:00 A.M.–4:00 P.M.

# Census Maps and Questions

Adapted from AniMap County Boundary Historical Atlas

### The 1790 census recorded

- name of town, city
- name of head of the family
- number of free white males of 16 years and upward
- number of free white males under 16 years
- number of free white females (not divided by age)
- number of all other free persons
- number of slaves

**1800**

Northwest Territory

(Part of Mass.)

Indiana Territory

Mississippi Territory (Claimed by Ga.)

*Adapted from AniMap County Boundary Historical Atlas*

## The 1800 census recorded

- name of county, parish, township, town, or city where the family resided
- name of the head of the family
- number of free white males
     under 10
     of 10 and under 16
     of 16 and under 26, including heads of families
     of 26 and under 45, including heads of families
     of 45 and upward, including heads of families
- number of free white females
     under 10
     of 10 and under 16
     of 16 and under 26, including heads of families
     of 26 and under 45, including heads of families
     of 45 and upward, including heads of families
- number of all other free persons, except Indians not taxed
- number of slaves

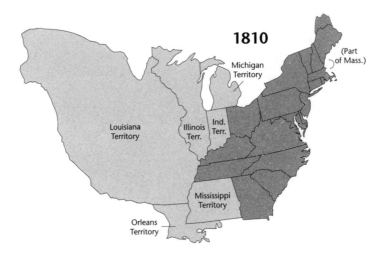

*Adapted from AniMap County Boundary Historical Atlas*

### The 1810 census recorded

- name of county, parish, township, town, or city where the family resided
- name of the head of the family
- number of free white males
    - under 10
    - of 10 and under 16
    - of 16 and under 26
    - of 26 and under 45
    - of 45 and upward
- number of free white females
    - under 10
    - of 10 and under 16
    - of 16 and under 26
    - of 26 and under 45
    - of 45 and upward
- number of all other free persons, except Indians not taxed
- number of slaves

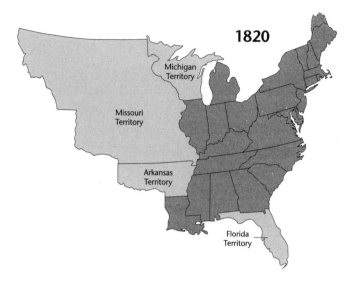

**1820**

Michigan Territory

Missouri Territory

Arkansas Territory

Florida Territory

*Adapted from AniMap County Boundary Historical Atlas*

## The 1820 census recorded

- name of county, parish, township, town, or city where the family resided
- name of the head of the family
- number of free white males
    - under 10
    - of 10 and under 16
    - between 16 and 18
    - of 16 and under 26
    - of 26 and under 45
    - 45 and upward
- number of free white females
    - under 10
    - of 10 and under 16
    - between 16 and 18
    - of 16 and under 26
    - of 26 and under 45
    - 45 and upward
- number of foreigners not naturalized
- number of persons engaged in agriculture
- number of persons engaged in commerce
- number of persons engaged in manufactures

- number of male slaves
    - under 14
    - of 14 and under 26
    - of 26 and under 45
    - of 45 and upward
- number of female slaves
    - under 14
    - of 14 and under 26
    - of 26 and under 45
    - of 45 and upward
- number of free colored males
    - under 14
    - of 14 and under 26
    - of 26 and under 45
    - of 45 and upward
- number of free colored females
    - under 14
    - of 14 and under 26
    - of 26 and under 45
    - of 45 and upward
- number of all other persons, except Indians not taxed

*Adapted from AniMap County Boundary Historical Atlas*

## The 1830 census recorded

- name of county, city, ward, town, township, parish, precinct, or district
- name of the head of the family
- number of free white males
    under 5
    of 5 and under 10
    of 10 and under 15
    of 15 and under 20
    of 20 and under 30
    of 30 and under 40
    of 40 and under 50
    of 50 and under 60
    of 60 and under 70
    of 70 and under 80
    of 80 and under 90
    of 90 and under 100
    of 100 and upward
- number of free white females
    under 5
    of 5 and under 10
    of 10 and under 15
    of 15 and under 20
    of 20 and under 30
    of 30 and under 40
    of 40 and under 50

of 50 and under 60
of 60 and under 70
of 70 and under 80
of 80 and under 90
of 90 and under 100
of 100 and upward
- number of males slaves
    under 10
    of 10 and under 24
    of 24 and under 36
    of 36 and under 55
    of 55 and under 100
    of 100 and upward
- number of female slaves
    under 10
    of 10 and under 24
    of 24 and under 36
    of 36 and under 55
    of 55 and under 100
    of 100 and upward
- number of free colored males
    under 10
    of 10 and under 24
    of 24 and under 36
    of 36 and under 55
    of 55 and under 100

of 100 and upward
- number of free colored females
    under 10
    of 10 and under 24
    of 24 and under 36
    of 36 and under 55
    of 55 and under 100
    of 100 and upward
- number of deaf and dumb white persons (male and female)
    under 14
    of 14 and under 25
    of 25 and upward
- number of blind whites
- number of deaf and dumb slaves and free blacks
    under 14
    of 14 and under 25
    of 25 and upward
- number of blind slaves and free colored persons
- number of white aliens/foreigners not naturalized

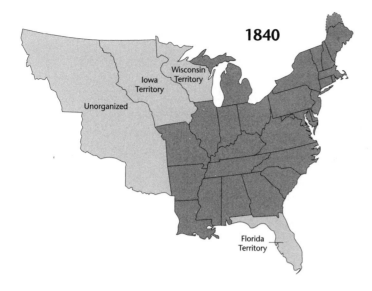

**1840**

*Adapted from AniMap County Boundary Historical Atlas*

## The 1840 census recorded:

- name of county, city, ward, town, township, parish, precinct, or district
- name of the head of the family
- number of free white males
    under 5
    5 and under 10
    10 and under 15
    15 and under 20
    20 and under 30
    30 and under 40
    40 and under 50
    50 and under 60
    60 and under 70
    70 and under 80
    80 and under 90
    90 and under 100
    100 and upward
- number of free white females
    under 5
    5 and under 10
    10 and under 15
    15 and under 20
    20 and under 30
    30 and under 40
    40 and under 50
    50 and under 60
    60 and under 70
    70 and under 80
    80 and under 90
    90 and under 100
    100 and upward
- number of free colored males
    under 10
    10 and under 24
    24 and under 36
    36 and under 55
    55 and under 100
    100 and upward
- number of free colored females
    under 10
    10 and under 24
    24 and under 36
    36 and under 55
    55 and under 100
    100 and upward
- number of male slaves
    under 10
    10 and under 24
    24 and under 36
    36 and under 55
    55 and under 100
    100 and upward
- number of female slaves
    under 10
    10 and under 24
    24 and under 36
    36 and under 55
    55 and under 100
    100 and upward
- number of persons employed in mining
- number of persons employed in agriculture
- number of persons employed in commerce
- number of persons employed in manufacturing and trades
- number of persons employed in navigation of the oceans
- number of persons employed in navigation of the lakes, canals, and rivers
- number of persons employed in learned professions and engineering
- names and ages of Revolutionary War or military service pensioners
- number of deaf and dumb whites
    under 14
    14 and under 25
    25 and upward
- number of blind whites
- number of insane and idiotic whites at private charge
- number of insane and idiotic whites at public charge
- number of scholars in universities and colleges, academies and grammar schools, and primary and common schools
- number of scholars at public charge
- number of white males over age twenty-one who could not read and write

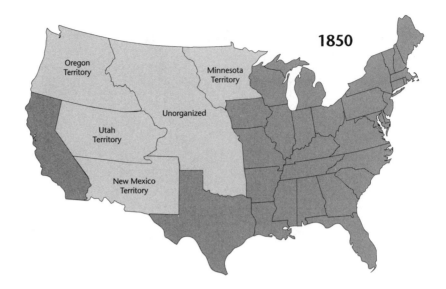

1850

*Adapted from AniMap County Boundary Historical Atlas*

## The 1850 free schedule recorded

- name, age, and sex of each individual in the household
- whether white, black, or mulatto
- profession, occupation, or trade of each individual over age fifteen
- value of the real estate owned by each individual
- state, territory, or country of birth
- whether married within the year
- whether attended school within the year
- whether could read and write, if over twenty years old
- whether deaf and dumb, blind, insane, idiotic, a pauper, or a convict

## The 1850 slave schedule recorded

- name of slave owner
- number of slaves, listed by age, sex, and color
- whether slave was a fugitive
- whether slave was deaf, dumb, insane, or idiotic
- number of slaves manumitted (granted freedom)
- number of slave houses owned

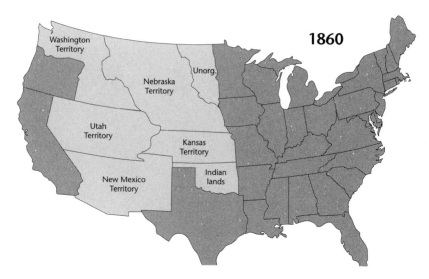

1860

*Adapted from AniMap County Boundary Historical Atlas*

## The 1860 free schedule recorded

- name, age, and sex of each individual in the household
- whether white, black, or mulatto
- profession, occupation, or trade of each male and female over age fifteen
- value of the real estate
- value of the personal property
- state, territory, or country of birth
- whether married within the year
- whether attended school within the year
- whether could read and write, if over age twenty
- whether deaf and dumb, blind, insane, idiotic, a pauper, or a convict

## The 1860 slave schedule recorded the following

- name of slave owner
- number of slaves, grouped by age, sex, and color
- whether slave was a fugitive
- whether slave was deaf, dumb, insane, or idiotic
- number of slaves manumitted (granted freedom)
- number of slave houses owned

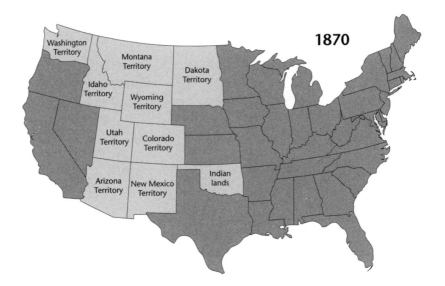

*Adapted from AniMap County Boundary Historical Atlas*

### The 1870 census recorded

- name, age, and sex of each individual in the household
- whether white, black, mulatto, Indian, or Chinese
- profession, occupation, or trade of each male and female over age fifteen
- value of the real estate
- value of the personal property
- state, territory, or country of birth
- whether married within the year
- whether attended school within the year
- whether could read and write, if over age twenty
- whether deaf and dumb, blind, insane, idiotic, a pauper, or a convict
- whether a male citizen over age twenty-one
- whether a male citizen over age twenty-one and right to vote had been denied or abridged on grounds other than rebellion or other crime

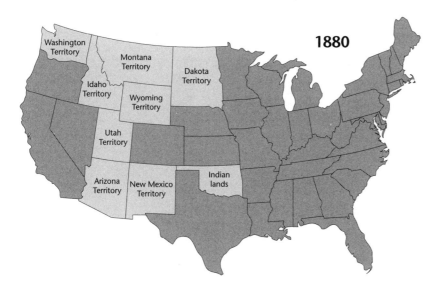

1880

Washington
Territory

Montana
Territory

Idaho
Territory

Dakota
Territory

Wyoming
Territory

Utah
Territory

Arizona
Territory

New Mexico
Territory

Indian
lands

*Adapted from AniMap County Boundary Historical Atlas*

## The 1880 census recorded

- the street name and house number in cities
- name, age, and sex of each individual in the household
- whether white, black, mulatto, Indian, or Chinese
- the month of birth, if born within the year
- relationship to head of household
- whether single, married, widowed, or divorced
- whether married within the year
- profession, occupation, or trade
- number of months unemployed during the census year
- whether sick or temporarily disabled so as not able to function normally, and if so, the nature of the illness
- whether blind, deaf and dumb, idiotic, insane, maimed, crippled, bedridden, or otherwise permanently disabled
- whether attended school within the year
- whether could read or write
- state, territory, or country of birth
- father's state, territory, or country of birth
- mother's state, territory, or country of birth

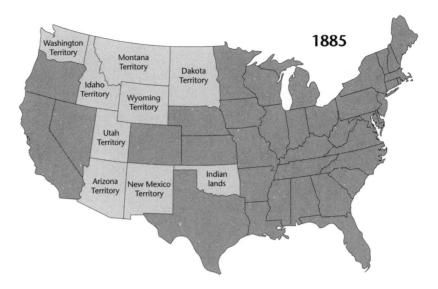

*Adapted from AniMap County Boundary Historical Atlas*

## The 1885 census recorded

- name
- color
- sex
- age
- relationship to head of family
- marital status
- occupation
- places of birth
- places of birth of parents
- literacy
- sickness or disability

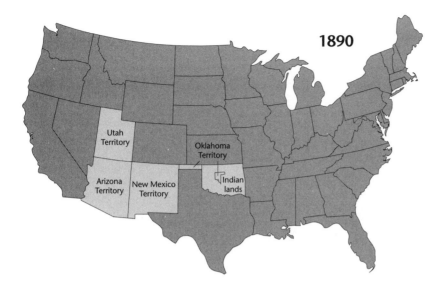

**1890**

*Adapted from AniMap County Boundary Historical Atlas*

## The 1890 census recorded

- the street name and house number in cities
- the number of families in the dwelling house and number of persons in the dwelling house
- the name, age, and sex of each individual in the household
- whether a soldier, sailor, or marine during the Civil War (Union or Confederate) or a widow of such person
- relationship to head of family
- whether white, black, mulatto, quadroon, octoroon, Chinese, Japanese, or Indian
- whether single, married, widowed, or divorced
- whether married during the census year
- mother of how many children, and number of these children living
- place of birth
- place of birth of father
- place of birth of mother
- number of years in the United States
- whether a naturalized citizen
- whether naturalization papers had been taken out
- profession, trade, or occupation
- number of months unemployed during the census year
- whether attended school during the census year
- whether able to read or write
- whether able to speak English; if not, the language or dialect spoken
- whether suffering from acute or chronic disease, with name of disease and length of time afflicted
- whether defective in mind, sight, hearing, or speech, or whether crippled, maimed, or deformed, with name of defect
- whether a prisoner, convict, homeless child, or pauper
- whether home or farm was rented or owned
- whether home or farm was free from mortgage

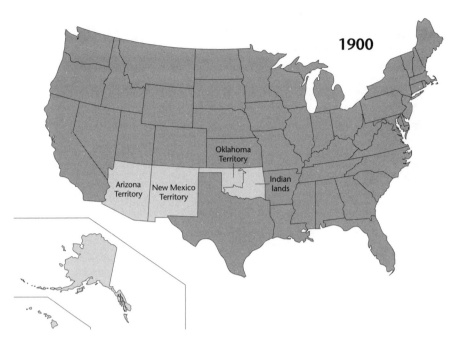

*Adapted from AniMap County Boundary Historical Atlas*

**The 1900 census recorded**

- street name and house number in cities
- Alaska only: month and year relocated to Alaska
- name and sex of each individual in the household
- relationship to the head of household
- color or race
- month and year of birth and age at last birthday
- whether single, married, widowed, or divorced
- number of years married
- number of children born to females, and the number of those children still living
- tribe and clan (Alaska only)
- place of birth
- father's place of birth
- mother's place of birth
- year of immigration to the United States
- number of years resided in the United States
- whether or not a naturalized citizen
- profession, occupation, or trade
- number of months unemployed during the census year
- whether attended school within the year
- whether able to read or write
- whether able to speak English
- whether family owned or rented their home, whether home was mortgaged, and if it was a farm or a house

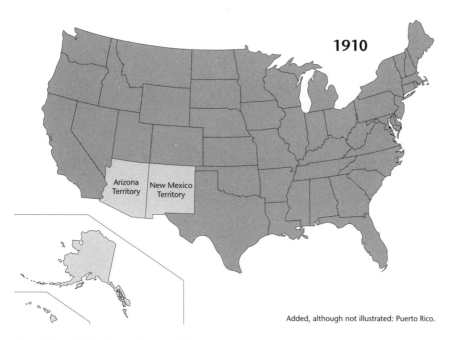

**1910**

Arizona Territory

New Mexico Territory

Added, although not illustrated: Puerto Rico.

*Adapted from AniMap County Boundary Historical Atlas*

## The 1910 census recorded

- street name and house number in cities
- name, age, and sex of each individual in the household
- relationship to the head of household
- color or race
- whether single, married, widowed, or divorced
- number of years in present marriage
- number of children born to females, and the number of those children still living
- tribe and clan (Alaska only)
- place of birth
- father's place of birth
- mother's place of birth
- year of immigration to the United States
- whether naturalized or an alien
- language spoken
- profession, occupation, or trade
- type of industry
- whether an employee, employer, or self-employed
- if an employee, whether or not currently employed, and number of weeks out of work in 1909
- whether attended school anytime since September 1909
- whether able to read or write
- whether family owned or rented their home, whether mortgaged, and if a farm or a house
- whether a survivor of the Union or Confederate Army or Navy
- whether blind, deaf, or dumb

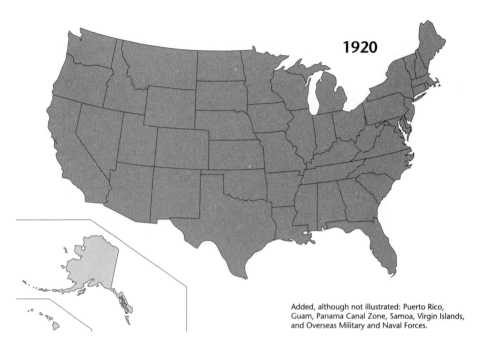

1920

Added, although not illustrated: Puerto Rico, Guam, Panama Canal Zone, Samoa, Virgin Islands, and Overseas Military and Naval Forces.

*Adapted from AniMap County Boundary Historical Atlas*

### The 1920 census recorded

- street or road name, whether a house number or if a farm
- name, age, and sex of each individual in the household
- relationship to the head of household
- whether owned or rented home and if mortgaged
- color or race
- whether single, married, widowed, or divorced
- year of immigration
- whether naturalized or an alien
- if naturalized, the year of naturalization
- whether attended school since September 1919
- whether able to read and write
- place of birth
- father's place of birth and mother tongue
- mother's place of birth and mother tongue
- whether able to speak English, and if not, language spoken
- profession, occupation, or trade
- type of industry
- whether an employee, employer, or self-employed
- if an employee, whether or not currently employed, and number of weeks out of work in 1919

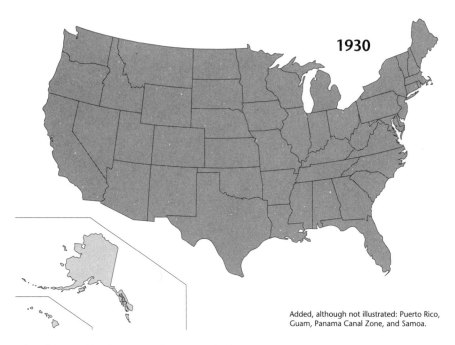

**1930**

Added, although not illustrated: Puerto Rico, Guam, Panama Canal Zone, and Samoa.

*Adapted from AniMap County Boundary Historical Atlas*

## The 1930 census recorded

- *street or road name, whether a house number or if a farm
- name, age, and sex of each individual in the household
- relationship to the head of household
- *whether owned or rented home and if mortgaged
- *value of home if owned or monthly payment
- *whether owned a radio set
- color or race
- whether single, married, widowed, or divorced
- *age at first marriage
- whether attended school
- whether able to read and write
- place of birth
- father's place of birth
- mother's place of birth
- *language spoken in home before coming to the United States
- year of immigration
- whether naturalized or an alien
- whether able to speak English
- type of profession or kind of work
- type of industry or business
- *class of worker
- whether worked yesterday or the last regular working day
- whether a veteran, and if so, what war

*These questions were *not* included in the Alaska census.

# *Abbreviations*

T hese abbreviations are divided into eight categories: (1) citizenship, (2) employment, (3) occupations, (4) ownership of home, (5) race, (6) relationship, (7) war, and (8) other abbreviations. For a comprehensive treatment of genealogical abbreviations, consult Kip Sperry's *Abbreviations & Acronyms: A Guide for Family Historians* (Orem, Utah: Ancestry Publishing, 2000).

## Citizenship

| | |
|---|---|
| A | Alien |
| NA | Naturalized |
| PA | First papers filed |

## Employment

| | |
|---|---|
| E | Employer |
| Em | Self-employed (1920) |
| Emp | Employer |
| NP | Unpaid family worker (1930) |
| O or OA | Own account |
| W | Wage or salary worker |

## Occupations

| | | | |
|---|---|---|---|
| Agric | Agriculture | FaH | Farmhand |
| Agt | Agent | FaL | Farm laborer |
| Ap | Apprentice | FaW | Farm worker |
| Asst | Assistant | Fi | Fireman |
| At | Attendant | He | Herder |
| Bar | Bartender | HGi | Hired girl |
| Bu | Butler | HH | Hired hand |
| Co | Company | Hk | Housekeeper |
| Coa | Coachman | Hm | Hired man |
| Comsn | Commission | HMaid | Housemaid |
| Dept | Department | Hw | Houseworker |
| Dla | Day laborer | Insr | Insurance |
| Dom | Domestic | La | Laborer |
| Dw | Dishwasher | Lau | Launderer |
| Emp | Employee | Man | Manager |
| En | Engineer | Merch | Merchant |
| Fcty | Factory | Mfg | Manufacturing |

| | | | | |
|---|---|---|---|---|
| Mfr | Manufacturer | | Sal | Saleslady |
| Nu | Nurse | | Sch | School |
| O | Officer | | Secy | Secretary |
| P | Patient | | Su | Superintendent |
| Pa | Partner | | Supt | Superintendent |
| Ph | Physician | | Teleg | Telegraph |
| Por | Porter | | Telph | Telephone |
| Pr | Prisoner | | Trav | Traveling or traveler |
| Prest | President | | Treas | Treasurer |
| Pri | Principal | | Wa | Warden |
| Prv | Private | | Wai | Waitress |
| Pu | Pupil | | Wkm | Workman |
| R.R. | Railroad or railway | | Wt | Waiter |
| Sa | Sailor | | | |

## Ownership of Home

| | |
|---|---|
| F | Free of mortgage |
| Fm | Farm |
| M | Mortgaged |
| O | Owned |
| R | Rented |

## Race

| | | | | |
|---|---|---|---|---|
| C or Ch | Chinese | | Ot | Other |
| B | Black | | I or In | Indian |
| Fil | Filipino | | Mex | Mexican |
| Hin | Hindu | | Mu | Mulatto |
| Jp | Japanese | | Neg | Negro (1930) |
| Kor | Korean | | W | White |

## Relationship

| | | | | |
|---|---|---|---|---|
| A | Aunt | | Cha | Chamber Maid |
| Ad | Adopted | | Cil | Cousin-in-law |
| AdCl | Adopted child | | Cl | Child |
| AdD | Adopted daughter | | Com | Companion |
| AdGcl | Adopted grandchild | | D | Daughter |
| AdM | Adopted mother | | Dl | Daughter-in-law |
| AdS | Adopted son | | F | Father |
| Al | Aunt-in-law | | FB | Foster brother |
| B | Brother | | FF | Foster father |
| BBoy | Bound boy | | First C | First cousin |
| BGirl | Bound girl | | FL | Father-in-law |
| Bl | Brother-in-law | | FM | Foster mother |
| Bo | Boarder | | FoB | Foster brother |
| C | Cousin | | FoS | Foster son |
| Cap | Captain | | FoSi | Foster sister |

| GA | Great-aunt | Ni | Niece |
| Gcl | Grandchild | Nil | Niece-in-law |
| GD | Granddaughter | Nl | Nephew-in-law |
| GF | Grandfather | R | Roomer |
| GGF | Great-grandfather | S | Son |
| GGGF | Great-great-grandfather | Sb | Stepbrother |
| GGGM | Great-great-grandmother | Sbl | Stepbrother-in-law |
| GGM | Great-grandmother | Scl | Stepchild |
| GM | Grandmother | Sd | Stepdaugther |
| Gml | Grandmother-in-law | Sdl | Stepdaughter-in-law |
| GN | Grand- or great-nephew | Se | Servant |
| Gni | Grand- or great-niece | SeCl | Servant's child |
| G | Governess | Sf | Stepfather |
| God Cl | Godchild | Sfl | Stepfather-in-law |
| GS | Grandson | Sgd | Stepgranddaughter |
| Gsl | Grandson-in-law | Sgs | Stepgrandson |
| GU | Great-uncle | Si | Sister |
| Gua | Guardian | Sl | Son-in-law |
| H | Husband | Sm | Stepmother |
| Hb | Half brother | Sml | Stepmother-in-law |
| Hbl | Half brother-in-law | Ss | Stepson |
| Hsi | Half sister | Ssi | Stepsister |
| HSil | Half sister-in-law | Ssil | Stepsister-in-law |
| Husb | Husband | Ssl | Stepson-in-law |
| L | Lodger | Ten | Tenant |
| M | Mother | U | Uncle |
| Mat | Matron | Ul | Uncle-in-law |
| ML | Mother-in-law | Vi | Visitor |
| N | Nephew | W | Wife |

## War (1930)

| Box | Boxer Rebellion | Phil | Philippine Insurrection |
| Civ | Civil War | Sp | Spanish-American War |
| Mex | Mexican Expedition | WW | World War |

## Other Abbreviations

| Dist | District | MCD | Municipal Civil District |
| Do | Ditto | NR | Not reported |
| DT | Dakota Territory | Twp | Township |
| IT | Indian Territory | | |

# *The Census on the Internet*

## Census Images and Indexes for Sale (CD-ROM, Microfilm)

ALLCENSUS
  www.allcensus.com/
Blue Roses Publishing Company
  www.angelfire.com/tx/1850censusrecords/cdrom/
Census4all
  www.census4all.com
Census View
  www.censusview.org/
FamilySearch
  1880  U.S. census and national index
  www.familysearch.org
Frontier Press
  www.frontierpress.com/frontier.cgi
Genealogy.com
  www.genealogy.com
Genealogical Publishing Company
  www.genealogical.com/
Heritage Quest
  www.heritagequest.com
S-K Publications
  www.skpub.com/genie/
Scholarly Resources, Inc.
  www.scholarly.com/
Willow Bend Books
  www.willowbendbooks.com

## Census Images Online

Ancestry.com
  www.ancestry.com
  Subscription required
Genealogy.com
  www.genealogy.com
  Subscription required
HeritageQuest Online
  www.heritagequest.com
  Subscription required
USGenWeb Census Project
  www.us-census.org/ and www.rootsweb.com/~census
  Free displays of census images

## Census Portals

Census Links
  http://censuslinks.com/
Census Online Links
  www.census-online.com/links/index.html
Cyndi's List
  www.cyndislist.com/census.htm
  Cyndi's List is the most famous and comprehensive genealogical portal, with over 100,000 links to genealogy Web sites. It has over four hundred links for "U.S. Census" and over one hundred links for "Census-Related Sites Worldwide." The U.S. census category is sorted into seven topics:
  1. 1890 Federal Census
  2. General Resource Sites
  3. Printable Census Forms
  4. Publications, Software & Supplies
  5. Soundex
  6. U.S. Census Indexes & Records (arranged chronologically and then alphabetically)
  7. USGenWeb Archives Census Project (alphabetical by state)
GenealogyPortal.com
  www.genealogyportal.com/
  GenealogyPortal.com features eight search engines—one of which is specific to census records.
USGenWeb Census Project
  Online Inventory of Transcribed Census Files
  www.us-census.org/inventory/
  Volunteers transcribed the census records posted at the USGenWeb Census Project. Each individual transcriber holds a copyright; therefore, the transcriptions may not be used for commercial purposes without written permission.

## Demographics

Demographia
  www.demographia.com
Integrated Public Use Microdata Series (IPUMS)
  www.ipums.org/
United States Historical Census Data Browser (1790 Through 1970)
  http://fisher.lib.virginia.edu/census/
The White House Social Statistics Briefing Room
  www.whitehouse.gov/fsbr/demography.html

## Enumerator Instructions

Enumerator Instructions, 1850 Through 1990
  www.ipums.umn.edu/~pipums/voliii/tEnumInstr.html

## Maps

AniMap Plus

www.goldbug.com

Over 2,300 historical maps displayed in color for consecutive years—not just the census years.

Animation of Boundary Changes

www.ac.wwu.edu/~stephan/Animation/animation.html

Oregon Counties: 1851–1917

Washington State Counties: 1844–1911

California Missions: 1769–1823

Formation of Contiguous United States: 1650–1907

United States Counties: 1650–1983

Library of Congress Map Collections: 1500–1999

http://lcweb2.loc.gov/ammem/gmdhtml/gmdhome.html

Perry-Castañeda Library Map Collection, University of Texas at Austin

www.lib.utexas.edu/maps/histus.html

Maps from The National Atlas of the United States of America (Arch C. Gerlach, editor. Washington, D.C.: U.S. Dept. of the Interior, Geological Survey, 1970) showing territorial growth 1775 to 1920. These maps can be viewed online. The university also provides links to several other Internet sites with historical maps.

## NARA Catalogs

*American Indians: A Select Catalog of National Archives Microfilm Publications* Revised. Washington, D.C.: National Archives and Records Administration, 1998. Online catalog is dated 1995; print catalog is dated 1998.

www.nara.gov/publications/microfilm/amerindians/indians.html

Microfilm Census Catalogs for Purchase

1790–1890, 1900, 1910, 1920, 1930

www.nara.gov/publications/micro.html#census

## NARA Genealogy Page

www.nara.gov/genealogy/genindex.html

## Orphans

Orphans' Home Web Site

http://freepages.genealogy.rootsweb.com/~orphanshome/

This new Web site is up and running *and* under construction, but it promises to be a great contribution to the genealogical field. Transcriptions are given of orphans, adoptees, and foster children who resided in orphanages, homes, and poorhouses as of U.S. and Canadian censuses. The site will also include orphanage fact sheets for each orphanage showing dates of operation and location of records. Orphanage rosters giving birth dates and other information on orphans will also be posted on the site.

## Soundex

NARA Soundex Indexing System
   www.nara.gov/genealogy/coding.html
Soundex Calculators
   National Archives: www.nara.gov/genealogy/soundex/soundex.html
   Family Tree Magazine: www.familytreemagazine.com/soundex.html
   RootsWeb: http://searches.rootsweb.com/cgi-bin/Genea/soundex.sh
   JewishGen: www.jewishgen.org/jos/

## U.S. Census Bureau

   www.census.gov/
Census Geographic Glossary
   www.census.gov/geo/lv4help/cengeoglos.html
How to Access and Use Census Bureau Data
   www.census.gov/mso/www/npr/access.html
State Data Center Program
   www.census.gov/sdc/www/
   State agencies and university facilities
Statistical Abstract of the United States
   www.census.gov/statab/www/

# *Bibliography*

The bibliography is divided into eleven categories, arranged alphabetically: American Indians (Native Americans); Black; Catalogs and Inventories; Finding Aids; General Reference: Books; General Reference: Journal Articles; Handwriting; Maps; Methodology: Journal Articles; NonPopulation Census; and State, Colonial, and International Censuses.

## AMERICAN INDIANS (NATIVE AMERICANS)

Ellsworth, Carole, and Sue Emler. *1900 U. S. Census of the Cherokee Indian Nation*. 5 vols. Gore, Okla.: Oklahoma Roots Research, 1982.

Hill, Edward E. *Guide to Records in the National Archives of the United States Relating to American Indians*. Washington, D.C.: National Archives and Records Administration, 1981.

May, Katja. *African Americans and Native Americans in the Creek and Cherokee Nations, 1830s to 1920s: Collision and Collusion*. Rev. ed. New York: Garland Publishing, 1996.

———. "Records of Native Americans." Chap. 11 in *Guide to Genealogical Research in the National Archives*. 3d ed. Washington D.C.: National Archives Trust Fund Board, 2000.

Prechtel-Kluekens, Claire. "American Indian Censuses, 1880–1920." *The Record* (May 1997): 21–22, 24.

Siler, David. *The Eastern Cherokees: A Census of the Cherokee Nation in North Carolina, Tennessee, Alabama, and Georgia in 1851*. New Orleans: Polyanthos, 1977.

Witcher, Curt B., and George J. Nixon. "Tracking Native American Family History." Chap. 14 in *The Source: A Guidebook of American Genealogy*, edited by Loretto Dennis Szucs and Sandra Hargreaves Luebking. Rev. ed. Salt Lake City: Ancestry, 1997.

## BLACK

Burroughs, Tony. *Black Roots: A Beginner's Guide to Tracing the African American Family Tree*. New York: Fireside Book, 2001.

———. "Finding African Americans on the 1870 census." *Heritage Quest Magazine* 17 (January–February 2001): 50–56.

Byers, Paula K., ed. *African American Genealogical Sourcebook*. Detroit: Gale Research, 1995.

Cerny, Johni. "From Maria to Bill Crosby: A Case Study in Tracing Black Slave Ancestry." *National Genealogical Society Quarterly* 75 (March 1987): 5–14.

Fears, Mary L., and Charles L. Blockson. *Slave Ancestral Research: It's Something Else*. Bowie, Md.: Heritage Books, 1995.

Frankel, Noralee. "From Slave Women to Free Women: The National Archives and Black Women's History in the Civil War Era." *Prologue* [Quarterly of the National Archives and Records Administration] 29 (Summer 1997): 100–101.

Heinegg, Paul. *Free African Americans of North Carolina and Virginia*, 3d ed. Baltimore: Clearfield Publishers, 1997.

Hoff, Henry B. "A Colonial Black Family in New York and New Jersey: Peter Santomee and His Descendants." *Journal of Afro-American Historical and Genealogical Society* 9 (Fall 1988): 101–134, and "Additions and Corrections," in vol. 10 (Winter 1989): 158–160.

May, Katja. *African Americans & Native Americans in the Creek and Cherokee Nations, 1830s to 1920s: Collision and Collusion*. Rev. ed. New York: Garland Publishing, 1996.

Mills, Gary B. "Tracing Free People of Color in the Antebellum South: Methods, Sources, and Perspectives." *National Genealogical Society Quarterly* 78 (December 1990): 262–278.

National Archives and Records Administration. "Records of African Americans." Chap. 12 in *Guide to Genealogical Research in the National Archives*. 3d ed. Washington, D.C.: National Archives Trust Fund Board, 2000.

Sanborn, Melinde Lutz. "Angola and Elizabeth: An African Family in the Massachusetts Bay Colony." *The New England Quarterly* LXXII (March 1999): 119–129.

Streets, David H. *Slave Genealogy: A Research Guide With Case Studies*. Bowie, Md.: Heritage Books, 1986.

Thackery, David T. "Tracking African-American Family History." Chap. 15 in *The Source: A Guidebook of American Genealogy*, edited by Loretto Dennis Szucs and Sandra Hargreaves Luebking. Rev.ed. Salt Lake City: Ancestry, 1997.

Witcher, Curt Bryan. *African American Genealogy: A Bibliography and Guide to Sources*. Fort Wayne, Ind.: Round Tower Books, 2000.

Woodtor, Dee Parmer. *Finding a Place Called Home: A Guide to African-American Genealogy and Historical Identity*. Rev. ed. New York: Random House, 1999.

## CATALOGS AND INVENTORIES

Cook, Kevin L. *Dubester's U.S. Census Bibliography With SuDocs Class Numbers and Indexes*. Englewood, Colo.: Libraries Unlimited, 1996.

Davidson, Katherine H., and Charlotte M. Ashby, comp. *Preliminary Inventory of the Records of the Bureau of the Census*. Preliminary Inventory No. 161. 1964. Reprint, Washington, D.C.: National Archives and Records Service, 1997.

National Archives and Records Administration. *American Indians: A Select Catalog of National Archives Microfilm Publications*. Rev. ed. Washington, D.C.: National Archives and Records Administration, 1998.

———. *Black Studies: A Select Catalog of National Archives Microfilm Publications.* Rev. ed. Washington, D.C.: National Archives and Records Administration, 1996.

———. *Guide to Federal Records in the National Archives of the United States.* 3 vols. Washington, D.C.: National Archives and Records Administration, 1995.

National Archives Trust Fund Board. *1790–1890 Federal Population Censuses: Catalog of National Archives Microfilm.* Rev. ed. Washington, D.C.: National Archives Trust Fund Board, 1997.

———. *The 1900 Federal Population Census: Catalog of National Archives Microfilm.* Rev. ed. Washington. D.C.: National Archives Trust Fund Board, 1996.

———. *1910 Federal Population Census: Catalog of National Archives Microfilms.* Rev. ed. Washington, D.C.: National Archives Trust Fund Board, 1996.

———. *1920 Federal Population Census: Catalog of National Archives Microfilms.* Rev. ed. Washington, D.C.: National Archives Trust Fund Board, 1995.

———. *1930 Federal Population Census: Catalog of National Archives Microfilms.* Rev. ed. Washington, D.C.: National Archives Trust Fund Board, 2002.

———. *Microfilm Resources for Research: A Comprehensive Catalog.* Washington, D.C.: National Archives Trust Fund Board, 2000.

## FINDING AIDS

Buckway, G. Eileen, et. al. *U.S. 1910 Federal Census: Unindexed States: A Guide to Finding Census Enumeration Districts for Unindexed Cities, Towns, and Villages.* Salt Lake City: Family History Library, 1992.

Bureau of the Census. *Heads of Families at the First Census of the United States Taken in the Year 1790.* 12 vols. Washington, D.C.: Government Printing Office, 1908.

*A Census of Pensioners for Revolutionary or Military Services,* 1841. Reprint, Baltimore: Genealogical Publishing Co., 1996

Church of Jesus Christ of Latter-day Saints. *Resource Guide: Accelerated Indexing Systems (AIS) Indexes to U.S. Censuses 1607-1906.* 4th ed. Salt Lake City: 1997.

Eales, Anne Bruner, and Robert M. Kvasnicka, eds. *Guide to Genealogical Research in the National Archives.* 3d ed. Washington, D.C.: National Archives and Records Administration, 2000.

Kemp, Thomas Jay. *The American Census Handbook.* Wilmington, Del.: Scholarly Resources Inc., 2001.

## GENERAL REFERENCE: BOOKS

Anderson, Margo J. *The American Census: A Social History.* New Haven: Yale University Press, 1988.

————. *Encyclopedia of the U.S. Census*. Washington, D.C.: C.Q. Press, 2000.

Anderson, Margo J., and Stephen E. Fienberg. *Who Counts? The Politics of Census-Taking in Contemporary America*. New York: Russell Sage Foundation, 1999.

*A Century of Population Growth From the First Census of the United States to the Twelfth*. 1909. Reprint, Baltimore: Genealogical Publishing Company, 1989.

Department of Commerce, Bureau of the Census. *Fourteenth Census of the United States, January 1, 1920: Instructions to Enumerators*. Washington, D.C.: Government Printing Office, 1919.

Dollarhide, William S. *The Census Book: A Genealogist's Guide to Federal Census Facts, Schedules and Indexes*. Bountiful, Utah: Heritage Quest, 1999.

Greenwood, Val D. "Census Returns" and "Using Census Returns." Chaps. 13–14 in *The Researcher's Guide to American Genealogy*. 3d ed. Baltimore: Genealogical Publishing Company, 2000.

National Archives and Records Administration. "Census Records" and "Cartographic Records." Chaps. 1 and 19 in *Guide to Genealogical Research in the National Archives*. Washington, D.C.: 1982,1985. Rev. ed. Washington, D.C.: National Archives Trust Fund Board, 2000.

Saldana, Richard H. *A Practical Guide to the "Misteaks" Made in the Census Indexes*. Salt Lake City: R.H. Saldana & Company, 1987.

Szucs, Loretto Dennis. "Research in Census Records." In *The Source: A Guidebook of American Genealogy*, edited by Loretto Dennis Szucs and Sandra Hargreaves Luebking. Salt Lake City: Ancestry, 1997.

Szucs, Loretto Dennis, and Sandra Hargreaves Luebking. *The Archives: A Guide to the National Archives Field Branches*. Salt Lake City: Ancestry, 1988.

U.S. Bureau of the Census. *200 Years of U.S. Census Taking: Population and Housing Questions, 1790–1990*. Washington, D.C.: Government Printing Office, 1989. [Earlier editions had different titles: *Population and Housing Inquiries in U.S. Decennial Censuses, 1790–1970* (1973) and *Twenty Censuses: Population and Housing Questions, 1790–1980* (1979).]

U.S. Congress Office. Eighth Census, 1860. *Eighth Census, United States— 1860. Act of Congress of Twenty-third May, 1850. Instructions to U.S. Marshals, Instructions to Assistants*. Washington, D.C.: G.W. Bowman, 1860. Enumerator's instructions for the 1860 census [omitted from *The History and Growth of the United States Census* compiled by Carroll D. Wright and William C. Hunt and *200 Years of U.S. Census Taking*.]

U.S. Congress, Senate. *The History and Growth of the United States Census*. Carroll D. Wright and William C. Hunt, comps. S. Doc. 194, 56 Congress, 1st session. Serial 385b. Reprint, 1967.

## GENERAL REFERENCE: JOURNAL ARTICLES

Anderson, Robert C., et. al. "Duplicate Census Enumerations." *The American Genealogist* 62 (April 1987): 97–105; 62 (July 1987): 173–81; 62 (October 1987): 241–44.

Blake, Kellee. "First in the Path of the Firemen: The Fate of the 1890 Population Census." *Prologue* [Quarterly of the National Archives and Records Administration] 28 (Spring 1996): 64–81.

Green, Kellee. "The Fourteenth Numbering of the People; the 1920 Federal Census." *Prologue* [Quarterly of the National Archives and Records Administration] 23 (Summer 1991): 131–145.

Joslyn, Roger D. "The 'Short-Form' 1880 and 1890 Federal Censuses." *The American Genealogist* 69 (October 1994): 231–233.

Parham, R. Bruce. "Finding People on the 1930 Census." Paper presented at the Family History Seminar, Family History Center, Anchorage, Alaska, March 24, 2001. Anchorage, Alaska: National Archives and Records Administration—Pacific Alaska Region, 2001. [Copies available from NARA's Pacific Alaska Region.]

Petty, Gerald M. "Virginia 1820 Federal Census: Names Not on the Microfilm Copy." *The Virginia Genealogist* 18 (1974): 136–139.

Pierce, Alycon Trubey. "In Praise of Errors Made by Census Enumerators." *National Genealogical Society Quarterly* 81 (March 1993): 51–55.

———. "Update: More Praise for Census 'Errors.' " *National Genealogical Society Quarterly* 82 (September 1994): 216–220.

Purdue, Bobbie. "Diary for 1910. Fleta M. Myers, Census Enumerator." *Orange County California Genealogical Society Journal* 33 (April 1996): 12–16.

Sipe, Karen V. "Hyphenated Names: A 'Modern' Problem in Historic Records." *NGS Newsmagazine* 27 (January/February 2001): 50–53.

Watts, Dorothy Chambers, and Harry A. Nelms. "Missing Households: Saint Clair County, Alabama, 1850." *National Genealogical Society Quarterly* 77 (March 1989): 66–67.

## HANDWRITING

Kirkham, Kay E. *Handwriting of American Records for a Period of 300 Years.* Logan, Utah: Everton Publishers, 1981.

Minert, Roger P. *Deciphering Handwriting in German Documents.* Woods Cross, Utah: GRT Publications, 2001.

Sperry, Kip. *Reading Early American Handwriting.* 2d ed. Baltimore, Md.: Genealogical Publishing Company, 2001.

Stryker-Rodda, Harriet. *Understanding Colonial Handwriting.* Baltimore: Genealogical Publishing Company, 1993.

## MAPS

Carpenter, Bruce. "Using Soundex Alternatives: Enumeration Districts, 1880–1920." *Prologue* [Quarterly of the National Archives and Records Administration] 25 (Spring 1993): 90–93.

Long, John Hamilton. *Atlas of Historical County Boundaries.* New York: Simon & Schuster, 1993.

————. *Atlas of Historical County Boundaries. Alabama.* Peggy Tuck Sinko, comp. New York: Charles Scribner's Sons, 1996.

————. *Atlas of Historical County Boundaries: Connecticut, Maine, Massachusetts, Rhode Island.* John Hamilton Long and Gordon DenBoer, comp. New York: Simon & Schuster, 1994.

————. *Atlas of Historical County Boundaries. Delaware, Maryland, and the District of Columbia.* New York: Charles Scribner's Sons, Simon & Schuster MacMillan, 1996.

————. *Atlas of Historical County Boundaries. Florida.* Peggy Tuck Sinko, comp. New York: Charles Scribner's Sons, 1997.

————. *Atlas of Historical County Boundaries. Illinois.* Gordon DenBoer, comp. New York: Charles Scribner's Sons, 1997.

————. *Atlas of Historical County Boundaries. Indiana.* Peggy Tuck Sinko, comp. New York: Simon & Schuster, 1996.

————. *Atlas of Historical County Boundaries. Iowa.* Gordon DenBoer, comp. New York: Charles Scribner's Sons, 1998.

————. *Atlas of Historical County Boundaries. Kentucky.* Gordon DenBoer, comp. New York: Simon & Schuster, 1995.

————. *Atlas of Historical County Boundaries. Michigan.* Peggy Tuck Sinko, comp. New York: Charles Scribner's Sons, 1997.

————. *Atlas of Historical County Boundaries. Minnesota.* Gordon DenBoer, comp. New York: Charles Scribner's Sons, 2000.

————. *Atlas of Historical County Boundaries. Mississippi.* Peggy Tuck Sinko, comp. New York: Simon & Schuster, 1993.

————. *Atlas of Historical County Boundaries. New Hampshire, Vermont.* Gordon DenBoer and George E. Goodridge, comps. New York: Simon & Schuster, 1993.

————. *Atlas of Historical County Boundaries. New York.* Kathryn Ford Thorne, comp. New York: Simon & Schuster, 1993.

————. *Atlas of Historical County Boundaries. North Carolina.* Gordon DenBoer, comp. New York: Charles Scribner's Sons. London: Simon & Schuster Prentice-Hall International, 1998.

————. *Atlas of Historical County Boundaries. Ohio.* Peggy Tuck Sinko, comp. New York: Charles Scribner's Sons, 1998.

————. *Atlas of Historical County Boundaries. Pennsylvania.* Gordon DenBoer, comp. New York: Simon & Schuster, 1996.

————. *Atlas of Historical County Boundaries. South Carolina.* Gordon DenBoer and Katheryn Ford Thoren, comps. New York: Charles Scribner's Sons, 1997.

————. *Atlas of Historical County Boundaries. Tennessee.* Peggy Tuck Sinko, comp. New York: Charles Scribner's Sons, 2000.

————. *Atlas of Historical County Boundaries. Wisconsin.* Gordon DenBoer, comp. New York: Simon & Schuster, 1997.

————. *Historical Atlas and Chronology of County Boundaries, 1788–1980.* Volume 1: Delaware, Maryland, New Jersey, Pennsylvania. John Hamilton Long, comp. Boston, Mass.: G.K. Hall, 1984.

Volume 2: Illinois, Indiana, Ohio. Stephen L. Hansen, comp. Boston, Mass.: G.K. Hall, 1984.

Volume 3: Michigan, Wisconsin. Hugo P. Learning and John Hamilton Long, comps. Boston, Mass.: G.K. Hall, 1984.

Volume 4: Iowa, Missouri. Adele Hast and John Hamilton Long, comps. Boston, Mass.: G.K. Hall, 1984.

Volume 5: Minnesota, North Dakota, South Dakota. Mark P. Donovan and Jeffrey D. Siebert, comps. Boston, Mass.: G.K. Hall, 1984.

National Archives and Record Service. *Cartographic Records of the Bureau of the Census*. Preliminary Inventory No. 103. Washington, D.C.: 1958.

Parker, J. Carlyle. *City, County, Town and Township Index to the 1850 Federal Census Schedules*. 1979. Reprint, Detroit, Mich.: Gale Research Company, 1994.

Thorndale, William, and William Dollarhide. *Map Guide to the U.S. Federal Censuses, 1790–1920*. Baltimore: Genealogical Publishing Company, 1987.

## METHODOLOGY: JOURNAL ARTICLES

Anderson, Joseph Crook, II. "Family Reconstruction Using Pre-1850 Census Returns: A Working Example." *The Maine Genealogist* 16 (February 1994): 19–25.

Barrows, Robert G. "The Ninth Federal Census of Indianapolis: A Case Study in Civic Chauvinism." *Indiana Magazine of History* 73 ( March 1977): 1–16.

Cerny, Johni. "From Maria to Bill Crosby: A Case Study in Tracing Black Slave Ancestry." *National Genealogical Society Quarterly* 75 (March 1987): 5–14.

Hoff, Henry B. "A Colonial Black Family in New York and New Jersey: Peter Santomee and His Descendants." *Journal of Afro-American Historical and Genealogical Society* 9 (Fall 1988): 101–134, and "Additions and Corrections" vol. 10 (Winter 1989): 158–160.

Mills, Donna Rachal. "Rachal 'Fanny' Devereaux/Martin of Alabama and Florida, A Free Woman of Color: Discovering a Name Change Through the Federal Census," *The American Genealogist* 70 (January 1995): 37–41.

Mills, Elizabeth Shown, and Gary B. Mills. "Those !#$%&! Census Traps— Here's Two We Can Avoid!" *National Genealogical Society Quarterly* 82 (December 1997): 243.

Mills, Gary B. "Tracing Free People of Color in the Antebellum South: Methods, Sources, and Perspectives." *National Genealogical Society Quarterly* 78 (December 1990): 262–278.

Sanborn, Melinde Lutz. "Angola and Elizabeth: An African Family in the Massachusetts Bay Colony." *The New England Quarterly* LXXII (March 1999): 119–129.

Winslow, Raymond A., Jr. "Some Observations on the Use of the 1850 Census,

With a Case Study of Proven Errors." *The North Carolina Genealogical Society Journal* 26 (February 2000): 37–71.


## NON-POPULATION CENSUS

Fishbein, Meyer H. *The Censuses of Manufactures, 1810–1890.* Reference Information Paper 50. Washington, D.C.: National Archives and Records Service, 1973.

Hatten, Ruth Land. "Finding 'Missing Men' on Early Census Records." *National Genealogical Society Quarterly* 81 (March 1993): 46–50.

————. "The 'Forgotten' Census of 1880: Defective, Dependent, and Delinquent Classes." *National Genealogical Society Quarterly* 80 (March 1992): 57–70.

Mills, Donna Rachal. *Florida Unfortunates. The 1880 Federal Census: Defective, Dependent, and Delinquent Classes.* Tuscaloosa, Ala. and Orlando, Fla.: Mills Historical Press, 1993.

Warren, James, W. *Minnesota 1900 Census Mortality Schedule.* St. Paul, Minn.: Warren Research & Marketing Publications, 1996.


## STATE, COLONIAL, AND INTERNATIONAL CENSUSES

Bureau of the Census. *Records of State Enumerations, 1782–1785.* 1908. Reprint, Baltimore: Genealogical Publishing Company, 1970.

Davenport, David P. "Duration of Residence in the 1855 Census of New York State." *Historical Methods* 18 (Winter 1985): 5–12.

Greene, Evarts B., and Virginia D. Harrington. *American Population Before the Federal Census of 1790.* 1932. Reprint, Baltimore: Genealogical Publishing Company, 1993.

Lainhart, Ann S. *State Census Records.* Baltimore: Genealogical Publishing Company, 1992.

Matthews, Raymond G., ed. *New York City 1915 State Census Street Address Index. Volume 2, Brooklyn.* Lois Owen and Theodore R. Nelson, comps. Salt Lake City: Family History Library, 1993.

Olmsted, Virginia Langham. *Spanish and Mexican Colonial Census of New Mexico: 1790, 1823, 1845.* Albuquerque: New Mexico Genealogical Society, 1975.

Smith, Daniel Scott. "How Half a Million Iowa Women Suddenly Went to Work: Solving a Mystery in the State Census of 1925." *The Annals of Iowa* 55 (Fall 1996): 374–393.

Wynne, Frances Holloway. *North Carolina Extant Voter Registration of 1867.* Bowie, Md.: Heritage Books, 1992.

# Index

# Get better research results with Betterway Books!

**Locating Lost Family Members & Friends**—Kathleen W. Hinckley combines her skills as a professional private investigator and Certified Genealogical Record Specialist to help you find the people you're looking for, no matter who or where they might be. She shows you how to access and use a broad range of resources to find names, addresses, phone numbers, occupations, and other current data.
*ISBN 1-55870-503-1, paperback, 176 pages, #70428-K*

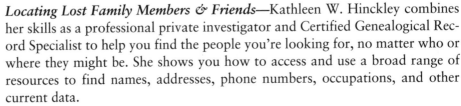

**Your Guide to Cemetery Research**—This comprehensive, in-depth reference illuminates the fascinating practice of cemetery research. From determining an ancestor's final resting place to decoding mysterious headstone symbols, Sharon DeBartolo Carmack shows you how cemeteries can help fill the holes in your precious family history. She also provides a thorough overview of American funeral and burial customs for a variety of ethnic and religious groups.
*ISBN 1-55870-589-9, paperback, 272 pages, #70527-K*

**The Genealogist's Computer Companion**—Master the basics of online research and turn your computer into an efficient, versatile research tool. Respected genealogist Rhonda McClure shows you how, providing guidelines and advice that enable you to find new information, verify existing research, and save valuable time. She also provides an invaluable glossary of genealogical and technical terms.
*ISBN 1-55870-591-0, paperback, 208 pages, #70529-K*

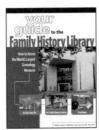

**Your Guide to the Family History Library**—The Family History Library in Salt Lake City is the largest collection of genealogy and family history materials in the world. No other repository compares for both quantity and quality of research materials. Written for beginning and intermediate genealogists, *Your Guide to the Family History Library* will help you use the library's resources effectively, both on site and online.
*ISBN 1-55870-578-3, paperback, 272 pages, #70513-K*

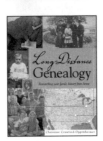

**Long-Distance Genealogy**—Gathering information from sources that can't be visited is a challenge for all genealogists. This book will teach you the basics of long-distance research. You'll learn what types of records and publications can be accessed from a distance, problems associated with the process, how to network, how to use computer resources and special "last resort" options.
*ISBN 1-55870-535-X, paperback, 272 pages, #70495-K*

*These books and other fine Betterway titles are available from your local bookstore, genealogy shop, online supplier or by calling (800) 221-5831.*